HOLD YE FRONT PAGE!

2,000 years of history in

By John Perry and
Neil Roberts

Foreword

• • • • • • • • • • • • • • • • •

THE tabloid Sun did not come into being until November 17, 1969 — which means about 14.5 billion years of the Earth's history went unrecorded in our pages.

This book attempts to right that wrong — and, with the world now celebrating the end of the second millennium since Jesus Christ's birth, we've decided to concentrate our coverage on those last 2,000 years.

In the next 144 pages you will find Sun front pages as we might have produced them the day after a great event.

We have also reproduced some of our most famous real front pages from the years since The Sun's debut in 1969. Each story has an accompanying piece on its left-hand page which sets it in its historical context and provides you with more information than can be conveyed in the few paragraphs that

Front page of first tabloid Sun: Nov 17, 1969

normally make up a Sun "splash". Often a story will end with a cross-reference to other pages inside the newspaper. Don't be fooled! These are merely for added authenticity, though occasionally the page WILL be followed by others related to it.

We make no claim for the stories we have picked being the definitive list of the most important in our history. Plainly some would be on such a list, but many just lend themselves more readily to headlines and pictures.

We have taken a few liberties — several of the pictures, for example, might well not have been available for the next day's edition. Many would simply not have been painted in time. We hope you find the book interesting, amusing, informative and a suitable, if sometimes irreverent, look back at the millennia we are leaving behind.

Words, ideas and research.....................**JOHN PERRY & NEIL ROBERTS**

Design...**PHIL LEACH**

Picture Research...**RACHEL WARD**

Photos..**STEVE LEWIS**

Apple-mac wizardry.................**EMMA HOLDER & COLIN PACKHAM**

Graphics...............................**KATHRYN GEORGE & ROY COOPER**

Contents

Dinosaurs lived from 260million to 65million years ago. Here are various museum reconstructions: Nest of hatchlings, Tyrannosaurus Rex (inset, left) Deinonychus (right)

1AD

BIRTH OF CHRIST

ABOUT a third of the Earth's population are Christians — the followers of Jesus Christ, whom they believe to be the Son of God and redeemer of mankind.

Our dating system is based on a Sixth Century calculation of when he was born, now accepted as being about three years out. Jesus was probably born around 3BC.

His life story is recorded in the New Testament gospels of Matthew, Mark, Luke and John, written towards the end of the First Century, plus the Epistles of Saint Paul and the Acts of the Apostles.

His existence is also confirmed by non-Christian historians.

This is the story of Jesus's birth, according to Matthew and Luke:

A virgin, Mary, was told by the Angel Gabriel that she would conceive solely through God's power.

She fell pregnant. Mary and husband Joseph then left their home in Nazareth, Judea, to visit Bethlehem, where Joseph had been born. This was to comply with a Roman decree that people had to return to the town of their birth to register for a census.

Every inn and house was full and the couple had to shelter in a stable, where Jesus was born. Mary wrapped him in cloths and used a manger as a cot. Angels appeared to shepherds in nearby hills and told them The Saviour had been born and was lying in a manger. The shepherds found Jesus in the stable, as predicted, and praised God.

Three Wise Men in the East saw a new star, indicating a new King of the Jews had been born.

They went to Jerusalem to see Herod, King of Judea, and asked where the baby was. Herod, fearing the baby would usurp him, sent the Wise Men to find Jesus.

The star led them to the house in Bethlehem where Mary, Joseph and Jesus were by this time staying.

The Wise Men were awestruck, worshipped the infant and gave him gifts fit for a king.

God warned them in a dream that Herod planned to kill Jesus, so they went home without reporting back to him.

In his determination to eliminate Jesus, Herod ordered his soldiers to kill every boy under two in Bethlehem. But an angel had already warned Joseph, who had fled into Egypt with his family.

After Herod's death, they travelled back to Mary's home in Nazareth, where Jesus grew up.

...Timeline...

All dates on this page BC . . .

14.5billion BC Big Bang creates the universe, which expands as matter hurtles through space (it is still doing so).

4.5bn Earth created — a mass of volcanoes, earthquakes and lightning storms without atmosphere.

2bn Bacteria and algae develop in sea, producing oxygen which gradually makes other life, including plants, possible.

600million Jellyfish, worms and coral develop in the oceans.

390m First known fish with backbones.

350m Insects and millipedes develop on land, sharks in sea.

300m Amphibians move on to land, mammals and reptiles appear.

260m First dinosaurs on land (Triassic period).

210m Start of the Jurassic period sees bird-like dinosaurs appear.

140m Start of Cretaceous period of dinosaurs.

65m Sudden extinction of dinosaurs — other animals gain prominence.

7m Apes and hominoids begin to evolve differently.

5m First appearance of Australopithecines in eastern Africa, apeman creature walking on two legs.

2.5m More humanoid creature, Homo Habilis, appears in Africa — makes primitive tools and shelters.

1.5m The more advanced Homo Erectus migrates out of Africa.

250,000 First appearance of Homo Sapiens in Africa, first incarnation being Neanderthal man.

70,000 Homo Sapiens Sapiens, our direct ancestor, appears in Africa, overlapping with Neanderthals.

30,000 Neanderthals die out, probably unable to compete.

20,000 Stone Age man creates intricate cave paintings and has primitive religion.

10,500 First known pottery appears, in Japan.

8500 People of modern-day Iraq begin to develop agriculture.

6000 New Stone Age — wheat and barley is cultivated, pigs and cattle domesticated, pottery is used.

4500 Egyptians bury dead with first known written documents.

4000 Population spurt in Mesopotamia leads to first towns; Bronze first used; Horse domesticated.

3500 City of Uruk founded in Sumer (Mesopotamia); Wheel invented there; Sail invented in Egypt.

2750 First literate civilisations under way — Sumerians and Egyptians.

2575 Egypt's King Cheops builds great pyramid at Giza, including the Great Sphinx.

2000 Stonehenge built in Wiltshire, possibly for sun worshippers.

1790 King Hammurabi founds the Babylonian empire.

1750 Greeks arrive in the Balkans and the middle east becomes mass of warring dynasties.

1200 Assyrians make first menacing appearance in middle east; Celts dominate central europe; The Trojan War (immortalised by poet Homer in the Iliad around 750BC); Israelites leave Egypt for Palestine.

1166 Death of last great Egyptian pharaoh, Rameses III.

1000 King David transforms Hebrews into formidable empire but it splits up under his successors; Assyrians ascend to military dominance of Middle East.

753 Traditional date given for the founding of Rome.

650 The first coins appear in Asia and Greece.

560 Series of revolts sparks downfall of Assyrian empire — it is replaced first by Babylonian empire, then Persian empire.

480 Persia attempts to conquer the city states of Greece but is defeated.

427 Birth of Greek philosopher Plato. Aristotle born in 384.

334 Rise of Alexander the Great, king of Macedonia, who invades Persia.

323 Death of Alexander, whose empire stretches from Egypt to India; Small Italian city state of Rome begins to expand.

300-200 Alexander's empire split by his successors. Rome conquers African state of Carthage and is leading power in western Mediterranean.

197 Rome goes to war with Macedonia and spends next 100 years fighting its way through Greece, North Africa, Southern France and Asia Minor.

58 Roman statesman Julius Caesar begins conquest of Celtic peoples in Gaul and crosses into Britain — series of civil wars leaves him master of the Roman world.

44 Caesar's assassination sparks another round of civil wars, from which his adopted son Octavian emerges triumphant.

27 Octavian adopts name Augustus and becomes first emperor — he later orders census throughout the empire.

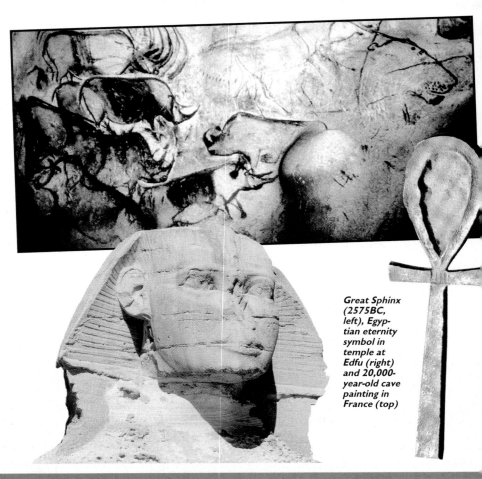

Great Sphinx (2575BC, left), Egyptian eternity symbol in temple at Edfu (right) and 20,000-year-old cave painting in France (top)

THE Sun

nday, December 26, 1AD   One bronze coin   THOUGHT: MUM AND CHILD 'STABLE'

A STAR IS BORN

Messiah claim as virgin has baby in stable

By FRANK INCENSE

A BABY born to a virgin mother was last night claimed to be the Son of God and the saviour of mankind.

He was discovered in a lowly cattle shed by three Wise Men who said an unusually bright star led them there.

They were so overwhelmed when they found the tot, named Jesus, they bowed down and handed him gold, frankincense and myrrh.

The baby was wrapped in cloth and lying in a manger, which his mum Mary and dad Joseph were using as a makeshift cot.

The stable was at the back of an inn in Bethlehem, Judea. It is believed the couple had to deliver the child there because the inn was chock-a-block with people in town for a census the Romans ordered.

SWADDLING

The baby was first found by a group of shepherds who said an angel tipped them off to his whereabouts while they were watching over their flocks by night.

The angel told the terrified men: "Fear not – I bring you good tidings of great joy. For unto you is born this day in the city of David a Saviour, which is Christ the Lord.

"Ye shall find the babe wrapped in swaddling clothes, in a manger."

The Wise Men behind yesterday's claims were sent to track down the baby by King Herod after he heard a new King of the Jews had been born. He is privately terrified of being ousted.

Herod: My Nightmare
- PAGES 4 &

Wise after the event . . . the three men hand gifts to newborn Jesus yesterday after finding him in a Bethlehem stable

718,347 DAYS TO GO

33
THE LIFE OF CHRIST

The Feeding of the Five Thousand, by 15th Century artist Joachim Patenier. One of Jesus's best-known miracles, it is said he fed a crowd with five loaves and two fishes

. . . Timeline . . .

9AD Romans axe plan to seize Germany when tribesmen kill 15,000 soldiers.

14 Death of the Roman Emperor Augustus.

17 Poet Ovid and historian Livy both die in Rome.

27 Approximate date of the start of Christ's ministry in Galilee.

After the resurrection the apostles were sent out to preach and perform miracles of their own. Left, Peter and John heal a lame man. Right, Sermon on the Mount

UNLIKE his birth, Jesus Christ's ministry and crucifixion are recorded in all four New Testament Gospels.

The earliest post-nativity episode described is in Luke, when at 12 Jesus disappeared for three days during a Passover festival visit to Jerusalem with his parents.

Mary and Joseph found him in the temple, talking with the country's wisest men. Scolded by a worried Mary, Jesus baffled her by saying she ought to have expected him to be doing his "Father's business."

The Gospels mention nothing of Jesus from then until the age of 30, when he was baptised by John The Baptist in the River Jordan and resisted the devil's temptations during 40 days' fasting and meditation in the nearby wilderness.

Then began his ministry — which saw him perform miracles, preach sermons and tell parables illustrating God's message of love.

He first picked 12 disciples — fishermen Peter and Andrew, their friends James and John, ex-tax collector Matthew, Thomas, Philip, Bartholomew, Simon, James, Thaddaeus and Judas Iscariot.

The first miracle came at a wedding he was invited to. The wine ran out, so Jesus produced more from six huge jars filled with water.

He later cured a leper by touching him, inspired a paralysed man to walk and calmed the raging sea of Galilee when it threatened to sink a boat containing him and his disciples.

Later, at the Feeding of the Five Thousand, Jesus miraculously used five loaves and two fishes to feed a crowd following him. He is later said to have brought a friend named Lazarus back from the dead to show God's power.

Among the parables is that of the Prodigal Son, in which a father forgives his son when he returns home broke but genuinely remorseful. Jesus said God would forgive sinners who repented.

In the Sermon on the Mount, Jesus recited the Lord's Prayer and a list of disadvantaged groups, including the meek, who were for varying reasons blessed.

Jesus's popularity grew — and he was seen as a threat by the local religious leaders, the Pharisees.

In Passover week, he entered Jerusalem on a donkey — greeted by enthusiastic crowds — drove traders and money-lenders from the temple and predicted his own death and resurrection.

Jesus ate a Last Supper with the disciples and said one would betray him. He urged them to eat bread and wine symbolising his body and blood — the "Eucharist", which is now the central Christian ritual.

Judas had agreed with the priests to hand over Jesus for 30 pieces of silver, and did so in the Garden of Gethsemane.

Jesus was tried by Jewish leaders, the Sanhedrin, and was condemned to death for blasphemy after insisting he was God's son.

The local Roman governor Pontius Pilate attempted to save Jesus, but then confirmed his sentence.

Jesus was crucified on a cross, with a robber on either side, on what is now marked as Good Friday.

He was laid in a tomb but was resurrected by Sunday (now celebrated as Easter Sunday) and appeared to the disciples, telling them to spread the word of God and perform miracles of their own. The Resurrection is a central plank of Christian belief as it gives humanity hope of life after death.

According to Luke, the disciples later saw Jesus ascend into heaven.

Leonardo Da Vinci's depiction of the Last Supper, at which Christ performed the Eucharist and predicted one of the disciples would betray him

THE Sun

FORGIVE US, LORD

Saturday, March 28, 33   Two bronze coins   THOUGHT: PILATE ERROR

This was the terrible moment that shamed mankind yesterday as Jesus Christ died on a wooden cross — his only crime to have preached a message of hope and love. Turn to Pages 2, 3, 4 and 5 to read about the harrowing last moments of the Son of God

Roman Emperor Tiberius, who died in 37, and (right) Emperor Claudius (41)

... Timeline ...

30-33 Resurrection of Christ, who appears to disciples.

37 Caligula becomes Roman Emperor on death of Tiberius; Nero born.

39 Increasingly-mad Caligula assembles army at Channel ports for invasion of Britain, then scraps the plan.

40 Mauretania is annexed by the Roman Empire.

41 Roman Emperor Caligula is murdered — Claudius takes over.

42 An attempted revolt against Emperor Claudius by the Roman governor of Dalmatia is put down.

43

INVASION OF THE ROMANS

THE invasion of 43 marked the beginning of almost 400 years of Roman rule in Britain. For the new Roman emperor Claudius the success of the mission was of supreme importance.

He was an uninspiring figure — a dusty academic rather than a charismatic politician — and his regime needed the prestige which military success would bring.

Claudius was also a great admirer of Julius Caesar, who had led two expeditions to Britain in 55 and 54BC.

During these, Caesar defeated the Celtic tribesmen who tried to stop him advancing inland, but neither was a serious attempt at conquest.

What better way for the sickly Claudius to prove his worth than to go one better than the mighty Caesar and conquer the Britons?

The Roman invasion fleet sailed from the area around modern-day Boulogne in the early summer of 43. Its ships were probably carrying almost 40,000 soldiers.

The legions are thought to have landed unopposed somewhere on the Kent coast, possibly at Richborough.

Caratacus, the war leader of the south-eastern Celtic tribes, sent his forces against the Roman general Aulus Plautius, but they were easily driven off.

At this stage the Dobunni tribe, based around the Severn valley, sent envoys to the Romans offering to surrender. The offer was accepted.

But Caratacus was made of sterner stuff.

He regrouped his forces, called up reinforcements and lay in wait for the Romans on the far bank of the River Medway, which they had to cross if they were to push further inland.

When the Romans reached the river they immediately attacked. Rather than waste time building boats or a bridge, Plautius ordered some of his veteran infantrymen to swim across wearing full battle gear.

They swam ashore in the middle of the British chariots, causing panic among the horses. Nevertheless the Britons held on and when night fell they were still in possession of the river bank.

The next day the Romans launched a renewed attack, Plautius throwing his reserves into the fray. The new onslaught turned the tide of battle in the Romans' favour and the British line buckled, then turned and fled.

The Romans pressed on towards the Thames, easily sweeping aside another army Caratacus had hastily assembled to oppose them.

By June they were ready to assault the large Celtic town on the site of modern-day Colchester. But Emperor Claudius wanted to be present in person for this and they had to wait for him to arrive.

Eventually he landed in Britain and during a 16-day stay saw his troops storm the town. He then returned to Rome, leaving Plautius with instructions to conquer the rest of the country.

The demonstration of Rome's military might convinced other tribes there was little point in prolonging the fight.

The Iceni of East Anglia and various tribes from Kent and Hampshire agreed to accept Roman rule. Even the powerful Brigantes, who lived around the Pennines, were alarmed enough to offer Rome the hand of friendship.

Caratacus realised the south was lost and retreated westwards.

He continued an increasingly futile struggle for a further eight years until he was captured by rival tribesmen, who immediately handed him over to the Romans.

Within 20 years of the invasion most of England was firmly under the control of the empire.

John's Gospel tells how apostle 'doubting' Thomas (kneeling, left) wanted physical proof of Jesus's resurrection. So Jesus got him to touch his crucifixion wounds. It convinced him

The Celtic lifestyle

THE Romans have left us a portrayal of the Celtic people of Britain as barbarian savages. According to some classical writers the Celts were war-mad fanatics who were quick-tempered, superstitious and utterly untrustworthy.

While there may be some truth behind these generalisations, they really only tell one side of the story.

The Celts were great artists renowned for their metalwork, as well as poets, lovers of songs and superb horsemen. Certainly some aspects of Celtic life were revolting to the modern mind. For instance, they liked to hang the decapitated heads of enemies from their horses — and their religion probably included human sacrifice.

But women in Celtic society enjoyed a much more prominent role than in the Roman world.

The Celts also took great pride in their appearance. According to Caesar, men who grew too fat could be punished by their tribe.

THE Sun

Tuesday, May 14, 43   Two bronze coins   THOUGHT: BYE CLAUDIUS

INSIDE SUN *Woman* TODAY

FROM HAGS TO RICHES

We give crone a make-over… now she looks like a million Denarii

SEND 'EM ROME

rave Brit warriors ready o hammer lousy legions

By HAYLEY CAESAR

THOUSANDS of brave British warriors were last night preparing to push Emperor Claudius's Roman invaders back into the sea.

Top general Caratacus has assembled a huge force of chariots to do battle with the Latin losers.

He plans to line his army up along the banks of the River Medway in Kent to stop the enemy from crossing.

Caratacus's bold battle plan comes just days after the Romans made a surprise landing on the Kent coast with more than 40,000 armed men.

Plucky local tribesmen tried to stop them marching inland, but were overwhelmed by sheer weight of numbers.

Last night a spokesman for Caratacus said: "We will defend our land to the last man."

They'll Make Us Have Baths — Pages Four and Five

Armoured robbery . . . one of the Roman invaders

ROMANS' REVOLTING HABITS

They'll make us have baths

Sick . . . Latins strip off their dresses and scrub themselves clean in public 'baths' like this o

EVIL WASHING PLOT

By LOU PHER

THE beastly Romans will scrap all of our good old British customs and force us to adopt their disgusting habits if their invasion succeeds.

One of the first things they will do is make everyone immerse themselves in **WATER** each day.

The Latin loonies call this bizarre practice "washing" or "having a bath".

They insist it is healthy — even though it is well-known that getting water on your skin weakens the body's natural defences.

The Roman custom of "bathing" takes place in special public buildings.

Inside, large holes in the ground are filled with tepid water. The Romans get into these, sometimes immersing themselves up to their necks.

Incredibly, they then systematically rub off all the protective layers of grime.

The Romans plan to inflict plenty more barmy ideas on us. They will:

● **MAKE** us swallow a vile intoxicating concoction made from squashed grapes and known as "wine".

● **ABOLISH** drinking from streams by building brick structures called "aquaducts" which ferry water into towns.

Threat

● **LITTER** the countryside with hideous carvings of famous Romans and construct buildings with fancy arches and columns.

● **PAY** Greek layabouts huge sums to create ugly pictures called "mosaics".

● **REPLACE** our dirt tracks with stone-built paths known as "roads", all of them tediously straight.

Last night the Druids launched a Keep Britain Celtic campaign to make people aware how dangerous the Romans are.

A spokesman said: "The people of Britain need to wake up — our entire way of life is under threat.

"Just look what's happened over the Channel. A hundred years ago the Gauls used to be just like us.

"Then the Romans invaded. Now half the country is speaking that Latin gobbledegook and some of the men

Run Roman . . . the invaders dash towards our men last nig

have even started wearing ridiculous Roman dresses called 'togas'. As if that's not bad enough they've planted those blasted grapes everywhere."

The Romans grow huge numbers of grapes to make the "wine" drink.

When the fruit is ripe it is picked and put in a large container. Then barefoot slaves tread on the grapes so the juice squirts out.

It is collected and stored in jars. The resulting drink is blood-red in colour and extremely sour in taste. Nevertheless, the Romans consume it in huge quantities.

The loopy Latins also have a mania for constructing useless items out of stone.

For example, they will spend a fortune creating aquaducts which stretch for miles from streams to towns.

They allow the water to flow downhill from the stream. The druids' spokesman added: "It's all very clever, but why bother when it's easier to walk to the stream and bring the water back in a pot like people have always done?"

The making of mosaics, bits of coloured stone arranged in a so-called pattern, is a particularly daft exercise.

Many are meant to represent people's faces or animals. But most of the time they look like something put together by a village idiot. And

the fools who spend th lives making these mosaics heralded as geniuses and p a fortune.

But perhaps the most po less Roman invention is road. These are identical the good old British m track — but with a covering stones and pebbles.

The druid added: "For the road is absolute proof Romans aren't all there.

"What is the point of cov ing a perfectly decent tra with something that see solely designed to make yo feet hurt?"

Reprisals

In the past many peop have been taken in by smooth-talking Romans.

They have abandoned th traditional ways and taken the newcomers' bizarre hab

But in time they have **A** lived to regret it.

One Gallic nobleman, w does not wish to be nam for fear of Roman repris said last night: "It seem great at first. But lately I begun to question it all.

"I mean they know how keep order, I'll admit that

"But they've done precio little else. Apart from sani tion, medicine, educatic wine, public order, irrigatic roads, the fresh water syst and public health . . . w have the Romans ever do for us?"

Turtle war . . . Romans make like a tortoise to protect themselves from our missiles

ROMANS' REVOLTING HABITS

Art attack . . . let Romans invade us now and our country will soon be filled with hideous carvings. Get a load of this oddball in one of their rather suspect 'toga' dresses

Ugly . . . Romans spend ages making mosaics — what's wrong with old-fashioned painting in animal blood?

Road to ruin . . . Romans will cover perfectly good mud tracks with stones. The dullards make all new roads straight

Brought of their minds . . . aquaducts costing a fortune will be built so lazy Romans don't have to walk to a stream to get their water

Beware bullies wearing togas

THE Romans are notorious for poking their noses into other people's business — then invading them if they object.

Up until about 200 years ago no one outside Italy had heard of them. Then the toga-wearing thugs suddenly decided a peaceful life was too boring and started causing chaos across Europe.

First they marched into North Africa — then Spain, Greece and the Middle East.

The Romans always use the same system. First they befriend a group of troublemakers in a nearby country. Then they contact the country's rulers and insist their friends be put in power. If their demands are refused they invade.

Infamous Roman thug Julius Caesar tried the same trick here about 100 years ago.

He invaded twice in two years — but both times was sent packing by our brave warriors.

Caesar was so unpleasant even his own people hated him. When he returned to Rome he was stabbed to death by men he thought were mates.

Bust of the infamous Nero, who took over as Roman Emperor in 54

61

REVOLT OF BOADICEA

BOADICEA — or Boudicca as she is often called nowadays — was Queen of a Celtic tribe called the Iceni who lived in settlements in East Anglia.

Her husband Prasutagus enjoyed a long reign, maintaining good relations with the Roman civil servants who ran Britain.

But when he died the unscrupulous Romans seized his territory. Boadicea was tortured and beaten and her two daughters were raped. Other members of the Iceni nobility were enslaved.

The Queen and her subjects responded by rising in rebellion.

Their first target was the Roman colony of Camulodunum (now Colchester). Many of the inhabitants were former Roman legionaries and their families.

The Britons hated these ex-soldiers, who treated them as little more than slaves, and were eager to settle old scores.

Their revenge was terrible. The Britons stormed the town, slaughtered the inhabitants and burned anything they could not loot.

The Romans immediately sent one of their vaunted legions to stamp out the revolt. But as it neared Colchester it was overwhelmed by Boadicea's forces and wiped out.

Her army, now said to have swelled to 100,000, followed up by attacking and burning the towns of Londinium (London) and Verulamium (St Albans).

More than 70,000 people are said to have been massacred.

The Britons seemed on the point of winning their independence. Many Imperial officials had already fled across the Channel to Gaul.

But Roman governor Paulinus Suetonius held his nerve.

When the revolt broke out he was on the island of Mona (Anglesey) suppressing the Druids. He gathered an army of 10,000 men and marched to meet Boadicea.

Suetonius chose his battleground carefully — lining his men up between two woods so they could not be surrounded.

The Roman historian Tacitus later claimed that before the Britons attacked, Boadicea made a stirring speech from her chariot.

She told them: "On this spot we conquer or die with glory. There is no alternative." The Britons charged towards the Roman line in a huge mob, screaming their war cries.

But the discipline of the legionaries held and they forced Boadicea's troops back. Then the Romans counter-attacked and the Britons broke and fled. Thousands were cut down as they stumbled over each other in blind panic.

Boadicea escaped — but committed suicide by swallowing poison rather than be taken prisoner.

Ancient coins

THE Celts had developed their own coins before the Romans came to Britain. The earliest types were simple bronze discs — but by the end of the First Century BC they were clearly copying Classical coins, stamping on them crude portraits of tribal leaders.

Once the conquest of Claudius had been completed, the Celts adopted Roman coins like the rest of the Empire.

The Roman system of coinage, originally based on Greek models, was diverse and sophisticated (see examples below).

The emperors minted a variety of coins using gold, silver, bronze and copper. In the early empire the main large denomination coins were the gold Aureus and the silver Denarius.

There was also a range of small coins, usually bronze, like the Sestertius and the As.

Successive emperors used their coins for propaganda.

Coin pictures would be used to represent Roman victories over their enemies.

And slogans like "Restorer of Liberty" would be used in an attempt to portray the empire as a champion of justice.

Archaeologists have found hoards of Roman and Celtic coins buried all over Britain, probably hidden during periods of conflict.

...Timeline...

54 Emperor Claudius dies — Emperor Nero takes over.

57 Approximate date of Buddhism reaching China after Han emperor Ming Ti dreams of flying golden deity.

59 Nero executes his own mother.

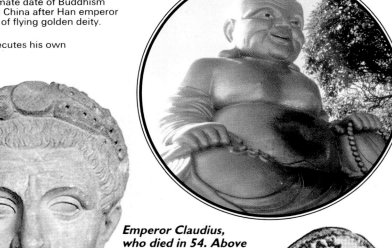

Emperor Claudius, who died in 54. Above right, Buddhism came to China around 57

THE Sun

day, August 28, 61　　2½ bronze coins　　THOUGHT: QUEEN B

Clarkson gives new chariots a woad-test

SEE PAGES 10 & 11

shiny . . . Roman money

GIRL POWER

Battling Boadicea bashes Latin louts

By BERNIE TOWNS

BRITAIN was up in arms against the hated Roman invaders last night — as Queen Boadicea destroyed THREE of their towns.

Flame-haired Boadicea first led her troops against the Roman colony of Colchester and burned it to the ground.

Then they massacred a legion of Latin louts sent to stop them — the Queen personally charging into the enemy in her chariot.

Finally Boadicea, Queen of the Norfolk-based Iceni tribe, attacked the Roman towns of St Albans and London, leaving them smouldering piles of rubble.

Last night thousands of Brits had flocked to join her forces.

Boadicea rebelled when the Romans seized her lands after the death of her husband King Prasutagus — and whipped her when she complained.

Full Story — Pages 4 and 5

Hell on wheels . . . Queen Boadicea charges into the Romans in chariot last night

ay No o single oman urrency

AY The Sun launches a ade to save the good British bronze coin.

oman bureaucrats t to SCRAP our money replace it with a single ency that can be used ver Europe.

ey reckon that trade in the Empire will be h easier if we all use s showing the head of Emperor.

ut The Sun is calling

ab . . our bronze coins

ts army of readers to us Save Our Coins. want you to join us for otest rally on the Ides arch in St Albans (as as the Romans have ilt it by then, folks!).

Sun spokesman said: is is one battle the ans must not win."

YOU THE JURY

AKE part in our You e Jury poll — and ll us whether you ink we should do way with our coins d replace them with e new Roman ones.

If you think No carry t the following sim- e procedure to regis- r your vote.

Find a dead animal d skin it. Dry the skin er a fire, then cut out square segment. Get piece of charcoal and ake these two marks it: N O

Then bring the skin us at The Sun, XII aesar Way, Londin- m. If you think Yes, ep your opinions to urself.

Victims at Pompeii were 'frozen' in ash after the eruption of 79. Excavations continue to this day

. . . Timeline . . .

62 Crazed Roman Emperor Nero executes his wife.

64 Great Fire of Rome — Nero is said to have recited poetry while watching it; Death of apostle St Peter.

66 Mass suicide of 1,000 zealots to avoid capture by Romans after siege of mountaintop fortress at Masada, Judea.

68 Civil war in Roman empire after Emperor Nero dies.

70 Romans destroy Jewish temple at Jerusalem.

79 Eruption of Vesuvius buries Pompeii, killing many — lava turns victims to stone.

80 Completion of Colosseum amphitheatre in Rome.

105 Approximate date for invention of paper in China.

116 Roman empire at its height under Emperor Trajan.

Roman emperor Trajan, who expanded boundaries of the empire (see 116)

Depiction of Mount Vesuvius erupting in 79. It buried the towns of Pompeii, Herculaneum and Stabiae. The ruins of Pompeii were not discovered until the 16th Century

122

HADRIAN'S WALL

THE Emperor Hadrian ordered the building of his famous wall during a visit to Britain in 122. He intended it to be an imposing frontier to stop the barbarian tribes of the North raiding the wealthier lands further south.

The brick wall was built by Roman soldiers and probably took about 16 years to complete.

Once finished, it was about 6½ metres high.

But a deep ditch about nine metres wide was dug on its northern side to make the barrier even more formidable.

The building of the wall was a powerful symbol of Rome's military might — and a sign that they were in Britain to stay.

Following the invasion of 43 the Romans had swiftly set about stamping out resistance from Celtic tribes in southern Britain.

Emperor Claudius sent about 40,000 soldiers to the new province and by a mixture of brute force and clever diplomacy they soon achieved their aims.

At first the Roman frontier stretched along the line of the Rivers Severn and Trent.

Most of modern-day Wales, northern England and Scotland were unconquered.

But the Romans had no intention of allowing these areas to remain under Celtic control for long.

They were particularly keen to get their hands on the mineral deposits — lead, iron, copper and even gold and silver — that the Celts mined in the West and North.

The second phase of the invasion began some ten years after the revolt of Boadicea.

By 78 the Romans had subdued Wales and pushed their frontier north to the River Tyne.

In the following six years the Roman governor Agricola launched his army into Scotland — penetrating even into the islands and highlands and inflicting heavy defeats on the Caledonian tribes.

But Scotland was never properly subdued. Over the next 40 years a bitter guerrilla war was fought out in the glens.

Time after time, the Caledonian tribesmen would strike at isolated Roman forts, then melt away into the mountains before reinforcements could arrive.

Then, in 117, Hadrian became the new Emperor — ushering in a totally new strategy for the Roman empire.

He abandoned his predecessors' policy of expansion in favour of an empire with strictly-defined borders.

One of these would be a mas-

A Roman centurion stands guard as Hadrian's Wall is built by his troops

sive wall across Britain between the Solway Firth in the west and the River Tyne in the east.

A Roman historian, writing a life of Hadrian, later said the Emperor wanted the wall "to separate Romans from Barbarians".

At the time Hadrian's Wall was a state-of-the art piece of military engineering. At every mile there was a milecastle guarded by at least eight men. Between milecastles were two turrets.

These enabled the soldiers to keep a close watch on the movement of goods, people and animals across the frontier.

In about 140 Rome again attempted to push north, establishing a new frontier in Scotland known as the Antonine Wall.

It was built of turf and stretched about 40 miles from the Firth of Forth to the Firth of Clyde.

But within 20 years the Antonine Wall — named after the Emperor Antoninus Pius — had been abandoned and the legionaries had returned to Hadrian's Wall.

For the next two centuries Hadrian's Wall remained Rome's imposing northern frontier, repelling raids from a new barbarian menace, the Picts.

Then in 410 the Romans pulled out of Britain, leaving the wall as testimony to their greatness.

XXL

VII

III

THE Sun

Tuesday, June 10, 122 · One sestertius · THOUGHT: WE'RE SCOT FREE

II

XIX VI

BONUS
XL

Did you win last night or was it a Nero miss?
CHECK YOUR LOTTO NUMBERS

WONDERWALL

Hadrian orders 80-mile barrier to beat raiders

By MILES ASTONE

THE Emperor Hadrian has ordered a huge wall to be built across Britain to stop the barbarians in the North making our lives hell.

The brick barrier — to be known as Hadrian's Wall — will stretch 80 miles from the east coast to the west. It will be about 15ft high and will have small castles situated at mile intervals. Each will be garrisoned by soldiers. Hadrian, 46, ordered the new wall after hearing how the savage Caledonian tribesmen regularly raid south, burning and plundering our farms.

A spokesman in the Emperor's office said last night: "The wall will certainly put a stop to the barbarians' antics.

"Nobody will be able to sneak across without us knowing."

Massive jobs boost for the North – See Page Two

564,145 DAYS TO GO

Left, St Augustine, the Bishop of Hippo in Roman Africa, who converted to Christianity in 387, and (right) St Patrick, said to have introduced the faith to Ireland in 432

455

VANDALS SACK ROME

THE Vandals were one of more than a dozen Germanic barbarian tribes who lived alongside the Roman empire in the Fourth Century.

Occasionally the tribesmen crossed the border — marked by the great Rhine and Danube rivers — and raided Roman territory.

But for much of the time the awesome military might of Rome was enough to keep them in check.

The situation changed dramatically around 360 as a terrible new force arrived in eastern Europe — the Huns.

The Huns, a nomadic people from the steppes of Asia, brought war and devastation to the region.

To escape from them the Germanic tribes began to force their way into the Roman empire.

At first the refugees lived in peace, but when unscrupulous Roman officials tried to extort money from them they rebelled.

In 378 the Roman army marched to confront 80,000 of these tribesmen — known as the Visigoths — but was utterly defeated at the Battle of Adrianople.

Much of the Roman army was destroyed and the Emperor Valens died on the battlefield.

The catastrophe of Adrianople left the Balkan parts of the empire undefended.

Over the next 30 years the empire descended into near-chaos as successive emperors tried to stop the Germans running amok. Then in December 406 disaster struck once again. The river Rhine froze and thousands of Vandal tribesmen and their families poured across into modern-day France — one of the Roman empire's richest provinces.

Within five years the Vandals had swept across France and carved out a new kingdom in Spain.

But still they were not finished. In 429 the Vandal king Gaiseric transported 80,000 of his people across the Straits of Gibraltar and into North Africa.

The ships were provided by a Roman official in charge of the wealthy Roman province of Carthage who was rebelling against the empire.

In 439 the Vandals took control of Carthage, the equivalent of modern-day Tunisia. Carthage supplied most of the grain Italy needed to feed itself — a situation Gaiseric was not slow to exploit.

He spent the next decade blackmailing the empire into giving him more and more territory by threatening to cut off Rome's grain supply.

The king also spent the time amassing a huge fleet. In 455 he put it to use, sailing his army to Italy to attack a defenceless Rome.

The raid proved just how powerless the empire had become in western Europe. Just 21 years later the last western Roman emperor was deposed.

... Timeline ...

166 Smallpox devastates the Roman empire.

180 Death of Roman Emperor Marcus Aurelius.

190 Chinese mathematicians calculate pi to five decimal places: 3.14159.

235 Beginning of new civil war in Roman empire.

238 Revolt in Africa against Roman rule begins half-century of unrest.

271 Chinese using magnetic compass; Aurelian walls built around Rome.

284 Diocletian becomes emperor of Rome, forms "Tetrarchy" of four emperors to rule empire together.

313 Christianity now tolerated throughout Roman empire.

314 Christian Constantine the Great becomes emperor of western half of Roman empire (sole emperor in 324).

330 Constantinople (now Istanbul) inaugurated on site of ancient Greek city of Byzantium in European Turkey.

360 Picts and Scots attack Britain; First invasions of Europe by Huns.

378 Romans defeated at Adrianople by Visigoths — Emperor Valens killed.

387 St Augustine of Hippo converts to Christianity.

395 Roman empire splits again into east and west.

410 Alaric, king of Germanic people the Visigoths, sacks Rome.

432 St Patrick introduces Christianity to Ireland.

445 Attila the Hun attacks western Europe.

450 Saxons from Germany launch an invasion of Britain.

The fearsome warrior Attila The Hun, who launched attack on western Europe in 445

Bust of the Roman Emperor Constantine the Great (314)

Vandal soldiers carry off loot and captives after attacking Rome. The Vandals were Germanic tribesmen who swept through France, Spain and North Africa

THE Sun

day, June 3, 455   2 sestertii   THOUGHT: SACKING OFFENCE

MINDLESS VANDALS

City in ruins . . . one of Rome's famous monuments yesterday. The damage can be clearly seen on the right of the picture

Barbarian yobs turn Rome into a smoking ruin

THE city of Rome was a smouldering ruin last night after it was attacked and plundered by barbarians called the Vandals.

The burly hooligans ran amok after breaking through the city wall.

Many of Rome's most famous monuments were damaged and its art treasures stolen.

The mindless barbarians also robbed citizens and set their homes ablaze. One senator fought back tears last night as he said: "They behaved like animals. The city will

From RAY PANPILLAGE in Rome

never recover from this." The Vandals have gained a fearsome reputation for thuggery and violence in recent years.

They sacked Rome after sailing up the River Tiber in large boats.

The beasts arrived just two days after Roman Emperor Petronius Maximus was killed while fleeing the city in panic.

Furious citizens learned he was abandoning them to the barbarians and attacked him with a shower of stones. He died when one hit him on the head.

Hun-called For — Page Seven

Hun-called For — Page Seven

The Byzantine Emperor Justininan I came to power in the year 527. This mosaic on display in Italy shows him surrounded by clergy, soldiers and other officials

. . . Timeline . . .

476 Germanic invader Odoacer expels Romulus Augustus, last emperor of Rome, and takes city. Western empire collapses, Byzantine (or eastern empire) now in full control.

500 Indian mathematicians introduce the zero; Ghanaian empire becomes the most important power in West Africa.

515 Huns destroy the powerful Gupta empire of India.

527 Beginning of reign of Byzantine emperor Justinian, who tries to unite east and west branches of Christian church.

529 St Benedict founds monastery at Monte Cassino, south of Rome.

552 Monks smuggle silkworms to Constantinople from China, launching Byzantine silk industry.

563 St Columba, from Ireland, founds monastery of Iona.

570 Mohammed, Prophet of Islam, is born in Mecca.

595 Indian mathematicians use decimal system.

597 Second St Augustine tries to convert Anglo-Saxons to Christianity.

600 First recorded sighting of the Loch Ness Monster, Scotland.

632 Death of Mohammed, Prophet of Islam.

640 Caliph Omar, a successor to Mohammed, conquers Egypt.

642 Arabs erect first mosque in al-Fustat, then capital of Egypt.

650 Revelations of Mohammed written and become the Koran.

664 Synod of Whitby in England; Roman Christianity chosen over Celtic.

670 Syrian chemist Callinicus invents highly-flammable liquid used by the Byzantine army in battle.

697 Arabs destroy Byzantine city at Carthage in North Africa; new city of Tunis built nearby.

732 Charles Martel, leader of the Franks, defeats Muslims at Poitiers in France, stopping Muslim advance northwards.

762 Abbasid dynasty ruling Iraq makes Baghdad its capital.

768 Charlemagne becomes king of the Franks.

784 Offa, king of Mercia in central England, builds defensive dyke between England and Wales.

793
VIKING RAIDS

THE Viking raids on Britain took the Anglo Saxons by surprise — and ushered in a new era of terror.

The first small-scale attack took place in 789. Four years later the Norsemen were back in force for their infamous assault on the island monastery at Lindisfarne, Northumberland.

The savagery of the raiders stunned the Anglo Saxons.

A chronicler wrote: "The harrying of the heathen miserably destroyed God's church in Lindisfarne by rapine and slaughter."

The sense of shock was captured by the Eighth Century scholar Alcuin, who wrote: "Never before has such terror appeared in Britain as we have now suffered from a pagan race.

"Nor was it thought possible that such an inroad from the sea could be made. Behold the church of St Cuthbert, spattered with the blood of the priests of God, despoiled of all its ornaments.

"A place more venerable than any other in Britain has fallen prey to pagans."

Within 40 years the Vikings were ravaging the south of England. In 835 they attacked the isle of Sheppey in Kent. From then on barely a year passed without a raid.

In 850 the Vikings changed their strategy. Instead of hit-and-run raids, they decided to spend the winter on the isle of Thanet.

Then in 865 a "great fleet of pagans" arrived in East Anglia. This was no raid — the Vikings had come to stay.

It was not only England that was tormented by the Vikingss. They plundered Ireland, Scotland and struck far into the interior of France by sailing their boats along the Seine and Loire rivers.

In the east the Swedish Vikings pushed south into modern-day Russia along the rivers that poured into the Baltic.

Eventually they formed a trading colony at Kiev.

All these expeditions were made possible by the Vikings' famous longships. These were made of wood and usually carried between 20 and 60 men. They were powered by a large square sail and oars.

The raiders themselves were usually armed with a sword or axe, a spear and a round shield. Wealthier warriors would have had a metal helmet and perhaps a chain-mail coat.

Some of the raiders were fanatics known as berserkers — a Viking word meaning "bear-shirt" and referring to the fact they often fought wearing an animal skin.

Before a battle these men would work themselves in a frenzy, then charge into the enemy.

The Dark Ages

THE Dark Ages is the traditional name given to the early medieval period which begins with the end of Roman rule in Europe in the Fifth Century.

The demise of Rome and the classical way of life led to a breakdown in civilisation and a steady decline in learning and art.

By the time of the first Viking raids, few apart from monks and clerics could read. Historians know relatively little about what went on in Britain between 400 and 1066 because few records were kept and hardly any survive.

The breakdown of learning was essentially a western European phenomenon. In the Byzantine empire and the Islamic dynasties of the Middle East, art and literature continued to thrive.

The Loch Ness monster is one of the great mysteries. The first recorded sighting, in 600, sparked centuries of debate and more 'appearances'. This photo is from 1934

Silkworms hit Constantinople in 552

THE Sun

Sunday, March 25, 793   **4 eggs**   **THOUGHT: NEVER THOR IT COMING**

MINDLESS VANDALS

Barbarian yobs turn Rome into a smoking ruin

Win a family day out at DRUID WORLD

...sh back . . . our last big story

Sun is crippled by news drought

By LES MAKEITUP

...Sun is getting smaller from ...week, folks — because we've ...out of news!

...'ll be cutting down to just ...pages a day due to the com... lack of interesting events ...g the Dark Ages.

...Sun spokesman said: "We're ... about this, but we really ... no choice.

...ince the Romans went home ...10 hardly anything seems to ...happened.

...esterday's Viking raid is the ...half-decent story in almost ...years. And that's probably a ...off."

Bargain

...st night pundits predicted ...the information famine could ...inue for another 82 YEARS.

...t don't fret — as soon as ...s DO pick up you'll be the ...to know.

...d at the bargain price of just ...eggs or 1½ turnips (depend-...n which system of barter your ...sagent uses) The Sun is still ...best value around.

... buy your super Sun every ... — and shine a little light on ...ry's darkest days.

COW HAS CALF

...ges 2, 3, 4 & 5

THE SEA DEVILS

Terror from the mist . . . Viking raiders leap from their longships yesterday before the looting of Lindisfarne

Vikings in raid on holy isle

By MAY HEMM

THEY came out of the mist yesterday in their ships of war — bringing death and destruction to a community of holy men.

The Vikings struck without warning as the monks on the island of Lindisfarne tended their flocks and toiled in the fields.

The heathen Norsemen came for plunder, protected by chainmail and shields and armed with spears and swords.

The monks defended themselves with only prayers and their Christian faith. It was not a battle, but a massacre. After barely an hour it was over.

Last night the church on the tiny isle off the Northumberland coast was still burning.

The monks' bloodstained bodies lay scattered around its walls.

The Vikings vanished as suddenly as they arrived — leaving nothing but blood and ruin.

And the terrible question: Will **OUR** *families be next to feel the wrath of the Sea Devils?*

409,697 DAYS TO GO

King Ethelwulf, who took the English throne in 839

King Egbert, who reigned in England from 822, and (above) Charlemagne, the powerful ruler of France, who was crowned Emperor of Rome on Christmas Day in year 800

878

ALFRED AND THE DANES

KING Alfred, dubbed Alfred the Great, was one of Britain's outstanding monarchs. He was a brave warrior who drove the Viking invaders out of England as well as a kind and literate man who encouraged education among his people.

Saxon Alfred was born in Wantage, Oxfordshire, in 849 and came to the throne at 22 when the Vikings were rampaging through England.

Alfred bought them off with a levy called the Danegeld but within five years they were invading further territories and forcing out the Saxon people.

Alfred used ships against the invaders in 875 — the origins of the Royal Navy.

In January 878 the Danes launched a surprise attack after which all the West Saxons surrendered, except Alfred and his men.

He retreated to a fortress at Athelney, Somerset, and began to put together an army comprising men from Somerset, Wiltshire and Hampshire.

It was during this time and while mustering his forces that Alfred's cake-burning incident is said to have happened.

In the summer of 878 Alfred defeated the Danes and seized their stronghold. He later captured back London and was recognised as King of all England.

The Vikings invaded again in 892 but Alfred forced them to leave after a four-year war.

But Alfred was not just a great leader of men — he was also a huge champion of education, beginning a school at his court and inviting scholars there.

He learned Latin and in 887 began to translate Latin books into English, ordering that all men of sufficient means must learn to read.

It is probably due to his encouragement of learning that the Anglo-Saxon Chronicle — one of the greatest sources of information about Saxon England — began to be written in 890. Alfred also instigated a series of laws protecting the poor and disadvantaged.

The Welsh scholar Asser wrote a biography of the King in 893. It contains the cake-burning story and a direct quote from the woman involved.

More importantly it reveals Alfred to have been attractive, wise, compassionate and learned.

Sir Winston Churchill, after World War Two, was called the greatest ever Englishman — but he is quoted as saying: ''No, the greatest Englishman that ever lived was King Alfred.''

Alfred the Great, a kind and literate King who sent the Vikings packing

. . . Timeline . . .

800 Pope crowns Charlemagne Emperor of Rome on Christmas Day in the city's St Peter's Church.

809 War begins between the Byzantine empire and the Bulgars.

811 Khan Krum of Bulgaria defeats Byzantines and kills their emperor.

814 Death of Charlemagne, Emperor of Rome.

820 Persian mathematician Musa al-Chwarazmi develops algebra.

822 Reign of King Egbert begins in England.

839 Beginning of the reign of King Ethelwulf.

841 Dublin is founded by the Vikings.

843 Frankish empire breaks up; Kenneth MacAlpin is first Scottish king.

844 Beginning of the rule of Rhodri Mawr, first Prince of Wales.

850 Maya civilisation in the southern lowlands of Mexico collapses, cities are abandoned.

858 Reign of King Ethelbald begins in England.

860 Reign of King Ethelbert begins; Vikings rule at Novgorod in Russia.

865 Great fleet of Vikings lands in East Anglia.

868 Another wave of Vikings invades England; The Diamond Sutra, the oldest printed book still in existence, is produced by wood block printing in China.

871 Beginning of the reign of King Alfred The Great.

A longship sails towards England in another raid. Viking forces first began plundering our coast in the 8th Century. Later they were repelled by Alfred

Chinese inventions

THE Chinese are arguably the most inventive nation in history. Long before the birth of Christ they had umbrellas, wheelbarrows, cast-iron ploughs, kites, the decimal system and paper.

In the early centuries after Christ, they invented the seismograph, matches, brandy, whisky, paper money, gunpowder and rockets — all long before they were seen elsewhere.

Even chess, believed to have originated in India in the Sixth Century, is thought to be based on an earlier Chinese game.

Travellers to China reported the use of toilet paper in the late 800s — but it was clearly in use well before then.

One Chinese scholar wrote in the Sixth Century: ''Paper on which there are quotations or commentaries from the Five Classics or the names of sages, I dare not use for toilet purposes.''

THE Sun

day, April 11, 878   4 eggs   THOUGHT: GIANT LEAK FOR MANKIND

CHINESE INVENT TOILET PAPER

Hygiene brainwave is a relief for us all

THE Chinese have invented toilet paper, it was dramatically announced last night.

The state-of-the-art hygiene solution was revealed by an Arab traveller to the far eastern country.

Amazingly, he was sneering about the Orientals' use of loo paper.

He told The Sun exclusively: "They do not wash themselves with water when they have done their necessities, they only wipe themselves with paper." But we reckon that's a great deal nicer than the **LEAVES** we've had to use for hundreds of years.

And last night The Sun despatched a reporter to China to see if they would lend us some.

He believes he can be back within just ten years — and may have several sheets with him.

China has always been ahead of the game when it comes to inventions.

They've been writing on paper for centuries — and they've already come up with matches for lighting fires.

They even have an early seismograph for predicting earthquakes.

A spokesman from King Alfred's office said last night: "We are, by comparison, a rather backward people."

Botever Next! — See Pages Four and Five

Royal roasting . . . peasant gives our Alfred a mouthful yesterday

Alfred the Grate

KING BURNS CAKES

A BUNGLING housewife told a guest off for letting her cakes burn yesterday — not realising he was KING ALFRED.

Brave Alfred, 29, was sitting by the fire of the peasant woman's home in Athelney, Somerset, preparing bows and arrows for another assault on the Danes.

The woman, wife of a local cowherd, saw them off the fire and ranted at the King:

"Can't you watch the cakes, man — don't you see them burning? I bet you'll eat enough of them as

soon as the time's come." The hapless woman was mortified with embarrassment when pals revealed who her guest was.

She was later given a stern ticking-off by her husband.

Alfred is busy in Somerset assembling an army to oust the Danes, who invaded our country seven years ago.

What's It All About, Alfred — See Page Seven

... Timeline ...

878 Alfred defeats Vikings under Gudrum at Ethandune — Treaty of Wedmore divides England between them.

891 Monks write the history of England in Anglo-Saxon Chronicle.

899 Reign of King Edward the Elder begins.

900 Magyars, a nomadic people from central Asia, invade Europe.

910 Benedictine Abbey of Cluny is founded in Burgundy, France.

911 Rollo, Viking chief, settles in Normandy.

924 Reign of King Athelstan begins in England.

936 Start of reign of Otto The Great, king of Germany.

937 Athelstan defeats large army of Scots, Irish and Danes at Battle of Brunanburh.

939 Start of the reign of King Edmund in England.

946 Beginning of the reign of King Edred.

950 Approximate date on which ancestors of the Maoris from the Cook Islands settle in New Zealand.

955 Germany's Otto defeats Magyars at Battle of Lechfeld and Slavs at Reichnitz; Reign of King Edwy begins in England.

959 Reign of King Edgar begins in England.

962 Otto is crowned Holy Roman Emperor.

969 Fatimid dynasty conquers Egypt and builds Cairo, which becomes capital.

970 Paper money introduced by the Chinese.

971 Fatimids build al-Azhar University, Cairo, one of the world's first universities and still in existence.

975 Reign of King Edward the Martyr begins in England.

976 Beginning of reign of Basil II, Byzantine emperor.

978 Reign of Aethelred the Unready begins; Vladimir is Grand Prince of Kiev.

983 China produces a 1,000-chapter encyclopaedia, the Taiping Yulan.

986 Eric The Red, Viking explorer, sets up a colony in Greenland.

987 Start of the reign of Hugh Capet, first Capetian king of France.

989 Vladimir of Kiev chooses Orthodox Christianity as his people's religion.

1000 Start of the rule of Stephen, first of Arpad dynasty of Hungary, who accepts Christianity for his people; Chinese perfect gunpowder and use it in warfare; Farmers in Peru grow sweet potatoes and corn; Viking explorer Leif Ericson reaches North America.

1014 Brian Boru, King of Ireland, defeats Vikings at Clontarf but is killed; Basil II defeats Bulgarians.

1016 Reign of King Edmund Ironside begins, but Viking Canute, who invaded in 1015, takes over.

King Canute, the Viking who invaded England and seized the throne in 1016

Crowning of Germany's King Otto as Holy Roman Emperor in 962

Edmund I — 'The Deed-doer' — whose reign as King of England began in 939

1034

KING CANUTE

KING Canute is one of those shadowy figures from the Dark Ages — like Arthur and Alfred the Great — who has passed into legend.

Countless generations have heard the story of the ruler who shamed his flatterers by proving he could not hold back the tide as they claimed.

The truth is that Canute was also one of the most gifted and astute rulers of his age.

He began life as a minor Viking prince and ended it as ruler of an empire that included England, Denmark and Norway.

Canute first came to England in 1013 in the army of his father, the Danish king Svein Forkbeard.

Within a few months Svein and Canute conquered most of England. Its king, Aethelred, often called The Unready, fled to Normandy.

But Svein died the next year and Aethelred seized the chance to regain his throne.

He returned from Normandy and managed to expel the Danish army and its new leader Canute.

But Canute had not given up. In 1015 he returned with another army to renew the struggle. In April 1016 Aethelred died and was succeeded by his son Edmund Ironside.

Edmund and Canute fought a bitter campaign over the next few months with first one side getting the upper hand, then the other.

But in the autumn at Ashingdon, Essex, Edmund's army was overwhelmingly defeated. Within a month Edmund was dead and Canute was England's first Viking king.

Two years later Canute's brother King Harald of Denmark died. Canute travelled to Denmark and quickly secured his hold over the country.

In 1028 he attacked Norway after spending years undermining the position of its ruler.

He managed to persuade a number of local chieftains to come over to his side and was proclaimed king.

Canute died in 1035, aged about 40, and was buried in Winchester. His heirs lacked his political genius and on his death the Anglo-Scandinavian empire he had built began to break apart.

Perhaps Canute's greatest achievement was that he gave England more than 20 years of much-needed peace.

As ruler of the Viking homelands of Norway and Denmark, he was able to stop their attacks.

Under his kingship art, trade and Christianity all flourished.

He also had great respect for the old English laws, to which he added a keen sense of justice and a regard for individual rights.

Canute was also eager to promote himself as an 'English' king. This prompted him to do penance for the wrongdoings of his Viking ancestors by building new churches or making generous gifts to existing ones.

Painting of a Viking raiding fleet racing across the North Sea. The Vikings were great explorers and warriors and it was around the year 1000 that Leif Ericson became probably the first-ever European to set foot on North American soil, possibly at Nova Scotia

Maoris during tribal war shortly after settling in New Zealand (950)

THE Sun

day, October 11, 1034   One farthing   THOUGHT: SHORELY SOME MISTAKE

YOU CANUTE BE SERIOUS!

Daft King's bid to hold back waves

By SANDY BEACH

DAFT King Canute gets a soaking yesterday — as he sits on a beach and ORDERS the waves to stay away from his feet.

The potty monarch tried to command the sea after flunkeys insisted he was so powerful that even the tide would obey him.

Vain Canute, 39, decided to test their theory and made aides carry him and his throne down to the beach.

As the waves rolled in he raised his right hand and bellowed: "Halt!"

But the water kept on coming and swamped the Royal toes.

Last night a team of spin doctors were doing their utmost to spare the King's blushes — by claiming the whole thing was a **STUNT.**

FOOLISH

They insisted Canute was play-acting because he wanted to show the world that his simpering courtiers were foolish flatterers.

A spokesman said the Royal Family was confident that the farce would not affect his popularity.

He added: "The King would not really try to stop the waves — he is an intelligent and God-fearing man.

"I'm sure his many wise deeds will be remembered long after everyone has forgotten this silly business with the tide."

FULL AMAZING STORY
— Pages 4 and 5

1066

BATTLE OF HASTINGS

The city walls at Marrakech, Morocco, which was founded as capital of the Almoravides in 1062. Now a major trade centre, it has a population of more than 1.5million

...Timeline...

1035 Reign of King Harold I Harefoot begins in England.

1040 Beginning of reign of England's King Hardecanute.

1042 Saxon King Edward The Confessor reigns (he is made saint in 1161).

1054 Split between Catholic church of Rome and Orthodox Christian church of Byzantium.

1062 The Moroccan city of Marrakech is founded.

1065 Consecration of Westminster Abbey; Muslim Seljuk Turks invade Asia Minor.

1066 King Harold II takes throne on death of Edward the Confessor.

Edward the Confessor (1042), so called because of his deep religious devotion

King Harold Harefoot (left), King from 1035 and not to be confused with Harold of Hastings fame, and (right) King Hardecanute, who reigned for two years from 1040

THE year 1066 is probably the best-known date in history — and marks the last successful invasion of England.

William the Conqueror's decision to invade was born of a wrangle over who was the true successor of the English king Edward the Confessor.

When Edward died on January 5, 1066, the throne was taken by Harold Godwinson, the late king's brother-in-law and his closest adviser.

Harold had been ruling the kingdom in all but name for the previous few years and seemed the logical successor.

But he was not the only claimant to the throne.

Over the Channel, William, Duke of Normandy, believed HE was the rightful heir.

William was a blood relation of Edward and insisted he had actually been promised the throne by the King some 15 years earlier.

William also claimed that in 1064 Harold had sworn a sacred oath to accept him as overlord and support his claim to the throne.

So when Harold was crowned, William protested vigorously.

When his objections were ignored he began making plans to assert his claim by force.

Before William could launch his invasion Harold had to counter another threat — from Viking Harald Hardrada, of Norway, a third claimant to the throne.

Harald arrived with an army on England's north-east coast in mid-September 1066.

King Harold swiftly assembled his forces and marched day and night towards York to counter this new threat.

On September 25 the English intercepted their enemy at Stamford Bridge near York. The Vikings were utterly defeated, Hardrada himself among the dead.

But Harold's celebrations had barely begun before news arrived that William's 7,000-strong invasion force of archers, infantry and cavalry had landed near Pevensey in Sussex.

King Harold was forced to rally his weary troops for a gruelling 260-mile march south to meet the Normans.

The forces met near Hastings. Harold's army, half of whom were untrained peasants, were no match for William's archers.

Two of Harold's brothers were killed. Then the King himself was fatally shot in the eye by an arrow and William — later dubbed The Conqueror — was crowned King of England on Christmas Day.

Top, King Harold II, killed in battle against William of Normandy (above)

THE Sun

nday, October 16, 1066 — One farthing — THOUGHT: A PASTING AT HASTINGS

STORMIN'

Arrowing experience . . . King Harold is struck in the eye as the battle goes on around him. His death sparked panic among the English   **Picture stitched up by ANNE GLOSAXON**

NORMANS

One in eye for Harold at Hastings

By IRIS PAYNE

KING Harold was killed by an arrow in the eye as the invading Norman army stormed to victory at the Battle of Hastings.

Harold, 46, died as his brave English troops made a desperate last stand on a hill near the Sussex town.

Last night the 38-year-old Norman war leader Duke William was preparing to head for London.

Once there, he is expected to demand that he is immediately crowned the new

EXCLUSIVE

King of England. More than 4,000 soldiers are thought to have died in Saturday's epic eight-hour battle.

In the early stages King Harold's men — standing shoulder-to-shoulder on top of the hill — had the upper hand.

But late in the afternoon cunning William ordered forward his archers, who poured volley after volley of arrows into the helpless English.

One pierced Harold's right eye — fatally wounding him and sending panic through the English ranks. William ordered his cavalry to stage a full frontal attack. As

they advanced, most of the English army began to retreat. The retreat soon turned into a rout as men fled for their lives.

But Harold's personal bodyguard refused to move. They surrounded their dying King and fought almost to the last man before William called a halt to the slaughter.

After the battle the Normans were unable to discover which of the thousands of dead warriors lying on the hill was Harold.

Eventually his long-term mistress Edith Swan-Neck was brought to the site to identify his body.

Last night Harold's mother Gytha offered William her son's weight in gold in return for the right to bury him. William is thought to be considering the offer.

Harold KO'd By Will Power — Pages Two and Three

INVASION OF THE NORMANS

HAROLD KO'd BY WILL POWER

Conqueror's awesome army crushes King

We will not be moved . . . King Harold's men stand shoulder to shoulder

KING Harold did everything right at the Battle of Hastings but was still defeated by the terrible power of William the Conqueror's awesome army.

Harold had seen the Normans in action before and was well aware that William's fierce cavalrymen would cut down his mainly unarmoured soldiers in a straight fight.

So on Saturday he cunningly lined his men up for 800 yards along brow of a rise known as Senlac Hill.

Harold knew that if the Norman cavalry charged, the horses' momentum would be slowed as they came up the hill — making them less effective.

The battle began at about 9.30am with William's 7,000-strong army moving slowly towards Harold's men. The Normans advanced with archers in front, the heavier-armed foot soldiers behind them and the fearsome cavalry at the rear.

As the two armies got within about 100 yards of each other the English shuffled together, overlapping their shields so there was no gap for the enemy to penetrate.

The English line formed up 12 deep. In the front line were the famous Housecarls — hardened professional soldiers.

Panic

Behind them were the peasants and farmers called to arms by Harold to defend England.

William's attack began with a shower of arrows — an attempt to "soften up" the enemy. After this his infantry passed between the ranks of bowmen and marched up the slope for hand-to-hand combat with the English.

The fighting was grim and both sides suffered heavy casualties.

But the English had the advantage of the hill and eventually the Normans retreated.

As William rode up and down the line urging his men to stand firm he tumbled from his horse. Immediately word passed through the Norman lines that William was dead. Panic began to grip the army.

William scrambled back on to his horse and, lifting his helmet so all could see him, yelled: "Look at me! I am alive and through the grace of God shall conquer!"

So far the English discipline had been superb. But a large group of peasant spearmen were so delighted at the sight of the Normans falling back that they ran after them.

They soon found themselves isolated from the English lines and surrounded by Norman cavalry who swiftly cut them down. At about noon William decided to hurl his cavalry at the English. They

By ANNE ARCHER

charged up the hill and slammed into Harold's men. The line buckled but stood firm.

As the Normans and English traded deadly blows William's horse was killed under him.

He grabbed a young Norman cavalryman, dragged him from the saddle and took his mount before rejoining the fighting.

But it was clear the Normans were not going to break through, and the cavalry pulled back.

It was now around 2pm. Cunning William suddenly remembered how part of the English line had broken away when his troops retreated earlier and decided to try a repeat.

He ordered his men forward again, but after a few exchanges of blows a body of Normans turned and appeared to flee. Again a section of the English line broke away and chased them — only to be ridden down by cavalrymen.

Volley

William tried the trick a couple more times, each time weakening the English line.

Some time around 4pm the Norman archers came back into the attack — pouring volley after volley of arrows into Harold's men. One struck Harold in the eye and he fell dying to the ground.

Panic gripped the English force and they began to flee. William realised victory was close and launched his cavalry forward again.

On the hill the housecarls surrounded their dying King.

But they were exhausted and unable to stop a group of Normans from breaking through their cordon and hacking Harold's lifeless body to pieces.

Ready to rumble . . . the deadly Norman cavalry get set to charge up the hill towards the English battle line

NVASION OF THE NORMANS

Cutting edge of a killing machine

THE Norman army is feared throughout Europe for its savagery and ruthless efficiency.

It boasts large numbers of soldiers armed with bows — some of them the deadly new crossbow.

There are also thousands of infantrymen wielding spears and javelins.

But the backbone of the army is made up of cavalrymen who are covered in chain-mail armour and protected by a large kite-shaped shield.

In the past 20 years the Normans have inflicted a number of devastating defeats on the French.

And groups of Norman adventurers have even managed to carve themselves out a kingdom in southern Italy.

Fearsome

Most of Harold's army is made up of part-time soldiers — peasant spearmen who are called to the ranks when the king needs them. They are unarmoured.

The only truly professional soldiers are a body of Royal troops known as the Housecarls.

These men were originally Danish — and have kept Viking-style weapons. They are principally armed with a fearsome battle axe.

This is up to 5ft long and in the hands of a trained man can cut a horse and rider in two with one blow.

The Housecarls are also protected by a large shield and a knee-length coat of chain-mail.

The English have no cavalry, although sometimes the Housecarls ride to battle on horses, then dismount to fight.

ABBEY WILL MARK SITE

WILLIAM was last night said to be planning to build a huge abbey on the site of Saturday's battle.

He hopes it will make up for the slaughter that took place to further his claim to the throne.

The Normans are also believed to be planning to commemorate the battle with a huge tapestry that shows the fighting.

William secured the approval of the Pope before he launched his invasion. His Holiness even excommunicated King Harold.

sh of the titans . . . the soldiers exchange axe and sword blows as the Normans charge. Inset, the wife of an English soldier waits anxiously behind the lines

294,891 DAYS TO GO

1192

Metal cover and extract from Domesday Book, a remarkably detailed survey of England compiled by panels of commissioners working for William The Conqueror in 1086

. . . Timeline . . .

1071 Seljuks defeat Byzantine army at Battle of Manzikert.

1072 Norman armies begin to conquer Sicily.

1077 Pope Gregory expels Holy Roman Emperor Henry IV from church.

1078 King William begins building the Tower of London.

1086 Survey of England, by order of William, recorded in Domesday Book.

1087 William II (Rufus), son of William The Conqueror, is King.

1088 Bayeux Tapestry, depicting the Battle of Hastings, is completed.

1090 A water-driven clock is built in China.

1096 Christian rulers from Europe go on First Crusade to retake Palestine from Saracens.

1098 Monastery founded at Citeaux, France — marking start of Cistercian order of monks.

1099 Crusaders capture Jerusalem from Muslims amid terrible slaughter.

1100 King Henry I begins his reign after Rufus dies in hunting accident; Rise of Inca people, farmers and warriors, in Peru.

1115 Henry IV makes Paris centre of religious learning.

1119 Bologna University is founded in Italy.

1120 Chinese invent painted playing cards.

1124 King David I begins his reign in Scotland.

1135 Reign of King Stephen begins in England; Birth of Jewish philosopher Maimonides (Rabbi Moses ben Maimon).

1139 Alphonso I becomes first king of Portugal.

1144 St Denis Abbey, first Gothic church, completed in Paris.

1149 Christian armies of Second Crusade defeated by Turks in Asia Minor.

1150 Founding of the University of Paris.

1152 Start of the reign of powerful Holy Roman Emperor Frederick I, called Barbarossa (red beard).

1154 Beginning of reign in England of Plantagenet King Henry II — he reforms law and government; Nicholas Breakspear becomes Pope Adrian IV, only English pope.

1163 Birth of Genghis Khan, creator of Mongol empire; French begin to build Notre Dame Cathedral, Paris.

Left, the Muslim warrior Saladin (1171). Right, Thomas a Becket, killed in 1170

Bologna University, one of Europe's oldest and most famous, was founded in 1119

1170 Archbishop Thomas a Becket is murdered in Canterbury cathedral by knights of King Henry II, whom he opposed.

1171 Henry II invades Ireland and is accepted as its lord; Saladin, Muslim warrior and commander in Egyptian army, overthrows Fatimid dynasty and declares himself sultan of Egypt.

1173 Saladin begins conquest of Palestine and Syria, taking Damascus.

1175 First mention of football in English literature.

1180 Philip II Augustus begins rule in France, conquering Angevin lands in the west.

1187 Saladin defeats Christians at Hattin and takes Jerusalem.

1189 Reign of King Richard I "The Lionheart" begins.

1190 Teutonic Order of knights set up in Germany to defend Christian lands in Palestine and Syria.

1192 Truce between Richard I and Saladin ends Third Crusade.

RICHARD & THE CRUSADES

RICHARD I's exploits in the Third Crusade have left him one of England's most famous kings.

The crusades began in 1095 when the Pope called on the Christian nobles of western Europe to rescue the holy city of Jerusalem from the Saracens, the name given to the muslims living in the area.

A year later the First Crusade set out and in 1099 captured Jerusalem amid terrible slaughter. In 1148 the Second Crusade was launched, intending to add much-needed reinforcements to the small crusader kingdoms that had been set up in the Middle East.

Then in 1187 disaster struck when the army of King Guy of Jerusalem was destroyed by the famous Saracen general Saladin at the Battle of Hattin. Three months later Saladin captured Jerusalem.

The fall of Jerusalem stunned Europe. The Pope immediately called for a new crusade to retake the holy city.

In 1190 King Richard of England, known as the Lionheart because of his bravery in battle, set out for the Holy Land.

Richard, who stopped off on the way to conquer the island of Cyprus, arrived in June 1191. He discovered the crusader forces were besieging the coastal city of Acre and took command.

On July 12 Acre surrendered and Richard took almost 3,000 Saracen soldiers prisoner along with their wives and children.

He agreed to spare their lives in exchange for a large sum in gold. But when Saladin was late paying the money the prisoners were executed on Richard's orders.

Five weeks later the armies of Richard and Saladin clashed at the Battle of Arsuf. Richard was heavily outnumbered, but once again showed his military talent. He drew his knights up behind ranks of bowmen and spearmen and ordered them not to charge until he gave the word.

Wave after wave of Saracen cavalry attacks bounced off the disciplined Crusader lines. The attacks went on until the Saracens began to tire. At that moment a thousand crusader knights surged forward.

The terrified Saracens turned and fled — or were crushed beneath the knights' horses. The result was a total victory for Richard.

Most of Saladin's army was, however, still intact. On August 5, 1192, Saladin caught Richard by surprise outside the city of Jaffa. Saladin's army consisted of at least 7,000 cavalrymen.

Richard had about 2,000 infantry and just 54 knights, of whom only 15 had horses. He drew his men up shoulder-to-shoulder in a tight semi-circle. In front of them were hammered a line of tent-pegs designed to impale enemy horsemen who tried to break through their line.

The Saracens attacked seven times. Each time they were driven off by the small crusader force. As each attack pulled back Richard sent forward his archers to pour volley after volley of arrows into the Saracen ranks. As daylight began to fade Saladin realised the battle was lost and retreated.

The crusaders had won against all the odds thanks to Richard's tactical genius. But the King was still no nearer to capturing Jerusalem. To make matters worse he was ill with a fever — and there was unwelcome news from England that his brother John was stirring up trouble.

Reluctantly, Richard decided he must go home. On September 2 he signed a five-year peace treaty with Saladin. It allowed Christian pilgrims to visit Jerusalem — but the city was to remain in Saracen hands.

A month later Richard sailed away from the Holy Land. On his way home he was captured by his enemy Henry VI of Germany. Richard spent more than a year in jail until a huge ransom was paid.

After his release he spent five years fighting the French King Philip Augustus. It was during this conflict, on March 26, 1199, that Richard was killed by an arrow fired from a French castle he was besieging.

Origins of football

AN early type of football was often played on festival days in medieval England. Neighbouring villages staged matches with more than 50 a side, using an inflated animal bladder as a ball.

The game would start at the mid-point between the two villages and the teams would kick, punch, throw and carry the ball forward. Once they reached the outskirts of the rival village they had scored. The game was extremely violent. Serious injuries were common. Sometimes players died.

In 1389 Richard II banned the game because it interfered with archery practice.

rsday, August 6, 1192

SunSport — CRUSADERS 3 SARACENS 0

3 LIONS ON HIS TUNIC

Ruthless Rizza mauls heathens

By WILL LANCEM

KING Richard the Lionheart yesterday led his England team to its **THIRD** stunning Crusades victory over the Saracens.

Rizza, 34, amazed all the pundits with the latest win outside the city of Jaffa in the Holy Land.

The King was outnumbered by the forces of the Saracen commander Saladin — and had the disadvantage of playing away from home.

To make matters worse many of his best attackers, the heavily-armoured knights, had been left out because of injury.

But Rizza, who has already done the double over Saladin at the battles of Acre and Arsuf, defended brilliantly.

And when the Saracens began to tire after hours of fruitless attacks, the Crusader knights charged forward — and the Saracens turned and fled.

Proud Rizza said last night: "I'm over the moon. All credit to the boys, they played a blinder."

A Knight To Remember — Pages 46 and 47

VILLAGE FOOTBALL LATEST
Middle Wallop...1   Nether Wallop...0
(86 sent off, 12 dead)

TRIKER

MAN ON, RIZZA!

NO, NO, NOT ON ME 'ED SON!

HAVE MERCY

HE THINKS IT'S ALL OVER...

IT IS NOW!

1215

St Francis of Assisi, who founded the Franciscan order in 1209, was a great lover of nature. Here, he is depicted preaching to the animals he called his 'brothers and sisters'

. . . Timeline . . .

1196 Genghis Khan becomes leader of the mongols.

1199 Reign of King John begins in England — supposed lifetime of legendary outlaw Robin Hood.

1209 St Francis of Assisi founds Franciscan religious order.

1212 Christians defeat the Muslim Almohads at Las Navas de Tolosa, Spain.

KING JOHN & MAGNA CARTA

THE signing of the Magna Carta is traditionally seen as the moment when English kings acknowledged that even they must obey the law of the land.

The ceremony itself, on the banks of the River Thames at Runnymede, marked the climax of King John's struggle with his barons.

The dispute had its roots in the feudal structure of English society.

Under the feudal system relationships between the King and his barons were dictated by a complex list of rights and duties.

In simple terms, the barons provided military services to the King and he provided them with protection and grants of land.

The King was also supposed to consult his barons before raising taxes or demanding large amounts of military service.

The system worked well as long as the King was wealthy, powerful and successful in war. John, nicknamed Lackland because of his relative poverty, was none of these.

Nevertheless, he was determined to fight to hold on to his family's lands in France — territory the French king Philip Augustus was determined to take over.

John's early military campaigns in France failed, so he demanded more taxes and increased military service from the barons. By 1204 he had lost all his lands in France.

He responded by taxing his English subjects still higher without his barons' consent, which was against feudal law. In 1214 he again went to war with the French — but was once more defeated.

When he returned home and attempted to collect even more money to fund renewed campaigns in France the barons revolted.

The rebel lords raised an army and captured London. But in the spring of 1215 John agreed to make concessions and the two sides met at Runnymede.

The result was the Magna Carta — or Great Charter in Latin — in which John agreed to abide by feudal law and guarantee the legal rights of citizens.

But John had little intention of keeping his word. Almost immediately he asked the Pope to declare the document invalid.

He argued that his promise to uphold the agreement was extorted by force. The Pope agreed and announced the Magna Carta was null and void.

News of the annulment caused the barons to revolt again. In October 1216, while the conflict was still going on, John died.

Cult of the holy relics

THE collecting and hoarding of holy relics — usually the bones of dead saints — was an integral part of medieval Christian worship.

The relics, often finger bones or skulls, were brought back from the Holy Land by crusaders. Most of them were fakes. The relics, thought to have miraculous powers, were housed in churches across Europe. So eager was each church to have its own relic that clerics would often steal them from each other.

Once, a bishop of Lincoln who was paying his respects to the arm of Mary Magdalene at Fecamp in Normandy bit off a fragment of her index finger to take home.

Robin Hood (see 1199), meets Friar Tuck (left) and greets return of King Richard I (right, above left)

THE Sun

esday, June 16, 1215 · One farthing · THOUGHT: NOBLE GESTURE

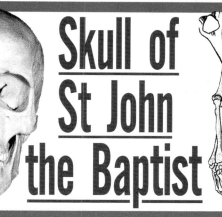

Skull of St John the Baptist

Bones of St Mark the Hermit

The Boots of St Angreavsie the pundit

INSIDE: ROBIN HOOD WRITES FOR THE Sun ... HE'S A PAL OF LITTLEJOHN

YOUR ROYAL SLYNESS

Crafty King will KO Magna Carta

By PIERS PRESSURE

TYRANNICAL King John solemnly pledged yesterday to rule England fairly — then immediately started making plans to break his word.

Angry barons made John, 48, sign a document called the Magna Carta which guarantees justice for all.

It stresses that no man may be imprisoned or outlawed on the whim of the King.

And it insists all subjects have the right to be judged "by the law of the land".

But last night Royal insiders claimed sly John intends to ask the Pope to declare the document invalid — because he was forced to agree to it.

One courtier said: "John never had the slightest intention of giving in to the barons.

WARS

"But he knew he had to do something to stop them declaring war, so he decided to agree to their demands just to gain some breathing space."

The document was signed at Runnymede, near Windsor. More than 20 of John's barons vowed to make him stick to the agreement — by force if necessary.

The barons acted after hard-up John imposed crippling taxes to fund his wars in France.

He ordered his men to attack or imprison anyone who resisted.

Last night a spokesman for the barons warned that there would be bloodshed if John broke his word. He added: "It will lead to a war that King John cannot win."

That Magna Carta In Full — in Latin on Page 11 and in English on Page 12

On the Runnymede . . . King John in negotiation with the barons yesterday before signing the Magna Carta

Jeremy Clarkson

When the cart really does come before the horse

IT'S all very well drooling over the latest two-seater Arab, with its leather seats and 40mph top speed, the simple fact of the matter is this: You need space for the family and the hay.

So while a Welsh cob can undoubtedly snap knicker elastic at 500 paces, you have to forget about horses and even donkeys. They're too fast, too expensive and too impractical.

That's why we're looking this week at the latest ox cart to hit the market square — the Magna Cart Deluxe.

Powered by two oxen, each of which does 40 miles to the flagon, it's cheap to run, but there's no shortage of power.

Even in the boggiest meadows of central London, the sheer torque coupled to the eight-leg-drive system means you're rarely stuck. Skinny 105 wheels on the trailer help too.

Mead

And then, once you're clear of the plague pits and in open country, you hold on to your sack-cloth and unleash the beasts. Magna's makers claim a top speed of 7mph, which puts Winchester just eight days away.

However, with the recent increase in mead-related accidents — and still no sign of that breathalyser Philippa Sorrester talked about on The Morrow's World — safety is important, especially if carrying children.

And I'm delighted to say the Magna is right up there with recent imports from the Vikings.

By making the cart from deformable willow rather than solid oak, passengers are surrounded by an effective crumple zone.

And if the driver has followed the instructions in the handbook and fed the oxen with beans, he'll be thrown forward on to what is basically a double gas

Quite a beast . . . Magna Cart Deluxe may not have the looks of the horse, but as a people-carrier it's spacious and very well-ventilated

bag. Of particular note is the forward-facing horn system, designed to pierce any oncoming lord.

Even the most arrogant, bray-ing Hooray Henry is going to look pretty silly when he crashes head-on into you and gets impaled on your ox's head.

''I had that Marquis of Blandford on the front of my cow last week'' . . .

Maybe this will slow the aristocrats down on their Hillhorse Hunters and Finger Gazelles.

As far as comfort's concerned, the Magna Deluxe is not good. Certainly, with those giant wooden wheels and cart springs, it's no match for the latest German machines. Compared to the Bavarian Mule Wagon, or BMW for short, the Brit is left far behind.

But the Magna does have some tasty optional extras. There's the ''Roman Feast'' paint scheme for a kick-off and, for just 1d a week extra, you can even have music on the move. He's called Marvin the Minstrel and he'll sit wherever you tell him to sit.

So, as a simple, cheap load-lugger with good, high driving position, the Magna is not a bad first-time effort.

Go cart . . . with a sporty paint job like t[...] hay won't be the only thing you're pullin[...]

QUICK GETA-BRAY

WITH the peasantry under the cosh from the nobles thanks to our feudal system, many country dwellers are on the lookout for good, used transport that's fast and agile.

When the lord comes rolling into the village on his armoured shire horse named Volvo (Latin for ''I roll''), you need to get away. And fast.

The mule is an obvious choice. With its fly-ridden bottom and stupid face, it is not cool enough for high society, so prices are depressed.

But with the pace of a horse and the stubborn determination of a horse, it makes a useful getaway tool.

I tested one last week and reckon it's good for 20mph. Prices start at 1 shilling but many dealers will take a hen or some beads in part-ex.

Mule . . . ideal workhorse

HONKING AT 4am

MOST of us are hard-pressed financially, what with paying all King John's new taxes, and theft is sadly becoming an all-too-common problem.

And whether it's youngsters after a joyride or the more determined thief who'll break up your transport for food, many victims are taking the law into their own hands.

But vigilante groups are warning against the use of

Goose . . . makes big din

geese. A spokesman said [...] week that while they do m[...] a loud whooping noise wh[...] ever someone comes ne[...] they will also cackle [...] idiots at four o'clock in [...] morning for no rea[...] whatsoever.

People worried about h[...] ing their oxen stolen sho[...] call the Lord, who'll sen[...] knight round to chop [...] head off.

Robin Hood's DIARY

HE'S A LAW UNTO HIMSELF

THE latest of our thrilling weekly instalments chronicling the life of the legendary Nottingham-based do-gooder . . .

MONDAY

AS usual the Merry Men and I begin the week with our wealth-redistribution scheme — or Robbing From The Rich, as we call it.

For the first time we are wearing our new uniform of Lincoln Green tunics and tights. These were Maid Marian's idea — she says they give us "corporate identity".

At 10am we rob some clergymen making their way through Sherwood and are about to run off when I notice Will Scarlett's missing.

We find him behind some trees, parading up and down and saying: "Does my bum look big in this?"

TUESDAY

THE second leg of the scheme, the bit known as Giving To The Poor — which frankly always depresses me.

I take two gold coins to the mad old bloke who lives on the edge of the forest.

I knock on his door and say: "I am Robin Hood, outlaw and righter of wrongs. I live in Sherwood Forest with my Merry Men and we take from the rich and give to the poor."

He answers: "If it's about the poll tax, I won't pay till me drains are fixed." Me: "No sir, you are missing the point. You're the poor and I'm giving you money." Mad bloke: "I don't want charity. And I'm not as poor or mad as you. You're the one living in a tree and wearing tights."

You'd never believe how ungrateful the poor can be.

WEDNESDAY

THE weekly Merry Men group therapy session.

Friar Tuck fears he may be bulimic. Apparently, for lunch yesterday he ate two chickens, a haunch of venison, two pheasants and a bowl of gruel with three pints of mead. Afterwards he felt a bit sick.

Little John is worried we may be giving ourselves a reputation as a soft touch by not inflicting enough violence during robberies. He suggests we dismember the rich.

Alan A Dale points out that such butchery could change our historical status from heroes to murderers, which if nothing else will put us in a different tax bracket. Nonetheless Little John is to do a feasibility study and report back.

THURSDAY

LUNCH with Sheriff of Nottingham at his castle. Over the cheese and biscuits he drops a bombshell — he wants to buy out the Merry Men and relaunch us as a profit-making body with each outlaw on commission. I promise to put it to the lads.

FRIDAY

I SPLIT up with Maid Marian again. She's been negotiating with a ballad writer for some songs based on our exploits, but he thinks it lacks love interest. So up she pipes: "Perhaps it would help if we got married."

Honestly, I should have seen it coming. It all comes out again . . . how she is 32 and still a maid, how her biological clock is ticking, etc, etc. Anyway, she packs and leaves.

SATURDAY

AS usual Saturday is devoted to sport, and today's our annual match against the Sheriff's team — a contest locals call Nottingham Forest v Nottingham County for some reason.

The first section is jousting — not our strong point as we have little need for horses in the forest.

Friar Tuck is unhorsed straight away by the Sheriff's champion Sir Roger de Linquant. The fans chant: "He's fat, he's round, he's fallen on the ground." 1-0 to them.

Next up, wooden stave fighting — Little John beats his opponent but then insists on cutting off his head and limbs. How many times have I told him about this? Our fans are delirious, though, and sing: "He's going home in a horse-drawn ambulance." 1-1 at half time.

Next, archery. I do brilliantly, notching three straight bull's eyes to give us a 2-1 lead as we head into the final game, the chivalry quiz.

The boys and I score high on questions about siege techniques and battlefield looting, less well on heraldry. It's level at 2-2, one question left. The quizmaster asks: "You storm a castle and find a damsel in distress. What is the correct procedure?"

Little John yells: "Strangle her, then cut off her head and limbs!"

You couldn't make it up. The Sheriff's men win 3-2.

SUNDAY

WALK to the village for the Sunday newsparchments, only to see a headline in the Feudal Times: "ROBIN'S MEN AIN'T MERRY — THEY'RE GAY! Maid Marian tells all".

Five pages of Marian's rantings about how I preferred to spend my time prancing about in a wood with the lads rather than with her.

Little John sees it and storms off, muttering about reporters and cutting off body parts.

Will Scarlett takes a job with William Tell's outfit and Friar Tuck tries to end it all by suffocating himself with a giant veal and ham pie.

Then the Sheriff scraps the buyout "in the light of adverse publicity." Let's hope next week's better.

LITTLE JOHN IS ON HOLIDAY

Our Robin . . . you couldn't make him up

Kublai Khan led the Mongol empire from 1260

1295

LIFE OF MARCO POLO

MARCO Polo made a vast fortune during his two decades travelling in China — and described the wonders of Asia to westerners for the first time.

He was born into a well-off merchant family in Venice, Italy, in 1254 — and when he was only six was left at home while his father Niccolo and uncle Maffeo went on the first of their long trips to China.

The Polo brothers knew they could earn huge sums importing exotic goods into Europe from the Far East along the so-called Silk Road from China. The key was to become trusted by the Mongol overlords — and this the Polos did.

Eventually they met China's Mongol ruler Kublai Khan, an intelligent man with a love of culture, and he warmly welcomed them.

In 1269 he sent the Polos back to Europe, instructing them to return with scholars who could tell him all about Christianity.

In 1271 Niccolo and Maffeo left Venice on a three-year trek back to the Khan's glittering palace — this time taking Marco, 17.

Khan liked Marco and made the young man with an inquiring mind a trusted aide. Marco was despatched far and wide as an ambassador and took detailed notes of everything he saw.

Of one province he wrote: "The silken fabrics and cloth of gold woven here are the finest ever seen. In the city of Tinju they make bowls of porcelain of incomparable beauty. Nothing lovelier could be imagined."

Marco, his father and uncle finally returned as rich men to Venice in 1295, long after they had been

Marco Polo, who spent two decades travelling in the Far East and writing

given up for dead by their family. Locals were spellbound by Marco's tales of the East and he was dubbed Marco Milione because of his millions of stories.

Four years later he was taken prisoner for a year during a local war and while there told his stories to a writer named Rustichello.

Rustichello published them in the 1299 book The Description of the World. It was a huge hit and later translated into several languages.

Marco returned to Venice and died in 1324. But the book of his life in China was for years a key reference for merchants, map-makers and mariners — including 15th Century explorer Christopher Columbus.

... Timeline ...

1216 Beginning of the Reign of Henry III in England.

1240 Russian Prince Alexander Nevsky defeats invading Swedes at the Neva river.

1249 University College, first college of Oxford University, founded.

1260 Genghis Khan's grandson Kublai elected Mongol ruler.

1262 Iceland and Greenland come under Norwegian rule.

1265 First English parliament meets in Westminster.

1272 Edward I is crowned King in England.

1273 Rudolph I becomes first Habsburg ruler of Austria.

1284 Edward conquers Wales; Peterhouse, first college of Cambridge University, founded.

1291 Three Swiss cantons join to begin struggle for independence from Habsburgs.

Photo from 1938 movie Alexander Nevsky, based on battle of 1240

Invention of spectacles

SEVERAL people are credited with having invented glasses — although at the time they were believed to be the devil's handiwork.

It is believed that glass had been used to magnify objects as early as the 10th Century.

But Italian monk Salvino degli Armati is thought to have developed the first spectacles to correct poor eyesight some time around 1290.

A translation of the words on his headstone reads: "The inventor of spectacles. May God pardon his sins. AD 1317".

The Oxford-based Franciscan monk Roger Bacon, who lived from 1210 to 1294, was also credited with the invention. But he wrote that specs originated in Italy.

Bacon was accused of witchcraft for his dabblings with lenses, mirrors and light — and served ten years in jail.

First known painting of man in specs

Oxford University's first college, University College, which was founded in 1249. Peterhouse, the first college of Cambridge University, was founded 35 years later

THE Sun

Saturday, December 10, 1295   One farthing   THOUGHT: VENETIAN BLINDER

Polo's made mint

Hattaboy .. Marco last night

EXPLORER'S RICH AFTER 24yr TREK

By RICHIE PICKINS

EXPLORER Marco Polo, who was missing presumed dead in China, has returned home out of the blue after 24 years — and he's LOADED.

The Italian, 41, has now been nick-named "Marco Millions" since he arrived back in Venice laden down with treasures.

And crowds are gathering at his house to hear the astonishing tale of his travels, which included journeying across the Gobi desert.

Marco set off on the jaunt with his jewel merchant dad when he was only 17 — and went on to become a favourite of China's powerful Mongol ruler Kublai Khan. He even toured the country as Khan's ambassador.

One Venetian said yesterday: "He is a man with a million stories."

He Made His Marco — Pages 4 and 5

A SIGHT FOR POOR EYES AS SPECS ARE INVENTED

By DI FOCALS

A CRAFTY monk has fixed his dodgy sight by making glass lenses to look through.

Salvino degli Armati — who became short-sighted while conducting physics experiments — now reckons he can see perfectly.

It is believed that the thick glass somehow "bends" light.

Armati, of Pisa, Italy, has nailed two lenses together so they fit over both eyes. Other more stylish models are now being made.

Mel Gibson, in his Oscar-winning movie Braveheart, starred as the Scottish warrior William Wallace, who routed the English army at the Battle of Stirling Bridge in 1297

1348
THE BLACK DEATH

THE plague known as the Black Death was the greatest catastrophe to hit mankind — killing more than 20 million people.

The epidemic, which began in rats and was spread by the fleas which lived on them, broke out first in central Asia.

By 1346 it had spread to the Crimea. By 1347 it had travelled along the trade routes to Asia Minor, Egypt, Sicily and Italy.

In 1348 it spread to France, Spain and England before sweeping into Germany, Russia, Scandinavia and the rest of Europe.

The death toll from the Black Death, or bubonic plague, was huge. In 1348 in Cairo 7,000 people were said to be dying every day.

In Europe the plague is estimated to have killed a third of the population in just three years.

In England, where it probably arrived in June 1348, the death toll is thought to have been as many as 1.4million.

About 30,000 people are believed to have died in London. Certain professions, including doctors and clergymen who came into contact with the sick, suffered an even higher death rate.

The bubonic plague virus was spread by fleas that were living on infected black rats and feeding on their tainted blood. When the fleas came into contact with humans they would bite them, passing on the disease.

A more infectious form of the Black Death — the pneumonic plague — was spread by coughing.

Symptoms included high fevers and vomiting of blood. Another characteristic was a swelling of the lymph nodes in the neck, armpits and groin. These swellings expanded until they eventually burst. Death followed rapidly.

The cycle of the disease, from fever to death, took only three or four days. Its swiftness and the terrible pain and grotesque symptoms it caused all served to make the plague terrifying to medieval man.

Not surprisingly there was panic as the epidemic spread. Many townspeople fled into the countryside when it arrived — often carrying the disease with them.

At the time it was widely believed the plague had been sent by God to punish mankind for its sins.

This belief led many to attempt bizarre acts of penance. One result was the strange sect of the flagellants. These were groups of people, sometimes 1,000 strong, who wandered from town to town whipping themselves in public.

. . . Timeline . . .

1297 William "Braveheart" Wallace and his men rout English army at Battle of Stirling Bridge.

1300 Incas begin to expand empire throughout central Andes.

1305 First private postal service in Europe.

1307 Beginning of the reign of Edward II in England.

1314 Scots defeat English at Bannockburn, led by Robert Bruce.

1325 Aztecs found Tenochtitlan (now Mexico City).

1327 Edward II murdered in castle dungeon by the insertion of a red-hot poker — reign of Edward III begins.

1328 England recognises independence of Scotland.

1330 Birth of Edward, the Black Prince, who wore black armour in battle.

1337 Edward III claims French throne, leading to 100 Years' War.

1339 Kremlin, originally made from wood, rebuilt in brick in Moscow.

1346 English defeat the French at Battle of Crecy.

1347 Black Death devastates Egypt and reaches Italy.

Robert the Bruce led the Scots in another rout of the English at Bannockburn in 1314

The tomb of Edward, the Black Prince, who was born in 1330, and (above) an illustration of the Kremlin palace in Moscow, originally made from wood but rebuilt in brick in 1339

THE Sun

Garry BUSHELL
ON THE POX
See Page 11

Wednesday, June 25, 1348   **One farthing**   **THOUGHT: FLEA FOR YOUR LIFE**

'BLACK DEATH TO KILL MILLIONS'

Terror plague hits Britain

Swift and deadly . . . man carries young plague victim

By PHIL GRIMM

A PLAGUE which experts predict will kill **MILLIONS** across Europe has claimed its first victims in Britain, it was revealed last night.

The pestilence, for which there is no known cure, has struck in Bristol and Dorset.

The epidemic, known as the Black Death, has already wiped out hundreds of thousands of people in Italy, Greece, France and Eastern Europe. It is thought to be passed on by rats and fleas and is highly contagious.

The first symptoms are fever and stomach cramps. Then painful black swellings appear over victims' bodies. Most die within four days.

How To Spot A Plague Victim — Pages Eight and Nine

King Richard II, with his patron saints behind him. He came to throne in 1377, aged only ten, so the country was run by nobles led by his uncle John of Gaunt, Duke of Lancaster

... Timeline ...

1354 Several die in three-day "town ver-sus gown" battle between Oxford residents and students — there is still tension in the city today.

1358 The Jacquerie Revolt by French peasants.

1364 Birth of Sir Henry "Harry Hotspur" Percy, who inspired Shakespeare's Hotspur in Henry IV.

1370 Geoffrey Chaucer writes Book of the Duchess, his first work.

1373 Treaty of Anglo-Portuguese friend-ship — England and Portugal are still allies today.

1377 Richard II is crowned King in England.

1380 Foundation of Kongo kingdom in Congo region of Zaire, Africa.

Geoffrey Chaucer, who wrote his first work, Book of the Duchess, in 1370 and went on to write the Canterbury Tales

1381
PEASANTS' REVOLT

THE Peasants' Revolt led by Wat Tyler in 1381 was sparked by a series of unpopular taxes.

The first had been imposed four years earlier and demanded a groat (four pennies) from every adult.

This was followed in 1379 by a graded tax that ran from a groat for the poor to ten marks (a little over 13 shillings in medieval money) for the rich.

Then in 1380 a new poll tax was imposed — demanding a shilling from all men and women over 15.

The officials of the 14-year-old Richard II tried to soften the blow by saying that in each district the rich should help the poor to pay the tax.

Large numbers of people tried to evade payment, but tax collectors were sent to their homes to take the money by force.

The heavy-handed tactics back-fired — and in 1381 protests began among the peasants in Essex, Kent and other rural areas.

They soon became riots involv-ing looting, arson and murder.

The Kent rebels chose as their leader Walter Tyler, known as Wat, who was from the gentry.

In fact many of the rioters were reasonably well-off men and women who had scores to set-tle against local officials.

The other leaders of the revolt were Jack Straw, about whom little is known, and the former clerics John Wrawe and John Ball. On June 7, Tyler and his followers took control of Canterbury, opened Maidstone Jail and marched towards London.

Just under a week later Tyler's men met the Essex peasants outside London and stormed into the city at Aldgate.

The rebels burned John of Gaunt's London palace, along with Fleet Prison and a hospital.

On June 15 the young King rode to Mile End to hear the rebels' demands.

Tyler stood before the King and asked for the scrapping of the poll tax, abolition of serfdom and the right to rent land at four pence an acre.

During the conference Tyler argued with one of the King's valets and drew a knife. William Walworth, mayor of London, intervened and Tyler was killed.

His body was carried to a hospi-tal. But it was found by Walworth who had the corpse dragged out and beheaded.

Meanwhile the peasants agreed to disperse after the King promised to grant their demands.

Once the danger had passed the King changed his mind.

There were a few further out-breaks of trouble among the peas-antry throughout June and July, but by the end of the summer the great Peasants' Revolt was over.

Wat Tyler, leader of Peasants' Revolt, is killed after drawing a knife during a confrontation with young King Richard. Tyler's corpse was beheaded (1381)

THE Sun

Friday, June 14, 1381   **One farthing**   THOUGHT: A GREEN AND PEASANT LAND

POLL TAX RIOTERS GO ON RAMPAGE

By ROB M BLIND

HUNDREDS of peasants ran amok through the streets of London yesterday after a poll tax protest exploded into violence.

They set light to a number of buildings in the Aldgate area, including a prison, a hospital and the house of a nobleman.

Some lawyers and Government officials were attacked and wounded. A few were last night fighting for life. Most of the rioters are from Essex or Kent.

The peasants were whipped into a frenzy by ex-priest John Ball, who made a speech saying God intended all men should be equal. He added: "When Adam dug and Eve span, who was then a noble man?"

LETS GIVE 'EM WAT FOR

Sun backs revolt by peasants

THE Sun today urges all its readers to join our campaign backing the rebel peasants and their leader Wat Tyler.

Young King Richard's decision to impose a poll tax on every adult has left many serfs penniless.

Now, following a series of poll tax riots, Richard has agreed to meet Wat and discuss the peasants' grievances.

And we need **YOU** to help us make the King realise that the nation is backing Wat.

All you have to do to get the message across is wear one of our Wat Tyler T-shirts bearing the slogan: Life Ain't Pleasant For A Peasant. Turn to Page Nine to find out more.

...Timeline...

1386 Geoffrey Chaucer begins writing his Canterbury Tales.

1389 Christian Serbs defeated by Ottoman Turks at Kosovo in Serbia.

1390 Ottoman Turks complete the conquest of Asia Minor.

1394 The First English school is started at Winchester.

1397 Kalmar Agreement unites the three Scandinavian kingdoms of Denmark, Norway and Sweden under single king, Erik of Pomerania.

1399 King Henry IV, of the House of Lancaster, crowned in England.

1403 Ghiberti crafts realistic sculptures of human body in Florence, heralding Renaissance.

1413 Beginning of the reign of King Henry V in England.

1415 Henry leads outnumbered English force in famous rout of huge French army at Agincourt.

1417 End of Great Schism in Catholic church as single Pope elected in Rome.

1420 Portuguese sailors begin to explore west coast of Africa.

1421 Estimated 100,000 drown as sea breaks through dykes at Dort, Holland.

1422 King Henry VI takes the throne in England.

1429 Joan of Arc leads French against occupying English army at Siege of Orleans.

1430 German metalworker Johann Gutenberg begins experimenting with printing using moveable type.

Kenneth Branagh, in movie of Shakespeare's Henry V, rouses his exhausted men with speech at Agincourt (1415). The English victory was thanks to the King's leadership

1431

JOAN AND 100 YEARS WAR

JOAN of Arc is one of the most remarkable women of all time — a peasant girl who inspired the French to victory over the English in the Hundred Years War.

Joan was born in Domremy in the Champagne region of France in 1412. She had no formal education. By the time she was 13 she had begun to hear voices.

She soon became convinced that the saints were speaking to her — urging her to rescue her homeland from the invading English.

In 1429 she persuaded the local commander of French troops to take her to see the Dauphin — the future Charles VII — who had yet to be crowned king of France because of the war and England's claims to the throne.

Charles had heard of the peasant girl who claimed to be guided by God and, according to legend, decided to test her. He disguised himself as a courtier and ordered that Joan be led into the room.

She walked straight up to Charles. Her recognition of him was seen as confirmation of her claims and a sign of divine approval of his claim to the throne.

Joan was given her own troops and armour and was allowed to join the army which was attempting to rescue the city of Orleans from an English siege.

On April 29, 1429, she forced her way into the city. A little over a week later the English retreated.

Joan then led Charles in triumph to the city of Reims where he was crowned king of France.

But despite her victory at Orleans Joan was unable to persuade Charles to attack Paris, which was in English hands.

When she set out on her own to take the town of Compiegne in 1430 she was captured and handed over to the English commanders.

After a lengthy trial she was found guilty of heresy and sorcery.

Joan of Arc is burned at the stake in Rouen for heresy, clutching a cross

Joan was burned at the stake in Rouen on May 30, 1431. The church retried her case 25 years later and pronounced her innocent. In 1920 she was declared a saint.

The Hundred Years War resulted from disputes between the Royal families of France and England.

The main bones of contention were over who owned various lands in France — and who were the true heirs to the French throne.

The English won three great victories — at Crecy, Poitiers and Agincourt — but were unable to completely crush the French.

After the rise of Joan of Arc the French slowly began to turn the tide. The war finally ended in 1453 after the English were defeated at the battle of Castillon.

Later painting of the pilgrims in Chaucer's Canterbury Tales, begun in 1386, a collection of stories told en route to the shrine of Thomas a Becket (see 1170) in Canterbury

THE Sun

esday, May 29, 1431   **One farthing**   THOUGHT: BLAZE OF GLORY

Hundred Years War to over-run by 16 years

THE Hundred Years War is due to over-run by a stunning SIXTEEN YEARS, The Sun can reveal.

The war, which broke out between England and France in 1337, was scheduled to finish around Easter in six years time.

But sources close to King Henry VI have revealed the finish date has been moved back to 1453 because there is no chance of making the deadline.

One courtier said: "It's an absolute disaster. For the first 40 years or so we were bang on schedule — then things started to go wrong.

"Battles that were supposed to take a few hours lasted two days and a spell of rainy weather around 1415 made one siege drag on forever."

Hundreds of history books have already been written claiming the war lasted exactly 100 years and ended in an English victory. Now experts say even a 1453 ending is only possible if the French win.

GUILTY

- ## Crazed French army girl Joan is to be burned alive
- ## Court convicts peasant 'saint' of heresy and sorcery

From PAULA SMOKE in Rouen

MAD French army girl Joan of Arc will be burned at the stake tomorrow after being found guilty of heresy and witchcraft.

The 19-year-old was condemned to death by a court yesterday for blasphemously insisting God and the Saints ordered her to fight the English.

Joan (pictured left), who dressed in armour like a man to lead the French army, also claimed God had been sending her messages since she was 13.

She told the court in Rouen, Northern France: "The first time I heard this voice I was a young child — I believe it was sent to me from God."

WRANGLING

Joan, acclaimed as a saint by her followers, used sorcery to bewitch the English army, prosecutors claimed.

They said it was the only way the peasant girl could have led the French to victory over the vastly superior English army at the siege of Orleans.

Yesterday's verdict ends an amazing 15 months of questioning and legal wrangling which was dubbed the Trial Of The Century by churchmen.

Afterwards chief prosecutor Pierre Cauchon said: "This was a dangerous and deluded woman."

Full Story — Pages 2, 3, 4 and 5

German Gutenberg nicks *Sun's* printing idea - Pages Eight and Nine

196,404 DAYS TO GO

Left, an engraving of Richard Neville, the Earl of Warwick, later dubbed Warwick the Kingmaker after putting the Yorkist King Edward IV (right) on throne in 1461

1462
PRINCE VLAD & DRACULA

VLAD Tepes, or Vlad the Impaler, is one of history's most murderous figures — and the inspiration for Count Dracula.

The Romanian prince was behind countless acts of unspeakable barbarity and ruthlessness.

His favourite method of murder was impalement — in which victims were lowered on to sharpened stakes, suffering an agonising death as their weight pulled them down.

Vlad was born in late 1431. His father, also Vlad, was military governor of Transylvania and belonged to the Order of the Dragon, a band of knights whose duties included crusading against Turks.

Vlad senior was given the surname Dracul because it means dragon in Romanian. Dracula is a diminutive form.

At 11 the young Vlad was seized by Turks and spent six years in captivity in Turkey, during which time he grew into a monster without compassion.

While he was away his father was overthrown as prince of the Romanian province of Wallachia and murdered, along with Vlad's older brother.

At 25, Vlad killed his father's murderer Vladislav II and seized power. Thus began a six-year reign of terror.

Vlad took revenge on those who helped topple his father by impaling the older ones and forcing the younger ones to march 50 miles to another town. There they were made to build him a fortress — and many died in the process.

Vlad was a law and order fanatic. Petty criminals were impaled. Merchants who flouted trade laws were impaled. Pretty much anybody Vlad disliked was impaled. He considered all poor people thieves. Once, he invited a crowd of them to a feast at his court in Tirgoviste. When they had finished he had the hall locked and burned to the ground with them inside, saying they were scroungers.

On another occasion he is said to have rounded up peasants and driven them off a cliff, beneath which he had placed row upon row of sharpened stakes.

Once, two Turkish ambassadors came to his court. Asked to remove their turbans, they refused on religious grounds — so Vlad got his guards to nail them to the screaming Turks' skulls.

Vlad had a particular hatred for Germans, and many of his worst atrocities are depicted in German propaganda printed on the newly-invented press.

One shows Vlad's most appalling act of savagery, which came in 1462 as his heavily-outnumbered army fled through Romania from Turkish invaders.

Along the way Vlad torched his own villages and poisoned wells so the chasing Turks had nothing to eat or drink.

At Tirgoviste, he impaled 20,000 Turkish prisoners and ate as he watched them die.

The Turkish soldiers who found the "Forest of the Impaled" were so distraught they gave up the chase and went home.

Vlad was assassinated in 1476 — but 400 years on his bloodthirsty deeds provided the inspiration for Dracula, a fictional character literally thirsty for blood.

The ghoul first appeared in the 1897 novel Dracula by Irish writer Bram Stoker and has made dozens of movie appearances since.

. . . Timeline . . .

1434 River Thames is recorded as freezing over.

1453 End of 100 Years' War as English expelled from all France except Calais; Ottomans capture Constantinople, ending Byzantine empire.

1454 Birth of Italian explorer Amerigo Vespucci, after whom America was named.

1455 Print pioneer Johann Gutenberg produces his first Bible.

1456 Hungarians storm Belgrade and drive out Turks.

1457 The first mention of golf in literature.

1460 China is making and exporting its exquisite Ming pottery.

1461 Baron Richard Neville champions Yorkists in Wars of the Roses and helps Edward IV become King — 28,000 die in deciding battle at Towton, North Yorks.

1462 Beginning of Reign of Ivan III (the Great), Grand Prince of Muscovy.

Left, a page from first Bible produced by German printing pioneer Johann Gutenberg (1455). Right, Ming china (1460)

THE Sun

nday, March 29, 1462   1½ farthings   THOUGHT: HOW DO YOU LIKE YOUR STAKE?

POINT TAKEN VLAD!

'Dracula' Prince impales 20,000

By RUTH LESSE

EVIL Romanian prince Vlad "Dracula" Tepes impaled 20,000 Turkish prisoners on stakes — then had his tea in front of them, it was revealed last night.

Vlad, nicknamed The Impaler, ate as he watched the captives dying in agony. Then he fled with his men.

When the invading Turkish army later arrived at Tirgoviste, Romania, they found a scene of horror they described as the "Forest of the Impaled." They were so sickened they went home.

The massacre is only the latest atrocity carried out by vicious Vlad, 31.

He has had people skinned, boiled, decapitated, blinded and buried alive.

He once nailed turbans to the heads of two Turkish ambassadors who refused to remove them in his presence.

And the potty Prince once invited a group of peasants to a feast — then burned them alive for "scrounging".

Vlad To The Bone — Pages 4 and 5

Beast's feast . . . dying see Vlad dine

1486
TRAGEDY OF THE PRINCES

1480 saw the Catholic Spanish Inquisition, in which victims were interrogated on their religious beliefs under torture. Illustration above shows a suspect being 'questioned'

... Timeline ...

1469 Birth of Guru Nanak, founder of Sikhism.

1470 King Henry VI back on throne after Edward IV is deposed.

1471 Edward reigns again after crushing Lancastrians at Barnet and Tewkesbury — Henry murdered.

1476 William Caxton prints first book in England.

1477 Letter believed to be first-ever Valentine, sent by Margery Brews to John Paston in Norfolk.

1478 Renaissance art patron Lorenzo de Medici rules Italy.

1479 Ferdinand and Isabella unite Spanish crowns of Aragon and Castile.

1480 Spanish Inquisition introduced to expose heresy.

1483 Young Edward V proclaimed King, but Richard, Duke of Gloucester, seizes throne to become Richard III. He imprisons Edward and young brother Richard in Tower and they are never seen again.

1485 Henry VII becomes first Tudor king after defeat of Richard at Battle of Bosworth, where Richard was killed.

THE mystery of who killed the Princes in the Tower has fascinated historians for generations. The terrible murder of the two young boys came as England was in the grip of civil wars known as the Wars of the Roses.

These were a series of conflicts between the nobles of the house of Lancaster and their rivals from the house of York over who was to rule England.

By 1471 the Yorkists had the upper hand. The Lancastrian King Henry VI was murdered and replaced by the Yorkist Edward IV.

But in 1483 Edward died, leaving the country in political turmoil.

His son and heir, Edward V, was just 13 and the Yorkists feared that their grip on the crown was too weak to allow a boy King to rule.

The young Edward was therefore deposed by his uncle, Richard of Gloucester.

Richard, soon to be crowned Richard III, did this by declaring that both Edward and his 10-year-old brother Richard, Duke of York, were illegitimate.

The two boys were removed to the Tower of London in 1483 — and were never seen again.

Richard III reigned for just 18 months.

A Lancastrian claimant to the throne, Henry Tudor, was soon mustering an army. And on August 22, 1485, the Yorkist and Lancastrian forces met for the last battle of the War of the Roses, at Bosworth, Leicestershire. The Lancastrians were victorious, Richard dying on the battlefield. Soon afterwards the victor was crowned as Henry VII.

No trace of the young Princes was found. They were assumed to have been murdered and the finger of suspicion pointed at Richard.

During Henry's reign, his propagandists did everything in their power to blacken Richard's name and portray him as a monster.

In fact, during his lifetime Richard built a reputation as a just ruler.

As Duke of Gloucester he was often called on to settle disputes because of his record of dealing fairly with defendants and plaintiffs, irrespective of rank. As King he introduced trial by jury.

Richard's guilt over the Princes' death has certainly never been proved. Indeed, many historians have suggested Henry had a much greater motive for killing two young boys from a rival faction — both of whom had claims to the throne.

Did Richard kill the Princes shortly after seizing power? Or did Henry find them still alive after Bosworth and decide to remove his potential rivals as quickly and secretly as possible?

It is unlikely that the truth will ever be known.

In 1674 workmen discovered some bones in the Tower. They were declared to be the remains of the Princes and were reburied in Westminster Abbey.

Renaissance art

SANDRO Botticelli, who was born in Florence in 1444, is one of the outstanding geniuses of the artistic and intellectual movement known as the Renaissance.

The movement, which began in Italy in the 14th Century before spreading throughout Europe, traditionally marks the end of the medieval age.

The word Renaissance, which means rebirth, was used to describe how Italian artists began to reject the strict, formal nature of medieval painting and sculpture and return to the more realistic styles of the ancient Greeks and Romans.

This included an increased artistic interest in the nude.

Among the best examples are Botticelli's Birth Of Venus and Michelangelo's statue of David. Other great Renaissance figures include Leonardo Da Vinci and Titian.

Caxton, who printed England's first book in 1476. He set up a press in Westminster after learning the trade abroad and later printed the Canterbury Tales

Tower of London, where Henry VI was killed and where Edward V and brother disappeared, never to be seen again

Henry VI was restored to the throne in 1470

THE Sun

day, June 2, 1486   1½ farthings   THOUGHT: THOSE POOR KIDS

Was it King Richard or was it King Henry?

Suspect . . . Richard III   Suspect . . . Henry VII

WHODUNNIT

She's got a smashing Botticelli

★ **SAY** hello to lovely Venus — a girl who's really come out of her shell.

★ Venus, 23 — seen here in a picture by the Italian master Sandro Botticelli — has one of the most heavenly bodies we've clapped eyes on in a long time.

★ And she's just one of the luscious lovelies competing today to be Sun Page Three Girl of the Year.

★ Turn to Pages Four and Five for your chance to check out Venus and a galaxy of other beauties battling for the coveted title.

Mystery over which Royal killed Princes in the Tower

By KIT NAPPER

THE Sun today asks the question which has been haunting the nation: Who is the pitiless monster who murdered the young Princes in the Tower?

It is now exactly three years since 13-year-old Edward V and his brother Richard, ten, were last seen.

Although there has never been any trace of their bodies, no one doubts that these angelic children are dead. But who killed them?

The finger of suspicion has always pointed at their uncle, the late King Richard.

It was Richard who imprisoned the boys in the Tower Of London when he made himself King — after insisting the young Edward could not take the throne because he was illegitimate.

And after Richard was defeated and killed at the Battle of Bosworth most people assumed he **WAS** the guilty man.

DANGER

But now some Royal insiders have dared to suggest that our new King Henry may be the true culprit.

They claim that 29-year-old Henry, who is nine months into his reign, actually had the greatest motive for murder.

The sources say Henry's claim to the throne is weak — and if the young Princes had lived they would have been a very real danger to him.

A Royal aide said: "We will probably never know the truth — but it is likely that **ONE** of our Kings has the blood of children on his hands."

Slaughter Of The Innocents — Pages Eight and Nine

Victims . . . Richard, left, and Edward

Who's in the frame for our Page 3 girl of the year?

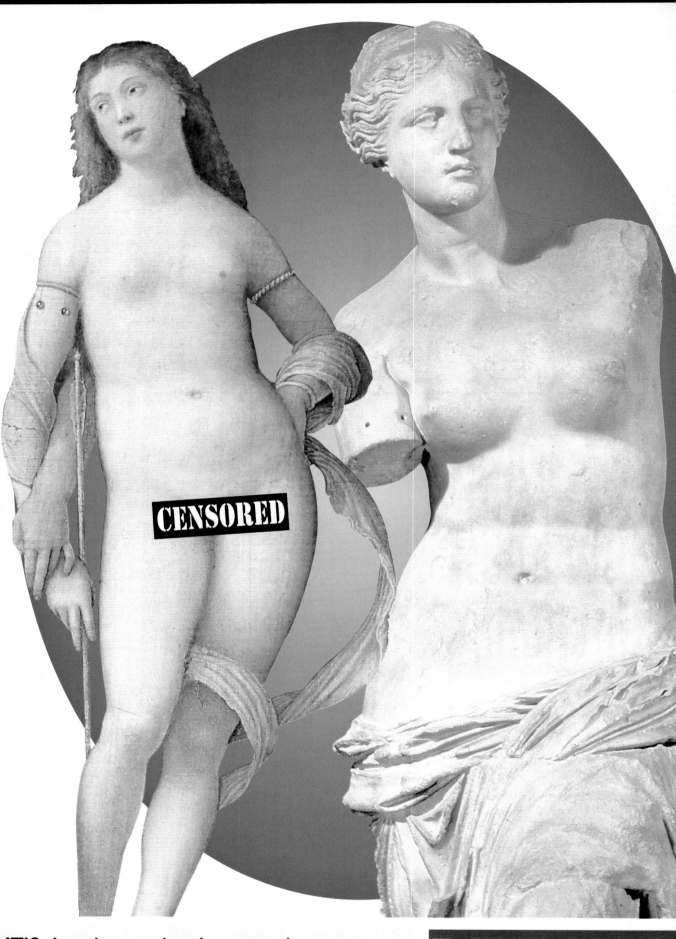

IT'S that time again when we ask you to vote for your Page Three girl of the year.

And what a year it's been on the most famous page in Britain's No1 newspaper! We've seen stunning Venus making her debut — while the original Page Three girl, Eve, is looking lovelier than ever.

First prize for the winning lass this year is a sitting with our top Page 3 painter Titian (steady, that's pronounced Tishan). So come on, get voting now!

VENUS

★ MEET a girl we always like t see plastered across Page 3 — voluptuous Venus, 23, from th Greek island of Milo.

Zeus's delicious daughter i famous for her statuesque figure, s we thought it would be a bit of arm less fun if she showed us her marb leous bust today. And just for Go measure there's another Venus pos on the far left.

CENSORED

FAITH, HOPE & CHARITY

⭐ YOU'VE got to admire the amazing Graces of our triplets Faith, Hope and Charity, from Italy.

The trio insisted on draping themselves with gowns before they posed outdoors in the cold — after all, what girl wants to get her Bottichilly?

CENSORED

CENSORED

EVE

⭐ CORE blimey! Here's A-dam fine figure of a girl . Eve, 22, from the Garden Eden. She appley dis-ayed her apeel for these ity pictures with a Granny ith and a snake — and we uldn't resist the temptation include them today. But hen we adder up her votes, ill her rivals pip her?

HOW TO VOTE

Place a tick in the box next to the girl of your choice. Tear out this panel and deliver it to The Sun, Wapping Village, Near London. ✓

VENUS ☐
EVE ☐
GRACE SISTERS ☐
BELLA ☐

BELLA

⭐ WELL oil be! Bella, from Italy, looks as pretty as a picture posing for us today. Our 22-year-old beauty won't sit for any old master — but she was easel-y persuaded to have a little brush with us on Page 3. Paint she sweet?

1492 saw the explorer Christopher Columbus (depicted above) reach the Americas. The Italian was the first European to do so in hundreds of years

...Timeline...

1486 Start of the rule of Aztec emperor Ahuitzotl in Mexico.

1487 Yorkist rebellion of Lambert Simnel, an imposter claiming to be heir to throne — he is defeated by Henry.

1490 Italian genius Leonardo Da Vinci draws Proportions of Man.

1491 Ruler of Congo kingdom baptised as Christian by Portuguese.

1492 Christopher Columbus lands on Bahamas and Cuba and thinks he's in India — first European to reach Americas since Vikings; Christians capture Granada, Spain, from Muslims.

1497 Englishman John Cabot is first European to find Canada; Portuguese explorer Vasco da Gama rounds Cape of Good Hope, South Africa, and sails on to India.

1498 Italian religious reformer Savonarola burned at stake.

1500 Lead pencils used in England; French exploration of Canada begins.

1502 Columbus begins fourth voyage, reaches Honduras, Nicaragua, Costa Rica, Panama and Colombia.

1504 Michelangelo finishes sculpture of David.

1506 Leonardo Da Vinci paints Mona Lisa; Columbus dies.

1507 Portuguese capture Sofala on Africa's east coast and found Mozambique.

1508 Michelangelo begins painting Sistine chapel, Rome.

1509 King Henry VIII takes the throne in England.

1510 First African slaves shipped to Caribbean by Portuguese.

1517 Martin Luther, German scholar, sparks Reformation by pinning his 95 objections to Catholic practices to the door of church at Wittenberg; Ottomans defeat Mamluks and conquer Egypt; Coffee introduced to Europe.

1519 Hernando Cortes, Spanish soldier-explorer, brings down the Aztec empire in Mexico; Charles, archduke of Austria and King of Spain, elected Holy Roman Emperor.

1521 Martin Luther is excommunicated by Pope.

1522 Ferdinand Magellan dies on voyage around the world after navigating the Pacific — crew complete the trek.

1527 Troops of Charles V, Holy Roman Emperor, sack Rome and capture Pope Clement VII.

1530 Birth of cruel Russian czar Ivan The Terrible.

1531 Polish astronomer Copernicus suggests Earth orbits sun.

1533 Spanish soldier Francisco Pizarro destroys Inca empire in Peru.

1534 Henry VIII breaks with Rome and makes himself head of English church.

1535 Henry executes ex-Chancellor Sir Thomas More for refusing to accept him as Church leader.

1540 First recorded race meeting, at Chester.

1541 Protestant John Calvin leads Reformation in Geneva, Switzerland.

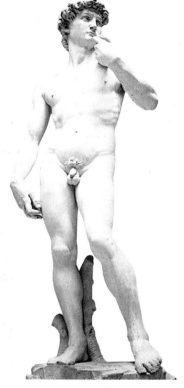

Michelangelo finished David (top) in 1504 and painted Sistine Chapel in 1508

1543
LIFE OF HENRY VIII

KING Henry VIII might be seen as a sex-mad murderer — yet he was popular and inspired great devotion.

He excesses — drink, food, women, war and general cruelty — have maintained people's fascination with him for 450 years.

His lasting legacy was to reform the Church by tearing England away from Catholicism, a split which came when he defied the Pope and divorced the first of his six wives.

Henry, the second son of Henry VII, was born in London on June 28, 1491. He was an intelligent, handsome child and a fine athlete.

His brother died and he came to throne in 1509 with England in crisis and isolated in Europe.

Henry married Catherine of Aragon, his brother's widow and daughter of the Spanish King Ferdinand, to forge an alliance with Spain. He then routed the French in battle.

Henry installed Cardinal Thomas Wolsey as head of his government, freeing himself from the tedium of daily administration.

The split with Catholicism came about for two reasons. Firstly, Henry desperately wanted a son — but five of his and Catherine's six children died and the other was a girl, Mary Tudor.

Secondly, by 1526 the King had fallen for Protestant Anne Boleyn and wanted rid of Catherine.

Henry argued that his children died because God believed the marriage to his brother's widow unholy. Wolsey was sent to Rome to persuade the Pope. He failed — and was replaced with Sir Thomas More, the Lord Chancellor.

More began to build a case — but Catherine appealed directly to the Pope, who backed her chiefly because her nephew Charles was Holy Roman Emperor. Henry retaliated by halting English bishops' payments to Rome and making them answer to him, not the Pope.

When Anne got pregnant in 1532, Henry was convinced the child would be a boy and was determined he would not be illegitimate.

He scrapped the Pope's power over marriage appeals in England and ruled they would now be decided by the Archbishop of Canterbury, a job he had already given Anne's friend Thomas Cranmer.

Cranmer granted the divorce in 1533. Anne had a girl, later to become Queen Elizabeth I.

The Pope excommunicated Henry, who declared himself head of the church in England and executed for treason anyone who defied him. Thomas More was among them.

Henry set about reorganising the church, maintaining Catholic practices but with himself as leader instead of the Pope.

He gradually began to strip the Catholic church of its vast wealth, seizing its land and property — monasteries included — and selling them to the nobility.

Henry's marriages are detailed on our next three pages. In short, Catherine of Aragon was divorced, Anne Boleyn beheaded, Jane Seymour gave Henry his only male heir (Edward VI) and died, Anne of Cleves was divorced and Catherine Howard beheaded.

Catherine Parr nursed Henry as his health failed and outlived him. He died on January 28, 1547.

Catherine married again the following year but died a week after giving birth to a daughter.

Da Vinci completed the Mona Lisa in 1506 and Proportions of Man in 1490. A painter, sculptor, engineer and architect, he was centuries ahead of his time

THE Sun

esday, June 12, 1543 **1½ farthings** **THOUGHT: TUDOR THOUGHT IT?**

I worry new hubby will cut off my head

Another tricky problem for Deidre's photo casebook — See Page 5

THE JOY OF SIX

ROYAL EXCLUSIVE

By BEA HEADER
Royal Reporter

KING Henry is to marry for the sixth time, The Sun can reveal.

His bride will be 31-year-old Catherine Parr, a twice-widowed country squire's daughter.

Last night sources close to the King at Hampton Court were calling Catherine "the bravest woman in Britain".

Her marriage, on July 12, will come only 18 months after Henry had fifth wife Catherine Howard beheaded at the Tower of London.

She was the second wife executed on the orders of the roly-poly Royal. He has divorced two others.

Catherine is said to be "bright, sensitive and caring".

And that might be just the tonic for 52-year-old Henry, who has been ill for some time.

One source said: "Maybe he's finally found the right woman. If she's lucky she might even survive him!"

Cath .. is she Miss Parr-fect?

Six maniac . . . Henry has already executed two wives, but now he's found another

King Henry to wed AGAIN

IS CATH FOR THE CHOP TOO? Pages 4 & 5

HENRY VIII AND WIFE No6

IS CATH HEADING FOR THE CHOP TOO?

ROYAL-watchers were amazed last night th King Henry had found yet another bride — a said: "She's really sticking her neck out."

But other experts said Catherine Parr could the perfect match — because she is meek and cari and will be a good "nurse" for sick Henry.

Last night a source close to brainy Catherine said: "S knows she'll have to tread carefully. But the King's not we what with his ulcerated leg and his obesity, and Cath wan to look after him.

"Plus, she's seriously into Protestantism, so she should in nicely." Catherine has already been widowed twice, wi first hubby Sir Edward Burough dying when she was ju 17. Her second husband, Yorkshire landowner Lord Latim also died last year before they could have kids.

Henry's love-life has been even more troubled. He had two wives beheaded and di-vorced two more. Another died after giving birth.

Wife No1 was Catherine of Aragon, daughter of Spain's King Ferdinand, who mar-ried Henry on June 24, 1509.

They were wed 24 years — during which time the randy Royal cheated on her with at least three women and Catherine lost five out of her six children.

The only one to survive was a girl — which infuri-ated the King, who was des-perate for a son.

Trumped

He began an affair with lady-in-waiting Anne Boleyn, and tried to divorce Cather-ine, who kicked up a huge stink about it with the Pope.

Henry decided to ignore the Pope and set himself up as head of the church in England — and got Anne's pal, Archbishop of Canter-bury Thomas Cranmer, to grant the annulment.

The Pope then excommu-nicated him. Meanwhile Henry had Lord Chancellor Thomas More executed for refusing to accept him as church leader.

By this time Anne was already **Wife No2**, because Henry had secretly married her in January 1533 before the annulment with Cather-

By BEA HEADER

ine was granted. But pre Anne didn't last long. S had a daughter and tw miscarriages — and fed Henry started to fancy lad in-waiting Jane Seymour.

Palace courtiers had An 29, tried on trumped-charges of adultery, ince and plotting against t King and she was execut at the Tower in 1536.

Henry got engaged to Ja within a day and she b came **Wife No3** two wee later. She had Henry's s Edward in 1537 but di within two weeks, aged from the strain of the bir

Henry made German roy Anne of Cleves **Wife No4** 1540 as a political move. thought Anne, 25, looked C in paintings — but when s arrived he thought she w hideous and branded her ' Flanders Mare".

The King, who alrea fancied a young lady-i waiting, Catherine Howa reluctantly married An anyway — on condition could divorce her quick This he did, and made year-old Catherine **Wife N**

Henry, 49, loved Catheri until he heard she was ha ing a fling. She was b headed for treason last ye

Now another Catherine set to be **Wife No6**. A Roy insider said: "Her head's the block if it doesn't wo out. But it's her funeral.

Executed . . . Lord Chancellor More refused to back the King

Henry's pad . . . Hampton Court Palace, on the Thames at Richmond, was built 30 years ago in the trendy modern 'Tudor' style and given to the King by government chief Cardinal Wolsey. Henry loved it so much he had it extended. Now it will be home to his sixth wife Catherine Parr

Deidre's Photo Casebook

No1

Divorced . . Catherine of Aragon

No2

Beheaded . . poor Anne Boleyn

No3

Died after birth . . Jane Seymour

BRIDE-TO-BE CATHERINE PARR GAZES FROM HAMPTON COURT WINDOW . . .

I do so love my Henry, but his temper is most fearsome and his affections are most fickle

LATER . . . WITH A FRIEND

I must make the right choice or 'tis my head upon the block

What she says is true. Look what happened to poor Anne Boleyn

I never laid a hand on those gentlemen

AT HENRY AND CATHERINE'S WEDDING FEAST, SHE WATCHES IN DESPAIR AS HE GETS DRUNK

Lawks! I knew he was not to be trusted. What will happen to me now?

LATER . . .

Mmm, that looks nice and sharp

DEIDRE SAYS: Catherine, it's only natural you have mixed feelings about marrying this man. On one hand, he's the King — on the other he's a fat, drunken, fickle, compassionless wife-killer and a serial seducer of young women. Make sure you talk through your worries with a counsellor — and insist the King comes along. If he shows no sign of understanding after that, run like the wind. My free leaflet Worried About Decapitation should point you in the right direction.

No4

Divorced . . . Anne of Cleves

No5

Beheaded . . Catherine Howard

No6

Alive . . . Catherine Parr's next

The Flemish baroque artist Peter Paul Rubens was born in 1577 and became a famous painter of voluptuous nudes, epitomised by The Judgment of Paris (about 1635, above)

... Timeline ...

1545 Tudor warship Mary Rose sinks in Solent — 700 drown.

1547 Edward VI crowned in England; Ivan The Terrible takes power in Russia.

1549 Church of England adopts Book of Common Prayer.

1553 Queen Mary I, or Mary Tudor — later dubbed Bloody Mary for her persecution of Protestants — is crowned.

1555 French astrologer Nostradamus publishes Centuries, string of prophecies many claim proved accurate.

1556 Worst earthquake ever kills 830,000 in Shaanxi, China.

1557 English mathematician Robert Recorde invents ''equals'' sign.

1558 Reign of Queen Elizabeth I, or Queen Bess, begins.

1561 Birth of Francis Bacon, statesman, writer, philosopher and Lord Chancellor of England.

1562 Sir John Hawkins starts taking African slaves to the Americas.

1564 William Shakespeare born; Naples bans public kissing, offenders face execution.

1569 Short-lived state lottery is launched in London.

1571 London Stock Exchange starts; Don John of Austria smashes Ottoman fleet at Battle of Lepanto.

1572 Massacre of St Bartholomew — 8,000 Protestants die in Paris.

1577 Sir Francis Drake begins to sail round the world; Birth of Flemish painter Pieter Paul Rubens.

1580 Britain's worst earthquake, in London, kills two.

1581 First major ballet is staged in Paris.

1585 Henry III of France fights ''War of the Three Henrys'' against Henry of Navarre; Simon Stevin publishes ''The Tenth'', explaining how to apply decimals to fractions.

Ivan the Terrible (1547) and Queen Mary I, who came to the English throne in 1553

The warship Mary Rose, pride of Henry VIII's fleet, sank in the Solent in 1545 — 700 died

1586
SIR WALTER RALEIGH

SIR Walter Raleigh led an extraordinary, privileged life as a soldier, explorer and poet — but also spent 13 years imprisoned in the Tower of London and was eventually executed.

He became a favourite courtier of Queen Elizabeth I and was famously reported as having spread his cloak over a puddle to stop her feet getting wet.

He is also the man credited with introducing potatoes and tobacco to England from the New World — though in fact it was more likely to have been the men he sent there, since the Queen often banned him from going on such hazardous missions.

Raleigh was born in 1552 in Hayes Barton, Devon, and grew to be 6ft, unusually tall then.

He fought in numerous campaigns, including against rebels in Ireland, before coming to the attention of the Queen.

Dashing Raleigh quickly became her favourite and she heaped favours on him — including a 42,000-acre estate in Ireland and monopolies on the export of certain goods.

Raleigh first sailed to America in 1578 and after returning home again arranged an expedition to claim some of the New World for his Queen.

He provided a ship, The Raleigh, and named the area it reached ''Virginia'' after Elizabeth — known as The Virgin Queen.

She knighted him in 1585 and made him Lord and Governor of Virginia as well as Captain of her guard.

Raleigh then sent settlers to colonise Roanoke Island, North Carolina, but the trip was catastrophic.

The group were unable to live off the land, fell out with the Indians they traded with and finally sailed home.

Further expeditions were sent — and from these it is believed that Raleigh's men Thomas Hariot and Sir John Hawkins brought back potatoes and tobacco.

They were discoveries which changed British life for ever. Hariot is said to have docked at Plymouth with potatoes on July 28, 1586. Some were then planted at Raleigh's Irish estate.

Raleigh first fell from favour when Elizabeth, who doted on him, discovered that he had married one of her maids of honour, Elizabeth ''Bessie'' Throckmorton.

Raleigh had kept this a secret from the jealous Queen, but the birth of his and Bessie's first son gave the game away.

Raleigh was thrown in the Tower and only released when one of his ships returned to England bearing a massive haul of Spanish treasure for Elizabeth.

Raleigh and Bessie retired to Dorset and built Sherborne Castle. The couple had three sons but only the second two, Walter and Carew, survived.

Raleigh's life fell apart when Elizabeth died in 1603 and King James I took the throne. James hated Raleigh — who was already unpopular for his arrogance and lavish spending — and accused him of plotting against the throne.

Raleigh was tried in Winchester and condemned to death. But moments before his execution James suspended the sentence and gave him life imprisonment instead.

Raleigh spent the next 13 years in the Tower, spending his time writing and earning himself a reputation as a leading intellectual.

He eventually convinced James to free him for an exploratory trip up the Orinoco river in Guiana, South America, which the King agreed to on the condition Raleigh would not upset the Spanish, who had settled in the area.

Disaster struck as Raleigh's son Carew and an aide attacked a Spanish settlement. Carew was killed in the assault.

Raleigh returned to England, where pressure from the Spanish persuaded James to invoke the suspended death sentence.

Raleigh was beheaded in 1618 and is buried in Westminster.

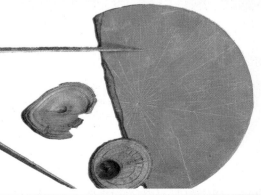

Relics from the Mary Rose, raised in 1982, provided historians with a mass of information on the Tudors

…day, July 29, 1586   One halfpenny   THOUGHT: SPUD WE LIKE

YOU'RE SPUDDY CLEVER, WALTER

Treat from New World

BRITAIN was in a frenzy last night over a major new food discovery called a "potato".

Experts predict the sensational vegetable, brought back from the New World by one of Sir Walter Raleigh's men, may change the face of the side dish.

They claim it can be boiled, cut up and eaten in chunks. It can also be ground down with a fork or other implement into "mash".

Some excited chefs believe the potato — dubbed "a spud" by wags — could be sliced and fried in

By MARIS PIPER

animal fat, producing a tasty snack they have nicknamed The Chip.

The first of the potatoes, which grow in the ground, have been planted at Sir Walter's Irish estate.

His pal Thomas Hariot, who scoffed several of them in the New World, said: "They are a kind of root of round form, some of the bigness of walnuts, some far greater.

"They are found in moist grounds, growing many together, and, being boiled, are very good."

Raleigh Tasty — See Page Nine

…but you can take that baccy where it came from

SIR Walter's men were branded "weird" last night over the bizarre practice of "weed-smoking" which they have brought back from the New World.

They claim natives there pick a plant called tobacco and stuff its leaves into clay

By NICK O'TEEN

pipes. Then they SET LIGHT to them and suck the smoke deep into their lungs, claiming it is good for them. Sir Walter, 32, originally

from Hayes Barton, Devon, is known be a keen smoker already. But a Sun reporter tried "smoking" and it made him feel sick.

He added: "It's a nasty habit and can't do you any good. Walter's got a hit on his hands with the potato — but tobacco sucks."

1588
ELIZABETH & ARMADA

St Louis, King of France And His Page was painted around 1588 by Greek-born master El Greco, whose dramatic style was not appreciated at the time

THE defeat of the Spanish Armada was a turning point in the histories of both England and Spain and one of the great achievements of Queen Elizabeth I.

It effectively destroyed the Spanish empire while establishing England as a world power with a superb Navy.

Spain's King Philip had decided to invade England for two main reasons. The first was to crush England's support for a Protestant uprising in the Netherlands, a land then controlled by Catholic Spain.

The second was to convert England back to Catholicism by ousting Protestant Elizabeth.

The plan was for the Spanish Navy and its army based in the Netherlands to join forces for a simultaneous assault on England.

In 1587 Philip prepared a force of 130 ships, carrying 30,000 men, for the invasion.

The English got wind of the plan and attacked the fleet in Cadiz, Spain, before it could sail — inflicting damage which set the Spanish assault back a year.

The Armada did finally set sail in 1588 and was first sighted off the Lizard, Cornwall, on July 29.

Admiral Lord Howard, with Sir Francis Drake as his vice-admiral, intercepted it with smaller and faster ships and fought battles off Plymouth, Portland Bill and the Isle of Wight.

But the Armada kept its formation and pushed on to Calais, ready to meet the land force coming from the Netherlands.

Here Howard struck the decisive blow. After Elizabeth's famous speech to her men, he sailed "fire-ships" into the Armada's midst. These were obsolete ships deliberately torched in the hope of setting light to the Spanish galleons. The Spanish panicked, scattered and eventually fled, with the English navy in hot pursuit.

Bad weather had cut off the Armada's route home via the Channel and they were forced to head north to sail back to Spain around Scotland and Ireland.

The English gave up the chase, but the Spanish still faced a gruelling voyage. Only 67 of the original 130 ships made it home — most of those badly damaged.

The defeat of the Armada was one of the defining moments of Elizabeth's extraordinary 45-year reign — which saw England enjoy an unprecedented period of economic and cultural prosperity and transformed into a world power.

Elizabeth, daughter of Henry VIII and Anne Boleyn, managed to unify a deeply-divided country by setting herself up as its glittering focal point.

Her bravery and cunning combined with her talent for self-display provided an inspirational figurehead.

Elizabeth firmly established Protestantism in England and brutally put down attempts to re-establish Catholicism. This included executing her cousin Mary, Queen of Scots, in 1587 after learning that plotters aimed to assassinate her and put Mary on the throne.

Elizabeth never married and was known as the Virgin Queen. In 1559 she refused a proposal from Spain's King Philip, who later planned the Armada.

Elizabeth's reign is also noteworthy for the most prolific period for literature in English history — thanks to writers such as William Shakespeare, Christopher Marlowe and Edmund Spenser.

... Timeline ...

1587 Elizabeth I executes Mary, Queen of Scots; Sir Francis Drake wrecks Spanish fleet at Cadiz; First performance of Christopher Marlowe's play Tamburlaine the Great.

1588 Birth of the English philosopher and political theorist Thomas Hobbes; Approximate date of El Greco's masterpiece St Louis, King of France.

Engraving of Mary, Queen of Scots, who was executed in 1587 after the discovery of a plot by Catholics to put her on the throne and assassinate Elizabeth I

Sir Francis Drake

SIR Francis Drake devoted his life to waging war on the Spanish and became England's first millionaire in the process.

Born near Tavistock, Devon, in around 1540, he commanded his first ship at 27. Spaniards attacked his ship on a slave-trading trip in the Gulf of Mexico — and his hatred of Spain was born.

He went on a string of voyages to the Caribbean and the New World, destroying and looting Spanish ships and ports and returning laden down with silver.

After one trip (1577-80) to the coast of the New World he returned by sailing west across the Pacific, rounding the Cape of Good Hope in Africa and thus becoming the first Englishman to sail round the world.

Drake's most daring feat was when, on the orders of Queen Elizabeth, he wrecked the Spanish fleet at Cadiz as it prepared for the Armada. He served as vice-admiral when the Armada attacked a year later — and is famously said to have carried on playing bowls after its first sighting.

In 1595 Elizabeth sent him on another expedition against the Spanish in the West Indies, where he caught dysentery and died.

THE Sun

May, August 9, 1588 — One halfpenny — THOUGHT: GO TO EL

SIMPLY THE BESS

QUEEN Bess gave Our Boys a rousing speech of encouragement hours before yesterday's stunning victory — insisting she would never let anyone invade Britain. She said:

❝ I know I have but the body of a weak and feeble woman, but I have the heart of a King, and of a King of England, too — and think foul scorn that any prince of Europe should dare invade the borders of my realms. ❞

Elizabeth . . stirring speech

Read her speech in full on Page 5

Hoe no you don't . . . Drake refused to budge

I'm finishing bowls first, insists Drake

SUPERCOOL Sir Francis Drake insisted on finishing off a game of BOWLS before finishing off the Armada, The Sun can reveal.

He and Lord Howard were playing at Plymouth Hoe, Devon, when they were told the Spaniards had been sighted for the first time off Cornwall.

Lord Howard said they should set sail at once to head them off.

But Drake, 48 — who has made a career out of bullying the Spanish — refused. He told his boss: "There's plenty of time to win this game and to thrash the Spaniards too."

Drakey Wakey — Page Five

Bowls to 'em . . . Sir Francis finishes his game

THE BIGGER THEY COME, THE ARMADA THEY FALL

Navy routs Spaniards in Channel

By WALTER E GRAVE

THE Spanish Armada was on the run last night after a devastating assault by our Navy.

Admiral Lord Charles Howard sent them packing with a stunning victory in the Channel at Gravelines, near Calais.

The Spaniards were already panic-stricken after Wednesday night's onslaught, when Howard sailed blazing ships into their midst.

But he struck the killer blow yesterday, the ninth day of the battle, sinking at least one galleon and crippling several others.

Last night dozens of the Spaniards' stricken ships were fleeing northwards with our fleet in hot pursuit.

Full Battle Report and Pictures — Pages 2, 3, 4 and 5

Wave bye bye . . . Spanish galleons still ablaze yesterday after Wednesday's 'fireship' attack

143,949 DAYS TO GO

Laurence Olivier as movie Hamlet. Shakespeare wrote play in 1599

1605

GUNPOWDER PLOT

THE Gunpowder Plot was hatched by a group of prominent Catholics who regarded King James I as a traitor for not granting them religious freedom.

The mastermind was Robert Catesby, a wealthy country gentleman who had been imprisoned for sheltering a priest.

Catesby first recruited his cousin Thomas Wintour and his friends Thomas Percy and John Wright. Then he recruited Guy Fawkes.

Fawkes, from York, was born into a Protestant family but converted to Catholicism.

He served in the Spanish army for a time before returning to England and throwing himself into Catholic politics with great zeal.

This fanaticism was fuelled by what Fawkes and his fellow plotters saw as the treachery of James I.

Before he came to the throne James had promised England's leading Catholics that, unlike Queen Elizabeth I, he would tolerate their religious beliefs.

But once James was in power he went back on his word and reintroduced some of the late Queen's anti-Catholic measures.

Catesby and his fellow plotters swore to get revenge by blowing up James when he attended the opening of Parliament at Westminster. They hired a cellar beneath the building, where they placed 36 barrels of gunpowder, hiding them beneath bits of wood.

But as their plans grew, more people were taken into their confidence — with disastrous results.

On October 26, 1605, ten days before Parliament was due to sit, an anonymous note was sent to the Catholic Lord Monteagle.

It warned him not to attend the opening of Parliament as ''a great calamity would consume it''.

Monteagle at once delivered the letter to the King's advisers.

The five chief plotters found out Monteagle had been tipped off, but when no action was taken against them they decided to carry on.

On the night of November 4, Fawkes was caught in the cellar with the powder. He intended to blow up Parliament the next day, November 5, which is still celebrated as Guy Fawkes' Night.

Fawkes was immediately marched into the King's bedchamber and questioned. Then he was tortured until he revealed the plot.

His four accomplices had fled. But on November 8, Catesby, Percy and Wright were found at a Warwickshire house. During a skirmish all three were fatally wounded.

Wintour was captured later. He and Fawkes were hanged, drawn and quartered on January 31, 1606.

...Timeline...

1589 Knitting machine invented by Englishman William Lee; First flushable toilet in use.

1593 Playwright Christopher Marlowe stabbed to death at pub in Deptford, South London, aged 29.

1596 Birth of French philosopher Rene Descartes.

1598 Henry IV, first Bourbon king of France, grants equal rights to Protestants; First Dutch trade posts are set up on the Guinea coast in West Africa.

1599 William Shakespeare writes his classic Hamlet.

1602 The Dutch East India Company is founded.

1603 Death of Elizabeth I marks end of the Tudor dynasty and beginning of the Stuart dynasty with King James I.

1605 Spaniard Miguel de Cervantes Saavedra publishes Don Quixote.

Shakespeare's later plays

BETWEEN 1603 and 1609 William Shakespeare wrote some of his most acclaimed plays. Into this period fall Measure For Measure, King Lear, Macbeth, Anthony and Cleopatra, Coriolanus and Troilus and Cressida.

Many of these works have a sombre tone — which has led academics to speculate that Shakespeare was in the grip of some personal crisis.

His problem was certainly not lack of popularity — his dramas were playing to packed houses and winning critical acclaim.

Shakespeare had also become a great favourite of King James I, who allowed his company to call itself The King's Men.

During this time Shakespeare's company averaged 13 Royal command shows a year. In Queen Elizabeth's reign they had averaged only three.

King James I took the throne in 1603. He was already James VI of Scotland

A later illustration of Don Quixote, hero of famous Spanish novel (1605)

Philosopher Rene Descartes (right) was born in 1596

Playwright Marlowe (left) died violently in 1593

THE Sun

May, November 8, 1605 — One halfpenny — THOUGHT: GUY FOR AN EYE

Knives out for Fawkes

Gunpowder plot beast to hang

GUY Fawkes is to be hanged, drawn and quartered for trying to blow up Parliament and kill King James.

The decision was taken after Fawkes yesterday confessed that he and four other disgruntled Catholics thought up the wicked Gunpowder Plot.

The 35-year-old ex-soldier was caught in a cellar beneath the Palace of Westminster on Monday night with barrels of gunpowder and

By BEN FIRENIGHT

fuses. He had planned to set off a huge explosion the next day as the King officially opened Parliament.

After his capture Fawkes was brought before His Majesty and asked why he had planned such hideous treason (pictured above).

The monster replied: "A dangerous disease requires a desperate remedy."

That Confession In Full — Pages Four and Five

SHAKESPEARE SHOCKER

By TOBY ORNOT

EATRE star Will Shakespeare's v thriller Macbeth features sicken- scenes of black magic and phic violence, The Sun can reveal. he play, set in medieval Scotland, tures at least SEVEN horrific ings — including the murder of a man and a child.

n one revolting scene three ches mix together parts of dead mals as they cast a spell. The X-

rated tale is a shock change of pace for Shakespeare, 41.

He is best known for costume dramas like Julius Caesar, touching romances like Romeo And Juliet or light-hearted comedies like The Merry Wives Of Windsor.

Many theatre insiders reckon that

Shakespeare wrote the gore-filled Macbeth after running out of ideas for storylines.

The Sun's drama critic Nick Fisher has had a sneak preview of the play — and last night predicted it will be a huge box office FLOP.

He said: "Will has clearly lost the plot with this one.

"Romeo and Juliet was a great weepie that you could take your wife

or girlfriend to. But I wouldn't take a woman along to see Macbeth, let alone children. It's too violent."

Shakespeare shot to fame during Queen Elizabeth's reign. His first play, Henry VI, received huge critical acclaim and played to packed houses at London's Rose Theatre.

Shakespeare is also a favourite of King James, who lets his actors call themselves The King's Men.

Shakespeare . . X-rated thriller

The Union Jack became the UK's national emblem in 1606 and combines the crosses of St George, St Andrew and St Patrick

...Timeline...

1606 Union Jack is adopted as United Kingdom's national flag.

1607 Jamestown Colony, first English settlement in North America, founded in Virginia.

1608 William Shakespeare writes Macbeth and King Lear; Quebec in Canada founded by French; Dutchman Hans Lippershey invents telescope.

1609 First regular newspaper in Germany; Song Three Blind Mice published in London.

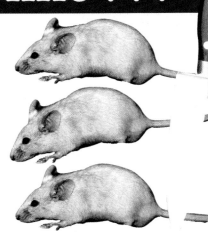

Song Three Blind Mice, in which rodents' tails are severed, was published in 1609

1609
LIFE OF GALILEO

GALILEO was not the first man to claim the Earth orbited the sun, but he was first who could prove it.

And the landmark discovery he made with his newly-built telescope changed the course of scientific thought.

Born Galileo Galilei in 1564 near Pisa, Italy, he was initially a physicist more than an astronomer and in his early life made a series of discoveries about gravity and motion.

He is reported to have once thrown two objects of different weights off the Leaning Tower of Pisa to disprove the theory of the ancient Greek philosopher Aristotle that the heavier would fall faster.

But Galileo's life changed direction when he was told that a Dutch optician had invented a crude telescope.

Based simply on what he had heard of it, Galileo made his own in 1609.

It was vastly better than the original, magnifying objects to 20 times their size.

He turned the telescope on the night sky and the discoveries began.

Galileo came to the conclusion that the movement of the planets which he observed only made sense if the Polish astronomer Nicolaus Copernicus (1473-1543) had been right in his theory that Earth moves around the sun.

Galileo's conclusions, published in March 1610 in his work The Starry Messenger, enraged traditional scientists, who still supported Aristotle's belief that the Earth was the centre of the universe.

They were further angered by Galileo's arrogance and open antagonism towards them — and they planted the idea in the mind of the Catholic church that Galileo's theory contradicted the Bible and amounted to heresy.

The Church insisted Galileo should abandon his theory — and the astronomer did indeed keep quiet on the matter for years.

But after repeating his belief in the 1630 book Dialogue on the Two Chief World Systems, he was summoned to Rome to stand trial.

He was forced to retract his theory and in 1633 was sentenced to life imprisonment, later commuted to house arrest.

Galileo died in 1642 — but 337 years later Pope John Paul II ordered an inquiry into the Church's treatment of him.

In 1992 the Vatican admitted the Church got it wrong.

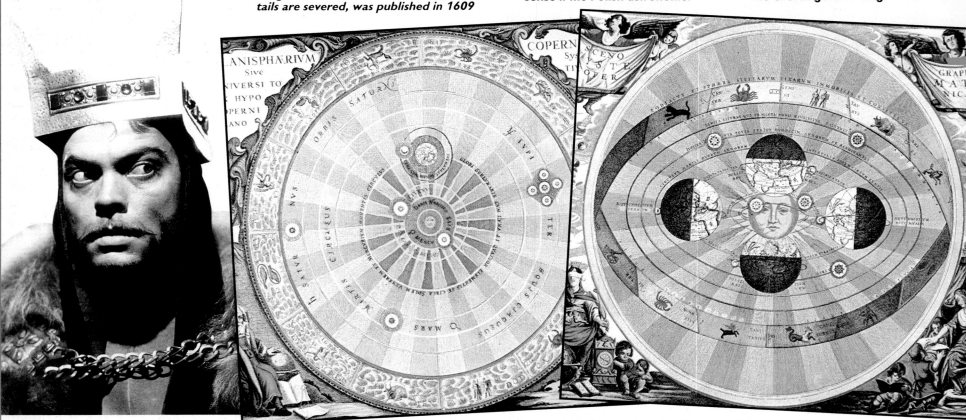

Orson Welles as movie Macbeth. Shakespeare wrote play in 1608

Early diagrams of solar system with the sun at its centre, illustrating theory of Copernicus which Galileo confirmed with telescope in 1609

THE Sun

Thursday, August 17, 1609 — One halfpenny — THOUGHT: GOOD SPOT, SON

This'll put 'em in a spin . . . controversial Galileo hard at work last night

LIFE REVOLVES AROUND THE Sun

Official verdict by Galileo, only bloke with telescope

'atch this space . . . astronomer Galileo demonstrates his unique telescope to crowd in Pisa

By TERRY SCOPE and UNA VERSE
sky news reporters

THE Earth revolves around the sun — NOT the other way round as we had all thought, it was confirmed last night.

And Galileo Galilei, the astronomer who's behind the groundbreaking discovery, knows what he's talking about — because he's the only man in the **WORLD** with a decent telescope.

Galileo has made a series of startling finds since he built his scope, which can magnify things to 20 times their size. He has revealed:

● The moon has craters and mountains.

● The milky way is made up of an enormous number of stars.

● The sun has spots — and Jupiter has four moons. Galileo plans to publish his findings in a book called The Starry Messenger.

They prove the controversial claims made a century ago by the Polish astronomer Nicolaus Copernicus.

Galileo, 45, of Pisa, Italy, has already been in trouble for chucking things off the top of the city's famous Leaning Tower.

And the new book is bound to cause him grief among other scientists and religious leaders, who hate any suggestions that the Earth moves around other planets.

They already dislike Galileo because he arrogantly picks fights with them and treats them like children.

Did The Earth Move For You? Spot Some Heavenly Bodies on the Centre Pages

---

Sun

A WACKY new drink called tea, being imported into Europe next year, is made from hot water and LEAVES, experts revealed last night.

Sun

THE Sun's suggestion that the first regular German newspaper, out this year, be called The Hun has been rejected by humourless bosses.

We're always at centre of the action . . .

IT'S DA BIZNISS LENNY!
We were first paper to print Mona Lisa in 1506

EXCLUSIVE: EDWARD THE CONFESSOR TELLS ALL (AGAIN)
Our fifth interview in 1043 with King Edward was by far his most explosive

PERU DARES WINS
We reveal Peru's destruction, 1533

BARD'S CHUM STABBED TO DEATH IN PUB
Sun was first with news of Christopher Marlowe's murder in 1593

The tea plant, which arrived in Europe from China in 1610

1620

THE PILGRIM FATHERS

THE Pilgrim Fathers are often thought to have been the first British settlers in America. They weren't — a settlement at Jamestown, Virginia, had been struggling for survival since 1607.

But the 102 men, women and children who arrived on the Mayflower in 1620 at the site of modern-day Provincetown, Massachusetts, did set up the first colony in New England.

And it is estimated that one million Americans can count these pilgrims as their ancestors.

The pilgrims' story began in the village of Scrooby, North Notts, in 1606. Dissidents there decided to break away from the Church of England because they felt it still had too many Catholic traits.

The group believed in religious and moral purity and became known as Puritans.

Disagreeing with the Church amounted to treason at the time because the Church and the King (James I) were deemed to be one. And the Puritans were so badly persecuted they fled to Holland.

They spent 11 years there but finally began to believe their traditions were being eroded by the Dutch — and Holland was under threat of war with Spain.

The Puritans decided to start their own colony in the New World. Their mission was backed by London investors who stood to get a ''cut'' of New World produce for seven years.

The group sailed from Holland in a ship called the Speedwell and arrived in England to rendezvous with the hired ship Mayflower.

Both ships were due to make the voyage, but the Speedwell proved unseaworthy and eventu-ally all 102 colonists set out from Plymouth in the 180-ton Mayflower. Of those, 35 were Puritans. The rest were hired by the investors to look after their interests.

The Atlantic voyage was hit by fierce storms. Conditions on the Mayflower were appalling and it was a miracle only two died.

The original intention was to land in Virginia, but the ship was blown off course and first sighted land 500 miles north-east, at present-day Cape Cod, Massachusetts.

On November 21 it dropped anchor off what is now Provincetown.

The colonists lived on the Mayflower for a month before scouting parties reported they had found a suitable site for the colony.

On December 16 they anchored there and named the place Plymouth after the port from which they had set sail.

The Pilgrims began building the settlement on December 26. They set up their own government and wrote the first constitution, the Mayflower Compact.

A harsh winter followed and almost half of the colonists died. While their homes were being built, their only shelter was on the Mayflower.

The colonists persevered and by March had been befriended by Indians who advised them which crops to plant and where.

Better weather led to an improvement in their health, too, and by April they were ready to let the Mayflower return to England.

The Pilgrims' Plymouth settlement survived and has now grown into a thriving coastal resort with a 46,000 population.

It is a mecca for tourists — many visiting the now-restored homes of the first colonists.

...Timeline...

1610 The tea plant arrives in Europe from China — and the cuppa is born.

1612 English settlers in Jamestown, Virginia, start growing tobacco.

1613 Fire guts the Globe Theatre in London during performance of a Shakespeare play; Michael becomes czar of Russia — beginning of the Romanov dynasty.

1615 The Dutch settle on Manhattan island, future site of New York.

1618 Beginning of the 30 Years' War in Europe.

1619 Doctor William Harvey, in London, discovers the circulation of the blood.

Doctor William Harvey, who in 1619 discovered blood circulation

London's Globe Theatre, restored in the 1990s, was gutted by fire in 1613 after a cannon set the thatched roof alight during performance of Shakespeare's Henry VIII

The first of the Puritan 'pilgrims', having anchored their ship the Mayflower off Massachusetts, get ready to step ashore from their lifeboat to explore the area

THE Sun

Wednesday, November 22, 1620 ½ penny **THOUGHT: BE CAREFUL OUT THERE**

QUAKE UP AND MAKE LOVE TO ME
Sizzling guide to Puritan passion
4-PAGE SPECIAL PULLOUT INSIDE

HAVE A NICE STAY
Pilgrims reach New World

Look after us, Lord . . . Pilgrims' first prayer in New World last night

THE Mayflower's 102 pilgrims arrived in the New World yesterday after an epic, storm-lashed voyage across the Atlantic.

They have dropped anchor in a sheltered harbour off a picturesque area they have named New England.

The men, women and children intend to live on the ship for a few weeks and send out scouting parties to find a decent place to site the new colony. The strait-laced colonists, who rebelled

By ELLEN DAMNATION

against Church of England practices, set off from Plymouth on September 16.

They intended to land in Virginia, where there is already a colony at Jamestown, but were blown off course by storms.

Two people died during the trip, which was financed by London investors. A third was blown overboard but was rescued.

A baby boy was also born on the Mayflower — the aptly-named Oceanus Hopkins.

Full Story — Pages Four and Five

1649

ENGLISH CIVIL WAR

One of history's greatest painters, the influential Dutch master Rembrandt is renowned for his brilliant character studies. This is Cornelis Anslo and Aeltje Schouten (1641)

...Timeline...

1622 Invention of the slide rule for mathematical calculations.

1625 Reign of Charles I begins; First blood transfusion, in France.

1626 Dutch found the city of New Amsterdam on Manhattan Island.

1627 Catholics besiege Huguenots in La Rochelle, western France.

1628 Petition of Right in England — Parliament curtails King's powers.

1629 King Charles I tries to rule without Parliament.

1633 Dutch artist Rembrandt (full name Rembrandt Harmenszoon van Rijn) paints Portrait of a Man and His Wife; First bananas on sale in Britain at London shop.

1636 Harvard is founded in Cambridge, Massachusetts, America's first university and still one of its most prestigious.

1640 Portugal gains its independence from Spain.

1642 Civil war breaks out in England, Scotland and Ireland between supporters of Charles I (cavaliers) and roundheads of Oliver Cromwell who support Parliament; Adding machine invented by Frenchman Blaise Pascal.

1643 Italian physicist Torricelli invents the barometer; Start of the reign of Louis XIV in France.

1644 Abel Tasman reaches Tasmania and then New Zealand, but is scared off by Maoris.

1648 Treaty of Westphalia ends Europe's 30 Years' War.

King Louis XIV of France, who came to the throne in 1643

Charles I was beheaded in January 1649 after standing trial on treason charges

THE English Civil War broke out between Charles I and Parliament in 1642 after the King had insisted on ruling the country on his own for more than a decade.

By 1640 he had been forced to summon the House of Commons in an attempt to raise enough money to fund a war in Scotland.

The Parliamentarians refused to co-operate and tension between the two increased. In January 1642 Charles left London and both sides began to prepare for war.

Royalist support came from Wales and the North and West of England. Parliament controlled the wealthier South and East — and London. It also controlled the navy.

The first major battle, at Edgehill in October 1642, was won by the King's men, known as cavaliers.

He followed this by marching on London, but was repulsed by the city militia and withdrew to Oxford.

For three years victories went one way then the other. The turning point came in 1645 with the formation by Parliament of a well-trained military force called the New Model Army or "roundheads".

This army, whose cavalry was led by Oliver Cromwell, won an overwhelming victory at Naseby on June 14, 1645. The next year Parliament captured Oxford and the last Royalist forces were disbanded.

Charles fled to the Scots, but they handed him over to Parliament.

Radical groups within the army now began to put forward their proposals for reorganising the State. The result was chaos, which was only remedied when Cromwell forcibly reasserted military discipline.

Meanwhile, Charles was ostensibly negotiating with Parliament over proposed reforms. But at the same time he was holding secret talks with the Scots, promising to establish Presbyterianism in England in exchange for military help.

His double-dealing sparked the so-called second Civil War, which was marked by a series of unsuccessful Royalist rebellions and a Scottish invasion in July 1648. The Scots were decisively defeated by Cromwell at the Battle of Preston.

The second Civil War left Cromwell the most powerful man in Britain. It also hardened attitudes towards Charles.

In January 1649 the King stood trial at the insistence of army radicals. The court called on "Charles Stuart, that man of blood, to account for the blood he had shed and mischief he had done".

Charles refused to recognise the court or speak in his defence. He was found guilty of high treason and condemned to death.

Cromwell was one of those who signed the death warrant. On January 30, Charles I was beheaded.

Explorer Abel Tasman reaches New Zealand (1644) but Maoris scare him off. He never sets foot there

Mathematician Blaise Pascal invented adding machine in 1642

Harvard University, founded near Boston, Massachusetts, in 1636

THE SUN

dnesday, January 10, 1649   One halfpenny   **THOUGHT: OLIVER TWISTED**

Sun asks the crucial question on Cromwell

Is this the most dangerous man in Britain?

Warts he playing at . . . Cromwell wants to execute our King Charles

PAGE ONE OPINION

THERE is much to admire in Oliver Cromwell — and The Sun has been among his greatest admirers.

He is a decent man. A modest man. A man of principle.

When King Charles opposed the wishes of the people's representatives in Parliament, Cromwell took up arms against him.

He did this not out of pride but to protect us from tyranny.

But now The Sun asks the question we never dreamed we would ask: Is Cromwell the most dangerous man in Britain?

For now the King is defeated Cromwell wishes not just to punish him — but to **EXECUTE** him.

So today The Sun gives this advice: Kings fall by the grace of God, not the whim of man.

And if Cromwell stains his hands with the blood of our King he will one day have to answer for it before the highest judge of all.

121,735 DAYS TO GO

India's Taj Mahal, built by the Mughal emperor Shah Jahan in memory of his wife, was completed in 1653 after 22 years. Some 20,000 men worked on the site every day

. . . Timeline . . .

1650 Oliver Cromwell conquers Ireland.

1652 Cromwell conquers Scotland; Dutch found Cape Town in South Africa.

1653 Cromwell dissolves Parliament, becomes Lord Protector of Britain, which now has written constitution; Taj Mahal completed in India.

1656 Formation of the Grenadier Guards regiment.

1660 Restoration of the Stuarts — King Charles II takes the throne after years of Cromwell unpopularity; Samuel Pepys begins his diary (it was not published until 1825).

1662 World's first bus service launched, in Paris.

1664 English capture New Amsterdam and rename it New York.

1666 King Charles II pioneers the waistcoat.

1656 saw formation of Grenadier Guards, still going strong

Samuel Pepys, who began his diary depicting upper-class life in London in 1660

A portrait by artist Pieter Nason of King Charles II, who took the throne in 1660

1666
THE GREAT FIRE

THE Great Fire of London began in the early hours of Sunday September 2, 1666, in the shop of the King's baker Thomas Farynor.

The blaze spread swiftly after sparks from the shop in Pudding Lane fell on hay in the yard of an inn next door.

Withing minutes the flames had reached the warehouses on the banks of the River Thames.

Many of these stored highly-inflammable goods like oil, spirits, timber and coal.

Most of the buildings were medieval — half-timbered, pitch-covered constructions that ignited at the touch of a spark.

By 8am the fire was half-way across old London Bridge.

The Mayor of London arrived on the scene and was asked for permission to pull down buildings in the path of the inferno to create gaps that the flames could not leap across.

He hesitated, fearing he would be held responsible for the cost of the rebuilding. By the time the order was finally given to start the demolition it was too late — the inferno was out of control.

As if things were not bad enough, the first efforts at demolition proved a disaster.

The houses chosen were too close to the fire and their wooden ruins were engulfed in flames before they could be cleared away.

The blaze finally burned itself out after five days. By that time much of the city had been destroyed, including more than 13,000 houses and 87 churches.

Amazingly, only six people were definitely known to have died in the flames. However, historians suspect the true death toll was much higher.

The devastation caused by the fire lasted for many years.

Though casualties were light, thousands were financially ruined, debtors' prisons became overcrowded and the capital was left scarred.

Sir Isaac Newton

SIR Isaac Newton is history's greatest scientist. He developed the three laws of motion — the basic principles of modern physics — and the theory of gravity. He also helped invent calculus and discovered the composition of light.

He carried out his research alone and was prone to terrible rages and sulks if criticised.

Newton was born in 1642 at Woolsthorpe, Lincs, and went to Cambridge University at 19. He graduated at 22 and returned to his mum's house in rural Lincolnshire to avoid the plague.

In her garden he saw an apple fall off a tree — and realised that the force which draws things to the Earth is a universal one which also governs planetary movements and tides.

Newton returned to Cambridge as a Fellow of Trinity College, shunning the curriculum to develop his own ideas.

Newton publicly announced his law of gravity in his 1687 work Philosophiae Naturalis Principia Mathematica.

It stated that every particle in the universe attracts every other particle with a force dependent on the product of their masses divided by the square of the distance between them. Newton died at 84 in 1727.

Newton watches apple fall. It did not hit him on the head, as popular myth has it

THE Sun

nday, September 3, 1666 · One halfpenny · THOUGHT: HOT CROSS BUNGLE

Core! Newton discovers gravity

BRILLIANT young scientist Isaac Newton has come up with a radical new physics theory after seeing an apple fall off a tree.

He has told pals a force called "gravity" draws everything on Earth to the ground.

The boffin, 24, believes it also affects everything in the universe. Friend William Stukeley said: "It was occasion'd by the fall of an apple, as he sat in contemplative mood.

"Why should that apple not descend sideways or upwards, but constantly to the Earth's centre?"

Feel The Force — Page 7

Newton . . . apple tumble

LONDON'S BURNING

Inferno is sparked by dozy baker

By STELLA LIGHT

DOZY baker Thomas Farynor may have sparked the fire by failing to make sure his oven was out.

He believed the oven was safely cooling down — but a few small embers are thought to have been still smouldering at the back.

Three hours after going to bed, Thomas, his wife and young daughter awoke to find their home in Pudding Lane full of smoke and flames.

Safe

The baker — who supplies bread to the King — managed to clamber to safety through an upstairs window with his family and a servant.

But his maid was too frightened to climb out and died in the flames.

A neighbour of Thomas's said last night: "It's a tragedy — he's such a nice man. He'll be absolutely distraught."

Panic in the streets . . . families flee from the fire towards the River Thames last night

Thousands flee from huge blaze

By DES ASTOR

LONDON was facing catastrophe last night as an enormous fire raged out of control.

Hundreds of houses have already been destroyed by the inferno, which is spreading by the second.

One terrified witness said: "There seems to be nothing anyone can do. Entire streets have been engulfed within a few minutes."

The blaze began at a baker's in Pudding Lane, East London, at about 1am yesterday.

Sparks ignited hay in the stables of an inn next door, then the flames spread to a church nearby.

WIND

A strong wind fanned the flames — and by 8am half of London Bridge was on fire. One person is known to have died so far and the death toll is expected to rise in the next few hours.

Last night King Charles ordered teams of soldiers to blow up wooden buildings in the fire's path in an effort to stop it spreading.

The London parishes are supposed to provide buckets and ladders for use in fighting fires. But yesterday many of them were found to have rotted through neglect.

More Amazing Pictures — Pages 2, 3, 4 and 5

1677
DISCOVERY OF DINOSAURS

THE thigh bone pictured in Professor Robert Plot's book The Natural History of Oxfordshire was the first dinosaur discovery ever documented.

Plot, head of the world's oldest museum — the Ashmolean in Oxford — had no idea what the bone was and it has since been lost.

But from the picture it appears to be from a Megalosaurus — which was one of the biggest of the reptiles that dominated the planet from about 260million years ago to their sudden extinction 65million years ago.

Major dinosaur discoveries and studies really only began in the early 1800s — 130 years after Plot's book — when the bones of another Megalosaurus and an Iguanodon were found in England.

About the same time, a young girl called Mary Anning discovered some of the first Ichthyosaur fossils in Lyme Regis, Dorset.

By 1842 the term dinosaur, meaning "terrible lizard", had been coined by the scientist Sir Richard Owen.

More complete skeletons were then found in New Jersey, U.S. and the hunt for dinosaur remains spread around the world.

A host of new varieties were discovered.

They ranged from the ferocious meat-eaters Tyrannosaurus Rex and Velociraptor to the vegetarian Stegosaurus and Triceratops.

Modern paleontologists are making new finds all the time. In 1983 a major new discovery, of a Baryonyx, was made in Surrey.

So far 350 dinosaur varieties have been unearthed, on all the continents of the world.

But scientists believe that is less then ten per cent of all the types that existed during the three main

Megalosaurus thigh bone in Plot's 1677 book was thought to be a giant's

ages of the dinosaur — the Triassic, the Jurassic and the Cretaceous periods.

Controversy still rages over how dinosaurs became extinct. Some scientists believe their population dwindled due to environmental changes.

But there is increasing evidence that they were wiped out when a giant asteroid or comet struck the Earth 65 million years ago.

It caused a widespread inferno, acid rain and a dust cloud which blocked out the sun for months.

That destroyed plants, the herbivorous dinosaurs which ate them — and the carniverous dinosaurs which ate the herbivores.

The theory is supported by the discovery in 1991 of a buried crater 125 miles wide in the Yucatan Peninsula of Mexico.

It is thought to have been caused by a gigantic asteroid.

Scientists have dated it to 65 million years ago — the same time the dinosaurs were wiped out.

This baby dinosaur fossil is one of most complete ever found. Inset, raptor claws

Nell and Charles

NELL Gwyn was an attractive, vivacious actress who was the mistress of King Charles II for about 16 years and had two sons with him.

From humble origins, she spent her childhood selling oranges outside London's Drury Lane Theatre.

She became an actress at 15 and rose to stardom thanks partly to roles written for her by the playwright John Dryden.

Nell became Charles's lover as a 19-year-old in 1669 and remained so until he died in 1685. She died two years later.

Nell is said to have persuaded the King to build the Royal Hospital in London's Chelsea for army pensioners.

Nell was 15 when she made her stage debut

Charles was Nell's lover for 19 years

. . . Timeline . . .

1667 John Milton's epic Paradise Lost is published.

1669 Actress Nell Gwyn becomes the mistress of Charles II.

1671 Irishman Thomas Blood steals crown jewels but is caught.

1674 Bones, believed to be of "Princes in the Tower" (see 1483), found and buried at Westminster Abbey.

1675 Architect Sir Christopher Wren begins rebuilding St Paul's Cathedral after Great Fire; King Charles lays foundation stone of Royal Observatory at Greenwich, South-East London.

Sir Christopher Wren (right) began rebuilding St Paul's Cathedral in 1675

THE Sun

Sunday, September 10, 1677 — Three farthings — THOUGHT: GWYN AND BARE IT

Nell's kiss and tell

MY NIGHTS WITH KING

★ NELL Gwyn lifted the lid last night on her naughty nights with King Charles. In an exclusive interview with The Sun, she told how she used her charms to rise from her humble background selling oranges on the streets of London to become the King's mistress.

★ Stunning actress Nell, 26, said: "Charles could watch me unpeeling all day long." But caring Nell also revealed her serious side — and how she wants her lover to build a hospital in London for disabled ex-servicemen.

Read Her Full, Frank Interview on Pages 4 & 5

WHAT'S THAT OSSIL BOUT

uld mystery ne be from ant lizard?

y TYRONE O'SAURUS

Oxford professor has arthed a major riddle t the history of the ld after discovering a BONE.

bert Plot is baffled by enormous fossil, dug up Cornish quarry and red in his new book.

thigh bone is 2ft round e end and weighs 20lbs. Plot believes it may be a giant who lived millions ears ago. Other scientists it is from an elephant the

nny bone . . . Prof Plot

ns brought here. A Sun t said last night: "It may e thigh bone of a terrify-zard which weighed sev-ons and became extinct 65 n years ago, probably due catastrophic impact of an id about 5½ miles wide landed in the Yucatan sula of Mexico."

of Contention — Page Seven

Buckingham ace to be built lans on Centre Pages

```
85,641  DAYS
        TO GO
```

American scientist and diplomat Benjamin Franklin proved lightning is electricity in 1752 by letting it flow down his kite and into a device for storing current

1765
JAMES WATT'S STEAM ENGINE

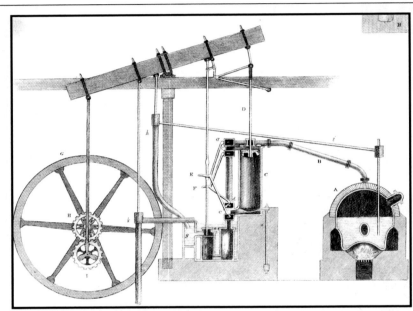

Diagram of James Watt's improved steam engine, which allowed the widespread use of steam as a power source for the Industrial Revolution

JAMES Watt's steam engine had an enormous influence on the Industrial Revolution and therefore on how the modern world was developed.

The popular misconception is that the Scottish engineer, born in 1736, invented the engine. In fact Englishman Thomas Newcomen did.

Newcomen's simple engine is still complex for the layman. Here's a basic explanation:

It was powered by steam, created in a cylinder by boiling water in a chamber under it. The pressure from the steam forced a piston inside the cylinder to move to the top. The piston was attached to a beam above it, so that moved too.

Next a jet of cold water was automatically sprayed into the cylinder, cooling it down, condensing the steam and thus lowering the pressure. With the pressure lower, the piston returned to its starting position, as did the beam above it.

The beam was attached to a rod, the up-and-down motion of which was used to work a pump.

Newcomen's engine was used to pump water out of mines, which allowed miners to dig much deeper for coal to fuel factories.

In 1764 Watt, an instrument maker at Glasgow University, was asked to repair a working model of Newcomen's engine.

As he did so he saw it wasted steam because its cylinder had to be alternately heated and cooled. So in 1765 he built an engine in which the main cylinder stayed hot but was attached to a second one which was kept cold.

This advance cut fuel consumption by 75 per cent. Watt refined the engine until it was efficient enough to run all sorts of machinery.

Thanks to Watt, steam powered the first railway engine in 1804. He died in 1819 and the electrical unit, the watt, was named after him.

... Timeline ...

1677 Buckingham Palace is built in London.

1678 John Bunyan's Pilgrim's Progress published.

1681 First street lamps are erected in London.

1685 James II crowned King; Johann Sebastian Bach born.

1688 Revolution in England against King James.

1689 William III (William of Orange) becomes King.

1690 Battle of the Boyne — William defeats Irish and French.

1692 Witchcraft hysteria in Salem, Massachusetts, gets 20 people executed after sham trials.

1701 Pirate Captain William Kidd hanged at Wapping, London.

1702 Queen Anne crowned; England's first daily newspaper issued, The Daily Courant.

1704 British take Gibraltar from Spain; French routed at Blenheim.

1705 Astronomer Edmund Halley discovers comet now named after him; Highway robber Dick Turpin born.

1707 Act of Union unites England and Scotland.

1712 Rob Roy (Robert MacGregor) leads uprisings in Scotland.

1714 George I becomes King; Typewriter patented in England; Thermometer is invented.

1715 First Jacobite rising attempts to restore exiled Stuarts to throne.

1720 South Sea Bubble scandal ruins thousands; Birth of German exaggerator Baron von Munchhausen.

1721 Robert Walpole becomes first and longest-serving British PM.

1724 Legendary lover Giovanni Jacopo Casanova born.

1725 Antonio Vivaldi composes The Four Seasons.

1727 Reign of George II begins; Europeans plant Brazil's first coffee.

1730 Founding of Methodism by John and Charles Wesley in Oxford.

1732 First performance of Handel's Oratorio, in London pub.

1734 Birth of legendary U.S. frontiersman Daniel Boone.

1740 Rule Britannia sung for first time in England.

1741 Anders Celcius devises the Centigrade temperature scale.

1745 Second Jacobite rising led by Bonnie Prince Charlie.

1746 English defeat Scots at Culloden; First reference to Yorkshire pud.

1748 Ruins of volcano-hit Pompeii discovered.

1752 U.S. scientist Benjamin Franklin flies kite during storm and proves lightning is electricity; Jockey Club founded;

Top, Liam Neeson as a movie Rob Roy (see 1712). Below, the sextant (1757)

England adopts Gregorian calendar.

1755 First smallpox outbreak, in South Africa, kills many.

1756 Black Hole of Calcutta — 123 British soldiers die after being locked by Indian troops in tiny dungeon overnight; Start of the Seven Years War — Prussia and Britain v France, Austria and Russia.

1757 Invention of the sextant enables sailors to navigate better.

1759 British Museum opens; Birth of Scottish poet Robert Burns.

1760 Reign of George III begins; All of Canada now in British hands.

1762 Jonathan Swift writes Gulliver's Travels; Start of the reign of Russian empress Catherine the Great.

The Earl of Sandwich

THE fourth Earl of Sandwich had an illustrious career in the Navy — but will always be known for inventing the snack which was named after him.

The Earl, real name John Montagu, was born in 1718 and educated at Eton. By the time he was 30 he was running the Navy as First Lord of the Admiralty.

Sandwich was notoriously corrupt and addicted to gambling. It is said that one summer around 1765 he spent 24 hours non-stop at a card table in a London pub.

He refused to get up for meals and when hunger finally overwhelmed him he ordered his servant to bring him cheese and meat between two slices of bread — a ploy to prevent his hands, and the cards, from getting greasy.

The snack was an instant hit — and quickly the sandwich spread.

THE Sun

Wednesday, July 10, 1765   Three farthings   THOUGHT: USED HIS LOAF

WATT LETS US IN ON STEAMY SECRET

INVENTOR James Watt has given exclusive details to The Sun about his latest project — which could change the course of history.

Mr Watt has made a fascinating improvement to the steam engine used for pumping water out of mines. It could mean the devices being used for a host of other applications. Glasgow-based Mr

Watt, 29, explained yesterday: "The idea came into my mind that, as steam was an elastic body, it would rush into a vacuum.

"If a communication were made between the cylinder and an exhausted vessel, it would rush into it, and might be there condensed without cooling the cylinder."

More Dramatic Revelations — Page Nine

3am news: Gambler Earl invents handy meal

Toff scoff . . . snack invented by the Earl, left. Note how the genius has placed the meat BETWEEN the slices of bread to avoid greasiness

Sun TOASTS THE SANDWICH

..and here's how you make one

MAKING a sandwich is a laborious process, but we think you'll agree it's worth it. Here's our four-step guide:

1. Take a loaf of bread, hack it into two pieces and put them down on a table.
2. Take some beef or ham, slice it up and put the slices down next to the bread.
3. Take the meat and place it between the slices of bread. If all has gone well, you should have a sandwich.
4. Pick up the whole thing and bite into it. Chew, swallow and repeat until it is gone.

We salute new snack

SAY hello to a mind-blowing new snack — dubbed The Sandwich.

It is the brainchild of the Fourth Earl of Sandwich, who invented it late last night during a marathon 24-hour gambling session in a London pub.

Fellow card-players were open-mouthed with astonishment at the simple brilliance of his concoction — a slab of beef and some cheese between two slices of bread. The gambling-addict Earl, 44, has been working

By ROLAND BUTTER

for months devising a tasty treat he could eat without leaving the table or getting his cards greasy.

He considered various options — two slices of meat with a slice of bread between them, two slices of meat with bread on top and two slices of bread with meat on top — before settling on his definitive version.

The Earl, who incidentally also runs the Navy, modestly refused to comment on his achievement.

Sandwich spread — Pages Four and Five

1770

COOK & AUSTRALIA

One of Britain's greatest poets, William Wordsworth, was born in Cumbria in 1770

The Venetian blind was patented in 1769, not in Venice, but in London

...Timeline...

1768 First Encyclopedia Britannica published; First of Captain James Cook's three voyages to the Pacific; Scottish explorer James Bruce travels in Ethiopia, attempting to reach the source of the Nile.

1769 Cook becomes first European since Abel Tasman to reach New Zealand — unlike Tasman (who was scared away by Maoris) he actually sets foot in the country; Venetian blinds patented in London.

1770 Poet William Wordsworth born; The eraser is invented.

James Bruce travelled in 1768 through Egypt, then Ethiopia, to find Nile's source

1770 was year the rubber was invented

CAPTAIN James Cook was one of the great explorers — and the first Briton to set foot in Australia and New Zealand.

His landing in Australia helped shape the country as it is today — because the prisoners Britain then decided to transport there formed its first non-Aboriginal colony.

Born a farm labourer's son in Marton, Yorks, in 1728, Cook joined the Navy in 1755 and rose swiftly through the ranks.

Between 1756 and 1767 he charted the waters off Newfoundland and Nova Scotia, Canada. Then in 1768 he was given the command of the ship Endeavour and began the first of his three great voyages in the South Pacific and off the North American coast.

He sailed to Tahiti before becoming in 1769 the first European to reach New Zealand since the Dutchman Abel Tasman 127 years earlier. Unlike Tasman, he also went ashore.

Cook and his crew sailed round the North and South Islands, charting them with remarkable accuracy.

Geographers of the time believed in a vast "unknown land in the south" — Terra Australis Incognita — which they thought balanced the Arctic in the North.

In 1770 Cook discovered a land fitting the bill. He landed on Australia's east coast on April 29 in a place he named Botany Bay due to its prolific vegetation.

Cook sailed north up the coast, which he also claimed for Britain and named New South Wales.

He returned to England in 1771 and was made Commander of another ship, the Resolution, in which he set out on his second voyage to the South Pacific in 1772.

He spent three years discovering and charting new islands, returning home in 1775.

Cook's third and last voyage, which began in July 1776, was an attempt to sail between the Atlantic and Pacific north of America. In

Cook and his crew inscribe the ship's name Endeavour on a tree at Botany Bay

the mid-Pacific, before searching in vain for this "North-West Passage", he charted the Sandwich Islands — naming them after his friend, the snack-inventing Earl of Sandwich.

Cook was killed when he returned to the Sandwiches (now Hawaii) in 1779 and had a row with villagers over the theft of a boat.

Four years later America gained independence from Britain and it was no longer possible to transport criminals there. So Britain decided to ship them to Australia instead.

In 1788 the first group of about 1,000 convicts — some innocent and many only petty criminals —

arrived at Botany Bay. Some modern-day Australians, nicknamed First Fleeters, are directly descended from those 1,000.

They settled near Botany Bay at Port Jackson, now the site of Sydney, and were the first people to settle in Australia since the Aborigines 40,000 years before.

Other Europeans emigrated there — and transportation was abolished in 1852. In 1901 the various Australian colonies joined up to form an independent nation.

The world's sixth largest country in area, Australia's population is now around 18.5million, about 94 per cent of European descent.

Life of musical genius Mozart

WOLFGANG Amadeus Mozart's great genius was only truly recognised after he died in poverty.

His prodigious talent as a child certainly amazed those who encountered it, but sustained popularity and success eluded him later on.

Mozart was born on January 27, 1756, in Salzburg, Austria. His musical ability was fostered by his father Leopold, a concertmaster and

violinist — and by six Mozart was composing and performing publicly.

But interest in his music waned as he reached adulthood. Partly because of his "difficult" personality, he struggled for greater recognition among influential figures.

Mozart achieved only fleeting successes — a fact which seems incredible now, given the quality and quantity of his output.

The most famous of his 600-plus

works include the operas The Marriage of Figaro (1786), Don Giovanni (1787), Cosi Fan Tutte (1790) and The Magic Flute (1791) as well as the Symphony No40 in G Minor (1788) and his Serenade in G Major, Eine Kleine Nachtmusik.

Mozart, plagued by illness throughout adulthood, died in Vienna on December 5, 1791, probably from typhoid. He was just 35. His grave is unmarked.

THE Sun

…day, April 30, 1770   **Three farthings**   **THOUGHT: STREWTH IS OUT THERE**

…ant…little Wolfgang

…hild …enius …rites …pera …t 14

…genius Wolfgang …eus Mozart has writ- … entire OPERA at 14. … latest work is called …dates, King of Pon- …nd was produced by …rilliant young musi- …n Milan.

… Sun has followed …gang's amazing … since he performed …ng George in London …ears ago.

… — in an exclusive …iew with the lad's …eopold — we were …rst paper to reveal …Volgang:

…as fluent on the vio- …, organ and clavier, …med all over Europe …ade up piano pieces … when he was SIX.

…arpsichord

…rote his first sonatas … violin and harpsi- …at only SEVEN. …mposed his first …mphony at EIGHT …n oratorio at TEN. …fgang is so talented …morises every note …composition — then …it out in one go on …script paper.

…t year he was made …rtmaster to the arch- … of Salzburg — his …town in Austria — …hen went to Milan, … he won an award …he Pope.

…h Operetta — Page 11

WIZARD OF OZ

G'day … Cook disembarks at Botany Bay shortly before sighting giant hopping rat-style creature (right)

Cook finds new land

Bay watch … Capt Cook

TOP explorer James Cook has discovered a new country full of weird animals and exotic plants, The Sun can reveal.

And last night the question being asked was: Has he found the lost land Terra Australis?

Captain Cook, 42, has encountered one strange furry creature, like a giant rat, which can hop 16ft in one bound and carries its babies in a pouch on its

By SIDNEY OPERA-HOUSE

stomach. And he was so impressed with the richness of the local plant-life he has named it Botany Bay.

Cook and his crew from The Endeavour have also met the country's native people, who don't seem very friendly.

Captain Cook, of Marton, Yorks, set out from Plymouth on August 26, 1768. He recently sailed around New Zealand and claimed it for Britain.

Cobber Load Of That — Pages 4 & 5

1776

WAR OF INDEPENDENCE

An anonymous painting of the Boston Tea Party, where defiant colonists protesting at the imposition of a tea monopoly hurled chests of British tea into Boston harbour

...Timeline...

1772 Cook's second voyage to the Pacific; London Credit Exchange Company issues the first traveller's cheques; First weighing machine with a dial is patented in London.

1773 Boston Tea Party; Emelian Pugachev leads uprising of Cossacks and peasants in Russia.

1774 Nursery rhyme collection, Tommy Thumb's Song Book, published — it contains Baa, Baa, Black Sheep; Sir Joseph Priestley discovers oxygen; Beginning of the reign of King Louis XVI of France.

1775 Birth of artist Joseph Turner in London; Submarine invented by American David Bushnell.

1776 Cook sets off on third voyage; San Francisco founded; First St Leger horse race at Doncaster.

The nursery rhyme Baa, Baa, Black Sheep was first published in 1774. It posed the question: Have you any wool?

THE Declaration of Independence, and the eight-year war which achieved its aims, was the birth of America as a nation.

It arose out of the resentment over British control which had been growing as the colonies expanded throughout the early 18th Century.

And it was fuelled by the imposition of new taxes by King George III's Government.

Breaking point came when Britain granted the East India Company a big tax break, giving it a monopoly on tea sales in the colonies.

The colonists were outraged. On December 16, 1773, a group disguised as Indians boarded three English ships and dumped 342 chests of tea into Boston Harbour.

This act of defiance — the "Boston Tea Party" — triggered war.

Britain sealed off the port and scrapped the local government's powers.

The state assembly refused to disband and urged locals to arm themselves ready for conflict.

In April 1775 British-appointed governor General Thomas Gage got wind of a haul of weapons stored at Concord, a few miles from Boston, and sent troops to destroy it.

They came under fire from local militia at Lexington. So began six years of fighting, at the end of which a highly-trained British army of about 42,000 men, plus 30,000 German mercenaries, were defeated by untrained militia who never totalled more than 20,000 at once.

Although superior militarily, the British underestimated hostility among civilians and the doggedness of the patriots.

At the Battle of Bunker Hill near Boston on June 17, 1775, a brazen British attack was defeated with terrible casualties because the militia refused to give up.

The British dismissively called the colonists "Yankees". But the revolutionaries proudly adopted the term and made Yankee Doodle a patriotic song. By June 1776 the Continental Congress decided to issue a mission statement. Drafted by the skilled writer and future President Thomas Jefferson, the Declaration of Independence comprised a vicious attack on the "tyrant" King George and a list of reasons why the colonists were splitting from Britain.

Many of its memorable phrases describe core beliefs for modern Americans. It was signed on July 4, a date Americans celebrate as Independence Day. It begins:

"We hold these truths to be self-evident, that all men are created equal, that they are endowed by their creator with certain unalienable rights, that among these are life, liberty and the pursuit of happiness.

"That whenever any form of government becomes destructive of these ends, it is the right of the people to alter or to abolish it and to institute new government."

The British won many battles during the war — but found that new pockets of resistance sprang back up as soon as they left a territory they had captured. They were also at a disadvantage being far from their own supply lines.

George Washington, a militia commander from farming stock, led the American army from July 1775 until the war's end in 1781 — when in one of his few victories his 16,000 men surrounded the 8,000 under General Charles Cornwallis, the British commander in the South, at Yorktown, Virginia.

Cornwallis surrendered on October 19 — and although the British were not entirely defeated the Government gave up the fight.

A peace treaty was signed on September 3, 1783, and Britain accepted America's independence.

Washington was sworn in as the first President on April 30, 1789, and the first Constitution was ratified on December 15, 1791.

The British artist Joseph Turner (right) was born in London in 1775. Above, his oil painting Dido Building Carthage, completed in 1815

John Trumbull's painting of the signing of the Declaration of Independence on July 4, 1776. It was drafted by Thomas Jefferson, later to become President

10 JOKES ABOUT THOSE SILLY HILLBILLIES

WE always suspected those Yankees were as thick as two short plankies — and now they've proved it. They **MUST** be dense to think they've got a chance of running their own country. Here are ten top gags about those dim-witted colonials:

★ A colonist was asked: "What's the capital of Virginia?" He said: "V".

★ What do you call the skeleton of a colonist in a cupboard? The world record-holder at hide-and-seek.

★ What's the difference between a colonist's wake and a colonist's wedding? One less drunk.

★ Did you hear about the tap dancer who came from the colonies? He broke

Moron . . make him President!

his leg . . . falling in the sink.

★ Why are jokes about colonists so short? So colonists can understand them.

★ A colonist kidnaps a child and writes a ransom note. Then he gives it to the kid and says: "Here, take this back to your parents."

★ How do you get a one-armed colonist out of a tree? Wave to him.

★ Two colonists on either side of a river. One says: "How do I get to the other side?" The other says: "You daft colonist — you're already on the other side!"

★ Did you hear about the colonist who took a ruler to bed? He wanted to know how long he slept.

★ How many colonists does it take to change a lightbulb? What's a lightbulb?

Colonic irritation . . . Thomas Jefferson and other cheesed-off bigwigs have another go at perfecting the wording of the Declaration

YANKED APART

Colonists go it alone

From BERTHA NATION
in the Colonies

DEFIANT colonists in America broke away from Britain last night and insisted they are setting up their own independent nation.

They issued an extraordinary statement which branded King George "a tyrant" who was unfit to rule them.

The Yankee colonists, who have been at war with Britain for almost 15 months, claim they have a right to scrap any government which denies them "life, liberty and the pursuit of happiness".

TROUBLESOME

Their so-called Declaration of Independence was voted through in Philadelphia yesterday by the Continental Congress, which represents the 13 colonies in North America.

A spokesman for our Government said last night: "This idiocy only goes to prove that we are right to be at war with them."

Meanwhile yesterday a 30,000-strong force of Our Boys landed on Staten Island, near New York.

They have orders to seize the city and cut off the troublesome patriots in New England from the rest of the colonists further south.

Full Story — Pages Four and Five

77,186 DAYS TO GO

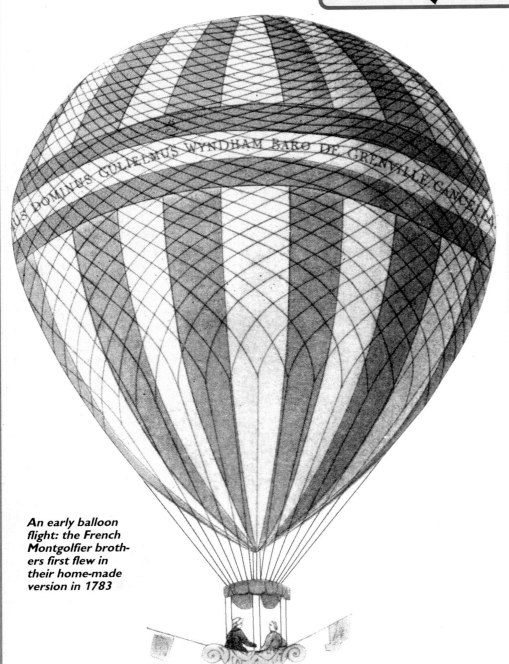

An early balloon flight: the French Montgolfier brothers first flew in their home-made version in 1783

1788

MADNESS OF KING GEORGE

KING George III's lapse into madness and the scandal caused by his son's various affairs threw Britain into crisis.

George became King in 1751. Unlike the first two Georges — who were from Hanover and spoke German rather than English — he was a popular monarch.

He and his wife Queen Charlotte seem to have been happily married and had 15 children.

George and Charlotte were both fairly strait-laced and shunned fashionable London society.

He also had a passion for agriculture — earning him the nickname of Farmer George.

The King's long and successful reign was repeatedly dogged by failing mental health.

In 1788 he began complaining of fever, insomnia and swelling in his limbs. His urine turned purple.

He was soon babbling incoherently and bursting into tears. He also made obscene comments about a female courtier.

The King's outbursts increased and became more violent. His wife refused to be alone with him.

The Royal doctors were puzzled. One even suggested the King's complaint was brought on by ''over-indulgence in fruit''.

In an attempt to find a cure, the King was bled, bathed in freezing and boiling water and put in a strait-jacket. All these ''cures'' failed.

He eventually recovered but in 1810 the madness returned. The next year his son George was made Prince Regent, a position he held until George III died in 1820.

The Prince, later to become King George IV, could not have been more different from his father. He was roundly disliked by the people, mocked by politicians and by cartoonists.

The Prince was seen as a ridiculous dandy, hopelessly spendthrift where his father was frugal.

He had numerous affairs with older women, his most infamous with Maria Fitzherbert, a Catholic widow six years his senior.

The Prince was said to have fallen in love with Maria after catching a glimpse of her at the opera.

He pursued her relentlessly but she was a decent, modest woman and refused to become his mistress.

Eventually he persuaded her to accept a proposal of marriage, even though it was illegal for the heir to the throne to marry a Catholic.

Maria immediately regretted what she had done and fled to France.

She did not see the Prince for more than a year — during which he wrote her scores of passionate letters begging her to marry him.

Maria eventually returned and in December 1785 they wed in secret in London.

The couple attempted to keep the secret by living separately.

But gossip soon began circulating that Maria was pregnant by the Prince — and it is possible the couple did have a child at the end of 1786.

Rumours of the secret marriage also leaked out. Questions were even asked in Parliament.

In 1795 the Prince reluctantly wed Princess Caroline of Brunswick — his first marriage being no obstacle as it was not legal. He disliked Caroline and refused to live in the same house as her.

When he became King in 1820 he offered her £50,000 a year to renounce the title of Queen.

She refused, so George began divorce proceedings — though public opinion was in her favour.

Caroline died shortly after his coronation. George died in 1830.

...Timeline...

1779 Captain Cook killed by islanders after landing on Hawaii.

1780 Steel pen points begin to replace quills; First Epsom Derby.

1781 British army chief Lord Cornwallis surrenders at Yorktown, ending American War of Independence; Frenchman Rene-Theophile-Hyacinthe Laennac invents stethoscope; Sir William Herschel discovers Uranus.

1783 French brothers Joseph and Jacques Montgolfier became the first humans to fly, in hot-air balloon; William Pitt the Younger becomes youngest PM at 24; U.S.

independence recognised at Treaty of Paris.

1785 Stagecoaches carry mail between U.S. towns; The beer pump handle is patented.

1786 Wolfgang Amadeus Mozart writes Marriage of Figaro.

1787 U.S. Constitution drawn up at convention led by George Washington, who is elected first President two years later.

1788 Marylebone Cricket Club sets up home at Lord's, establishes rules of game; First British convicts shipped to Botany Bay, Australia; The Times is born; Birth of poet George Gordon (Lord Byron).

George Washington led 1787 convention at which first constitution was drawn up

An early cricket match being played at Lord's, the North London ground which the Marylebone Cricket Club made its base in 1788 — it is still the game's home

William Pitt the Younger, who in 1783 became youngest-ever Prime Minister at 2

THE Sun

Tuesday, September 2, 1788   Three farthings   THOUGHT: BY GEORGE!

GEORGIAN MILDRED
Our great new AGONY AUNT

OT a problem that won't go away? Call for
orgian Mildred! Yes folks, our fabulous new agony
nt starts her column today. So turn straight to
ge Eight — it'll be a weight off your mind.

THEY'RE BOTH BONKERS

King goes mad and Prince has a 'love-child'

By MADGE JESTY and LOU KNEE

KING George has gone MAD — and his son and heir
may have had an illegitimate child, The Sun can reveal.

Royal sources say the King has been having violent
outbursts and keeps making obscene remarks to shocked
ladies-in-waiting.

The King's condition may have been aggravated by the scandal
surrounding Prince George, 26. He is rumoured to have fathered a
child by a Catholic widow called Maria Fitzherbert.

The Royals In Crisis — Pages 2, 3, 4 and 5

ing George . . . outbursts

Prince George . . . scandal

DEAR *Mildred*

OUR GREAT NEW AGONY AUNT

Dear Mildred

I'VE been having an affair with the best friend of the second cousin twice removed of the nephew of my sister-in-law's father — and I'm so confused.

He says he believes we are related and that we have to end the relationship immediately. I think he's using it as an excuse. What should I do?

MILDRED says: YOU'RE confused? I must admit I cannot work out what relation you are to this man. Be assured, though, that unless he's your brother you're in the clear.

Dear Mildred

I LOVE my girlfriend very much — but we've been drifting apart because of her strange obsession.

She thinks about nothing but ballooning ever since those terrible French brothers went up in their contraption a few years back.

As far as I'm concerned, if God had wanted us to fly, he'd have given us wings. What do I need to do to make her forget about it?

MILDRED says: Forget her. Find someone less flighty and more down-to-earth.

My missus is the William Pitts in bed

Dear Mildred

MY sex life is in ruins because my wife has a thing about our dashing young Prime Minister — and even yells his name when we're making love.

We have always been perfect together in the bed chamber.

But now, at the moment of ecstasy, she cries out: "Oh William, William Pitt The Younger!" It is utterly off-putting. And my name's not William. I have been trying my best to understand her.

She claims that when passion overwhelms her she doesn't know what she's saying. But I can't help feeling she has a thing for this Pitt.

I suppose I have to accept he's got something about him.

After all, he's very bright and was Prime Minister when he was only 24 — I doubt that will ever be surpassed.

He's still only 29 now, and still single, which worries me a bit (though actually, I don't think the little pipsqueak is even interested in women — politics seems to be the only thing that gets his blood racing).

What do I do? I am only a humble farm labourer — I'm no match for him.

MILDRED SAYS: It's an unusual problem that possibly has an unusual remedy.

My guess is that you spend much of your time tromping through the house with muddy boots and smelling of farm animals.

I think what your wife is searching for is someone a little more statesmanlike. Try saving up some money and hiring the finest ceremonial outfit.

Next, set up a large wooden box on a plinth in your bedroom. At bedtime stand behind it and, while thumping the box with your right hand, make a rousing speech fit for the House of Commons.

Mark my words, she'll soon be voting with her feet — and you won't exactly be leading the opposition!

HE'S SHIPPED OUT

Dear Mildred

MY sailor husband and I have been married for four years and everything was going fine — until he decided to go with his navy mates on a voyage to an exotic island, leaving me at home with the kids.

We have two small urchins and a nice hovel and my hubby has always been attentive and kind.

But last year his friend — whom I won't name (it sounds a bit like Fletcher Crispian) — talked him into going to Tahiti on a ship called The Bounty. My husband said it would be nothing but a long, hard voyage and that the Captain was a right so-and-so. But since he left I haven't heard a word from him.

To be honest, I don't trust my hubby when he's with this friend. The man is nothing but trouble and is always leading his pals astray.

Plus, he's single. At the first sight of those Tahitian girls in grass skirts he'll be off like a rabbit, encouraging all his mates to join him, married or not.

What should I do? My husband's never strayed before, but I'm going through sheer hell wondering what he's up to thousands of miles away.

P.S. What are breadfruit trees?

MILDRED says: I'm sure you're worrying about nothing.

You husband sounds like a thoroughly decent man — and remember, they've got a strict captain to keep them in check.

I'm sure your husband's not planning a mutiny!

As sure as eggs is eggs, he'll arrive back home in no time with exotic gifts for you and the family.

HELPLINES

OUR Mildred has written a range of numbered leaflets which give handy advice on a host of problems. They're all available free from your local town or village hall. Look for your problem below, then pick up the leaflet you need:

Trouble with smallpox? .... Leaflet

Bustle too big? .... Leaflet

Worried about your wig? .... Leaflet

Clothes look ridiculous? .... Leaflet

Hooked on ballooning? .... Leaflet

Depressed about U.S. Independence? ..... Leaflet

Up for a revolution in France? .... Leaflet

Jane MOORE

SHE TELLS IT LIKE THAT WHICH IT IS

What's next . . children out of wedlock?

KING George may well be mad. But his public are bloody furious. How many more Royal scandals do we have to endure?

Henry VIII, the serial wife killer. Queen Elizabeth and her series of affairs whilst supposedly being the "Virgin Queen". And now this.

The King is apparently prone to violent outbursts and making obscene suggestions to ladies-in-waiting.

And his son Prince George has clearly taken a leaf out of his father's book *(Do What You Want And Damn The Consequences, 1 shilling, Ye Olde Penguin).*

Parading his mistress along Brighton seafront in broad daylight . . . whatever next – future Kings refusing to give up their mistresses when they marry an innocent virgin?

Royal wives having their toes sucked by someone who's not their husband?

The son of a Royal mistress parading around the South of France and boasting about his drug-taking exploits?

The mind boggles.

Speaking about Prince George's "relationship" with Catholic widow Maria Fitzherbert, Charles Fox MP says: "This is a low and malicious rumour". Unfortunately, he isn't showing righteous outrage that the Prince is rumoured to be having an affair with this woman and has fathered a child by her. No. His indignation stems from the suggestion that they might tie the knot, because it's illegal for the heir to the throne to marry a Catholic.

With hypocritical views like this in the corridors of power, what hope is there for the rest of us?

Before you know it, the moral fabric of society will have unwoven to the extent where – God forbid – it's the norm to fornicate and bear children outside wedlock.

According to a Palace insider, the Prince's sexploits may have triggered his father's madness.

King George is "agitated" and "talks indecently" to the extent that Queen Charlotte refuses to be left alone with him.

Presumably this renders him incapable of performing Royal duties for fear he might insult dignitaries or the public.

Who knows? He might refer to the Chinese as "slitty-eyed" or insult deaf people on a visit to Cardiff. That would never do.

King George has gone from being a feisty monarch who was determined to bring Parliament to heel to a froth-mouthed loon who is even shunned by his own wife and children.

It's time to oust him in favour of the next in line. Trouble is, his heir Prince George is showing all the signs of being even more mad, bad, and dangerous to know.

God help us all.

The Gentleman Joke

A QUESTION: Why should one consider the possession of a simple farthing preferable to performing the act of love with a gentleman? **THE ANSWER:** A farthing will last one a great deal longer!

NOT the Gentleman Joke

A QUESTION: Why is it that a wife's feet are smaller than those of her husband? **THE ANSWER:** In order that she may stand nearer to the sink in the scullery.

76,870 DAYS TO GO

1789
FRENCH REVOLUTION

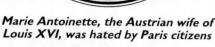

Marie Antoinette, the Austrian wife of Louis XVI, was hated by Paris citizens

Ailing France needed a dynamic leader but Louis XVI was weak and indecisive

THE storming of the Bastille on July 14, 1789, was seen by the French revolutionaries as a symbol of the fall of the old regime.

The pressure for widescale reform within France had been growing for more than 50 years.

A series of wars had proved to be an enormous drain on the country's finances. By the time Louis XVI took the throne in 1774 France was spiralling into bankruptcy.

The country needed a leader of genius to pull it out of the crisis. Unfortunately, Louis was a weak and indecisive man.

From 1776 a succession of finance ministers made the situation worse by operating a policy that relied entirely on the state borrowing money.

Within a decade the Government's credit was exhausted. In 1786 finance minister Charles Alexandre de Calonne came up with a desperately-needed programme of reform.

Central to it was the replacement of a series of taxes with a single universal land tax. But aristocrats refused to accept the reforms.

By the summer of 1787 Louis was in dire need of money. His new finance minister Lominie de Brienne tried to persuade the provincial Parlement of Paris to support tax reforms. But in

November the king lost his patience. He ordered armed troops to surround the building Parlement was meeting in and forced it to approve some loans he needed.

The move sparked fury among the people of Paris. Over the next few months royal edicts were ignored, royal officials were assaulted and pamphlets denouncing Louis as a despot were published all over France.

As the financial crisis deepened Louis summoned a meeting of the Estates-General.

This was a consultative body of representatives from France's three legally-defined social classes — clergy, nobility and commoners.

The Estates-General came together for the first time in almost 200 years on May 1, 1789.

After a few weeks of fruitless debate, the commoners — known as the Third Estate — decided to try to force the pace of political change.

In June its members, which now called themselves the National Assembly, met at an indoor tennis court and swore not to disband until a constitution had been established.

Rumours began to circulate that Louis was moving 16 regiments of foreign mercenaries to Paris to

overthrow the Assembly by force. The news incensed the poorer citizens of Paris, who were being stirred up against Louis and his unpopular Austrian wife Marie Antoinette by political agitators.

Crowds roamed the capital looking for arms to fight off a royal attack. On July 14 the mob attacked and captured the Bastille, a fortress that had once housed political prisoners.

At the end of August, the National Assembly issued its famous Declaration of the Rights of Man — a document that denied the king's right to rule.

On October 5 a Parisian mob marched to the king's palace at Versailles to protest at the high cost of bread. When Marie Antoinette was told of their protest she is said to have exclaimed: "Let them eat cake."

The demonstration became a riot. Louis and his family were forced to return to Paris with the mob.

With the royal family virtual prisoners, the Assembly set about debating reforms which would leave the king as head of a constitutional monarchy.

The debates were still going on when, in June 1791, the royal family was caught trying to flee France in

disguise and arrested. The failed flight inflamed revolutionary feeling and split the Assembly into radical and moderate factions.

In August 1792 a mob that supported the extremist Jacobins stormed the Tuileries Palace in Paris, hacking to death 600 soldiers.

Over the next few weeks Paris lurched into anarchy. On September 21 France was declared a republic. The Jacobins, led by the young lawyer Maximilien Robespierre, pressed for Louis to stand trial on treason charges. In January 1793 he was found guilty and guillotined.

By the summer, the government was effectively in the hands of a 12-man body called the Committee of Public Safety, with Robespierre at its head. The committee began executing anyone it deemed a threat to the revolution — ushering in a period known as The Terror.

Over the next months 17,000 were guillotined, among them Marie Antoinette. In July 1794 Robespierre and 82 followers were arrested during a coup and executed.

With his death, the revolution's radical phase ended. By 1799 France was being ruled by the brilliant young general Napoleon Bonaparte.

Mutiny on the Bounty

Captain Bligh and his supporters are seized by mutineers on the Bounty

IN 1787 William Bligh, a young Navy officer who had recently served with Captain Cook, was commissioned to travel to Tahiti in the HMS Bounty.

He and his crew were to obtain a large number of breadfruit plants which were to be transplanted to the Caribbean to provide food for slaves.

The voyage was long and bad feeling began to grow between Bligh and his crew.

After a long stay in Tahiti the Bounty began the second leg of the

trip to the Caribbean. On April 28, 1789, Fletcher Christian and 12 crew members led a mutiny, eventually setting Bligh and his supporters adrift in a small boat.

After incredible hardships they reached Timor in the East Indies on June 14, having travelled more than 3,600 miles.

Christian, once a close friend of Bligh's, set up home on Pitcairn Island with the other mutineers and some Tahitian men and women.

He is thought to have been killed by the Tahitians five years after the mutiny.

In a brilliant piece of seamanship, Bligh steered a small boat more than 3,600 miles across the Pacific

...Timeline...

1789 French Estates General meets for first time in almost 200 years; Formation of National Assembly; Members of France's Third Estate take the Tennis Court Oath; Louis XVI orders the Third Estate to disperse, its members refuse; Riots in Paris after price of bread doubles; Mob storms the Bastille following rumours that Louis is about to send troops into Paris.

THE Sun

Wednesday, July 15, 1789   Three farthings   THOUGHT: MOBS ROUT NOBS

MUTINY
Crew of Bounty ditch skipper

By IAN SURRECTION

BRAVE English Navy captain as survived 47 days adrift in e Pacific in a small boat ter his crew mutinied.

William Bligh, 35, and 18 of s men were forced off their ip HMS Bounty and dumped the ocean following a jour- ey to Tahiti.

The mutineers — led by the ip's first mate Fletcher hristian — did not expect ther their captain or his sup- orters to survive.

But in a brilliant display of amanship Bligh steered the aky boat more than 3,600 iles to land safely at Timor, ear Java.

Stern

News of the mutiny has ken almost two months to ter back to Britain.

The Bounty had sailed to hiti to pick up breadfruit ants and take them to the est Indies.

The cause of the mutiny and e current whereabouts of e rebels is not known.

Bligh, who has a reputation a strict disciplinarian, pre- ously sailed with the top ex- orer Captain James Cook.

Christian, 25, of ockermouth, Cumbria, rned down the chance of a iversity place to go to sea. He was once a close friend Bligh's and served under m on previous voyages.

Men overboard . . . Captain William Bligh and his valiant officers are set adrift in a small boat by callous Fletcher Christian and the mutinous crew

THE FRENCH ARE REVOLTING
(And we're not talking about their habits, folks)

in arms . . . Paris mob storms the Bastille yesterday

REVOLUTION erupted in France yesterday after more than 100 people died when a mob stormed a Paris prison called The Bastille.

Trouble began when rabble-rous- ers began stirring up low-paid workers, urging them to take up arms against King Louis XVI.

They began to run amok, ransacking homes and shops in a desperate search

From GILL O'TINE in Paris

for guns and swords. The mob soon began marching towards the Bastille, spurred on by rumours that weapons and ammunition were stockpiled there.

When the commander of troops at the prison saw the crowd he panicked and ordered his men to open fire. The

incensed mob managed to drag a cannon from a nearby barracks and blasted the prison until the soldiers surrendered.

The rebels hacked off the commander's head and paraded it through the city.

Last night there were reports of more violent clashes on the streets of Paris — and in other French towns and cities.

And Royal sources claimed the shocked King is planning to allow a sweeping programme of reforms in a bid to hold on to his crown.

Has Louis Throne It Away? — Page Eight

72,980 DAYS TO GO

1800

The head of King Louis XVI is held aloft after he was guillotined in January 1793 during the French revolution. His wife Marie Antoinette was also executed for treason

...Timeline...

1791 Mozart's The Magic Flute premieres in Vienna.

1792 First horse-drawn ambulance designed in France; Washington's White House is built.

1793 First free British settlers reach Australia; Louis XVI of France and wife Marie Antoinette — who said of the breadless poor "Let them eat cake" — beheaded for treason.

1795 British seize Cape Colony from Dutch; France overruns Netherlands — creates dependent Dutch republic.

1796 Gloucestershire doctor Edward Jenner discovers vaccination for smallpox which eventually eradicates the

disease; British conquer Ceylon; Scottish explorer Mungo Park travels through Gambia and reaches Niger.

1797 Top hat invented by London milliner John Etherington; Bank of England issues first £1 note; First parachute jump, from balloon above Paris.

1798 Franz Joseph Haydn composes The Creation.

1799 Wolfe Tone organises Irish revolt against English rule; Indian warrior Ranjit Singh seizes Lahore and founds Sikh kingdom in Punjab.

1800 London opens first soup kitchens for the poor; Britain's first Christmas tree goes up at Queen's Lodge, Windsor.

In 1796 Edward Jenner found smallpox vaccine

The fearsome Sikh warrior Ranjit Singh (1799)

The Christmas tree, which was first seen in Britain in 1800 at the Queen's Lodge, Windsor

THOMAS JEFFERSON

THOMAS Jefferson's love-child was the first sex scandal to rock a President — and has echoes of the Zippergate controversy that engulfed President Bill Clinton almost 200 years later.

Jefferson is believed to have had at least two children with slave Sally Hemings. But his career survived all the allegations because his supporters successfully argued that the newspaper which broke the story was politically-motivated.

The rumours have continued to this day, however — and genetics researchers in 1998 claimed to have proof that Sally's son Eston was fathered by Jefferson.

Eston was born long after her first son Thomas Woodston — who looked remarkably like Jefferson and whose family always considered him the President's son.

Sally was born into slavery on Jefferson's estate in 1774. She was the child of John Wayles, father of Jefferson's wife Martha, and a slave called Elizabeth Hemings.

The affair between Jefferson and Sally is believed to have begun after Martha's death and when Jefferson was sent to France as American ambassador in 1787.

Sally, then 13, went as an attendant to his daughter Maria. She is said to have become his "concubine" there and gave birth to Thomas shortly after they arrived back in America. But the scandal was a

mere detail in the life of a remarkably brilliant, energetic man who was a champion of democracy.

Jefferson, born in 1743 into a wealthy Virginia family, was a philosopher, scientist, musician, writer and inventor who said he found interest in the smallest blade of grass.

He invented the swivel chair, the dumb-waiter and a new type of plough. He designed houses and helped plan Washington DC.

As a young man, Jefferson studied law before entering politics in Virginia's general assembly.

He reached Congress in 1775 with a formidable reputation as a writer. The colonists, who were fighting for independence from Britain, chose Jefferson to write a statement detailing why. His Declaration of Independence is one of history's most famous documents.

Jefferson became Governor of Virginia in 1779 and the war ended in 1781. A year later his ailing wife Martha died aged 34.

Jefferson went on to serve in various capacities in government, including as Vice-President.

He was nominated for President in 1800 and inaugurated the following year, serving two terms, but refused to be the Republicans' candidate in 1808. At 65 he retired to his Virginia estate and died on Independence Day, July 4, 1826.

Electricity breakthrough

IT is now hard to imagine the world without electricity — it provides light and heat and powers transport, industry and countless devices we take for granted.

The major breakthrough in its development was made by physicist Alessandro Volta when he created the first battery.

Other scientists had experimented with electrical charges, but

Volta's "Voltaic Pile" was the first invention to produce a steady stream of current. Volta, born in 1745 in Como, Italy, was a physics professor at the University of Pavia.

He was showered with honours by various countries for the Voltaic Pile and was made a Count by Napoleon in 1801.

His name gave us the volt, the measurement of electrical charge.

A topping invention by London hatmaker in 1797

Silliest Dresser

Lifetime Achievement

Best Overall Act

Best Haircut

Best Gig

You what? Ludo bags five gongs

★ SEXY young composer Ludwig Van Beethoven has swept the board in the Bizarre Music Awards – despite the fact he's going DEAF.

Ludo, 30, won FIVE top honours including Best Overall Act, Best Newcomer and Hunkiest Composer.

★ Sun readers voted him the winner in the Best Single category — for his barn-storming anthem Trio in G Major for Flute, Bassoon and Piano (1791).

And the German genius also bagged the prestigious gong for Best Alive Act — thanks mainly to most of the competition being dead. The Best Gig award went to Austrian Wolfgang Mozart, for his Clavier Live! (at the Salzburg Hippodrome).

★ German Johann Sebastian Bach saw off stiff competition to win Best Haircut for the 100th year running.

The prize for Silliest Dress Sense went to Italian Antonio Salieri while Austrian Franz Joseph Haydn picked up the Lifetime Achievement award, for want of anything else to give him.

Results In Full –Pages 16 & 17

Volta ... battery boy

Bright spark Volta

ARKY scientist ssandro Volta has in- ted the first device r to produce a eam of electricity.

he 55-year-old Ital- 's "Voltaic Pile" is a mplex contraption in- ving metal discs and gy cardboard.

his somehow pro- es a flow of current, ch could one day be d to power a host of our-saving gadgets.

One scientist said: his is a breakthrough our evolution. It's the st we can do now to me a unit of electric- after him."

NIPPERGATE

President Jefferson had baby with teenage slave

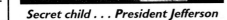

Secret child ... President Jefferson

By CLINTON ECHO

THE next American President Thomas Jefferson fathered a secret love-child with a 15-year-old slave, it was revealed last night.

Jefferson, 58, who will be sworn in as third President next year, got pretty Sally Hemings pregnant while he was in Paris

EXCLUSIVE

as ambassador to France. Their son, called Thomas Woodson, is now 11.

And it is believed widowed Jefferson is **STILL** having an affair with attrac- tive Sally, now 26.

Amazingly it was also revealed that Sally is the child of a slave woman and her owner — the father of Jeffer- son's wife Martha.

That makes Martha, who died in

1782, Sally's half-sister. The scandal is a big blow to Jefferson, from Virginia, who was elected only last month.

But political pundits last night pre- dicted it will **NOT** spell the end of his glittering career — because America needs his extraordinary talent.

Jefferson is a scientist, musician, architect and philosopher who wrote the Declaration of Independence.

He also has a sideline as an inven- tor — and dreamed up the swivel-chair and the dumb-waiter.

Slave To Love — Pages 4 & 5

1815
NAPOLEONIC WARS

NAPOLEON Bonaparte arose from the chaos of the French Revolution — transforming himself from a humble artillery officer into an Emperor.

His meteoric rise began in 1793 as revolutionary France fought a desperate war for survival against her enemies Austria, Britain, Prussia, Holland and Spain.

The British navy had seized the southern French port of Toulon. Napoleon, though only a 24-year-old junior officer, took charge of the siege and forced the British out.

Three years later he was a general leading the French army into Italy to fight the Austrians. The blitzkrieg campaign that followed was one of the most remarkable in history. Within weeks Napoleon had smashed the Austrian army and proved himself a military genius.

A campaign in Egypt in 1798 further enhanced his reputation.

With his victories came political success. In November 1799 he and two colleagues seized power in France. A few months later Napoleon, a Corsican by birth, was appointed First Consul — making him sole ruler in all but name.

In 1804 all pretence was dropped as he assumed the title of Emperor of France.

In the same year he revealed his plan to invade England, massing a vast army along the French coast in readiness.

But he was foiled because his ships could not wrest control of the Channel from the Royal Navy.

Napoleon's invasion dream was finally shattered in October 1805 when Admiral Horatio Nelson smashed the French navy at Trafalgar — giving Britain unchallenged mastery of the sea. On land

Napoleon enjoyed success after success. In December 1805 he defeated the Austrian army at Austerlitz. The next year the Prussians were humbled at the Battle of Jena.

In 1807 Napoleon beat the Russians at the Battle of Friedland and Tsar Alexander sued for peace. The same year Napoleon made his brother Joseph King of Spain.

By 1810 Napoleon was at the height of his power. His empire stretched from the borders of Russia to the southern coast of Spain.

But the cracks had already begun to appear. The British army in Spain, under the Duke of Wellington, was slowly but surely pushing the French back. Then in 1812 Napoleon invaded Russia with an army of 610,000 men.

The French captured Moscow — but the expedition ended in disaster when they were forced to retreat during a freezing Russian winter.

Just 20,000 men made it back to France. As the scale of the disaster became apparent the nations of Europe united against Napoleon.

For two years he fought on, but the odds were impossible. In April 1814 he abdicated and was exiled to the Mediterranean isle of Elba.

However, Europe had not heard the last of Napoleon. In March 1815 he landed in France, winning over the troops sent to capture him. He laid plans to defeat his old enemies before they could destroy him.

In June his army marched into Belgium, hoping to swiftly defeat the British and Prussian forces stationed there. But his gamble failed on the field of Waterloo.

He was exiled to Saint Helena, a remote island in the south Atlantic, where he remained until his death from stomach cancer in 1821.

Admiral Horatio Nelson (left) defeated French navy at Trafalgar (1805) and put an end to Napoleon's dream of invading Britain. Nelson died in the battle

. . . Timeline . . .

1801 First census puts Britain's population at 8,872,000.

1802 First race meeting at Goodwood, Sussex.

1803 Richard Trevithick builds first steam locomotive.

1804 Napoleon is French Emperor; First oil lamp made in England; Royal Horticultural Society founded.

1805 Admiral Horatio Nelson says "England expects that every man will do his duty" before beating French at Trafalgar — he is killed; First Trooping the Colour in London.

1806 Napoleon brings the Holy Roman Empire to an end; Carbon paper patented in London.

1807 First Ascot Gold Cup horse race; Britain abolishes slave trade; Pall Mall, London, is world's first street lit by gas lamps.

1808 British scientist John Dalton proves atoms exist; Ludwig Van Beethoven writes his famous Fifth Symphony; The saxophone is patented.

1809 Birth of frontiersman Kit Carson in America.

1812 First tin cans produced in England for preserving food; Grimm brothers' Fairy Tales published.

1813 Jane Austen's Pride and Prejudice published; English inventor William Hedley patents his "Puffing Billy", first steam locomotive to pull 50-ton coal wagons.

1814 Cape Colony in South Africa formally handed to Britain by Dutch; Francis Scott Key writes The Star-Spangled Banner, later to become American national anthem.

1815 Englishman Humphry Davy invents miners' safety lamp.

Napoleon moves among his troops during the closing stages of the Battle of Waterloo (1815). After his defeat he was exiled to the tiny isle of St Helena

NOT TONIGHT, JOSEPHINE
Boring Boney left me aloney

Stunner . . Boney's girl Josephine

She tells all – See Pages 4 & 5

NAPOLEON BLOWN APART

Wellington puts boot into the French at Waterloo

Down and out . . . French dictator Napoleon Bonaparte

From WARREN PEACE in Belgium

NAPOLEON Bonaparte was on the run last night after his army was smashed at the Battle of Waterloo by British general the Duke of Wellington.

Napoleon, 45, had to flee the battlefield to escape capture.

And French military sources now say the demoralised tyrant plans to surrender to Our Boys. The battle, which was fought about 10 miles from the Belgian capital Brussels, spells the end of Napoleon's 20-year reign of terror.

During that time he and his armies have waged war throughout Europe — from the frozen steppes of Russia to the sun-baked sierras of Spain.

Before yesterday's bloody clash Napoleon had been confident of victory.

He told his aides: "Wellington is a

EXCLUSIVE

bad general and the English are bad troops. It will be a picnic."

But the Corsican-born monster could not have been more wrong.

Wellington's 67,000 men — mainly British and Dutch — stood their ground despite taking a fearful pounding from 246 French cannons.

And when Britain's Prussian allies arrived behind Napoleon's right flank in the late afternoon it was the French who panicked and ran. Almost half of Napoleon's 74,000-strong army was either killed or wounded.

Up And At 'Em — Pages Two and Three

The safety pin was first seen in 1848

1848

BIRTH OF COMMUNISM

...Timeline...

1816 Bicycle invented by German Karl Sauerbronn.

1818 Mary Shelley publishes her novel Frankenstein.

1819 Peterloo Massacre sees 11 killed as troops disperse Manchester crowd demanding parliamentary reforms.

1820 Beginning of the reign of King George IV in England.

1821 John Constable paints Hay Wain; Poet John Keats dies aged 25; Michael Faraday invents electric motor.

1822 First photograph produced by Frenchman Joseph Niepce.

1823 Scot Charles Macintosh invents waterproof fabric for raincoats; Rugby invented at Rugby School, Warwicks.

1824 RSPCA and RNLI founded; Beethoven completes Ninth Symphony.

1829 George Stephenson builds Rocket locomotive; Gioacchino Rossini writes his William Tell overture; Metropolitan Police established; Typewriter invented in U.S.; Braille printing for blind invented by Frenchman Louis Braille; First Oxford-Cambridge boat race.

1830 William IV is oldest monarch to take throne, at 63; Isambard Kingdom Brunel designs Bristol's Clifton Suspension Bridge; Manchester to Liverpool Railway (England's first) opens; Mormon Church founded in U.S.

1832 First Yeti ''sighting'' in Himalayas, by Briton B H Hodson; First Great Reform Bill gives more men the vote; New Yorker Walter Hunt invents sewing machine.

1834 Sir Robert Peel is PM; Tolpuddle Martyrs, six Dorset farm workers, given seven years' hard labour for forming union.

1835 American Samuel Colt invents the revolver; Madame Tussauds founded; Britain bans cock-fighting.

1836 Texas wins independence from Mexico — Davy Crockett and Jim Bowie die during 12-day siege of the Alamo, which helps defeat Mexican army.

1837 Beginning of long reign of Queen Victoria; Pitman publishes a book on shorthand; Samuel Morse taps out his Morse Code on a new electric telegraph; London's first railway station, Euston, opens.

1838 Charles Dickens writes Oliver Twist; 4,000 Cherokees die on 800-mile Trail of Tears after being forced to move from homeland in the Appalachians to Oklahoma.

1839 First Grand National at Aintree; First Henley Regatta; Baseball invented at Cooperstown, New York.

1840 Queen Victoria weds cousin Albert, who becomes Prince Consort; Penny Black stamp transforms postal service; Use of boys as chimney sweeps banned in Britain.

1841 Birth of impressionist Pierre Renoir; Ninth President Henry Harrison catches fatal pneumonia making his inaugural address in rain without hat or coat.

1842 Christmas cards invented; Treaty of Nanking hands Hong Kong to Britain; Ether used as anaesthetic for the first time during operation in Georgia, U.S.

1843 Britain takes over Natal from the Boers; Nelson's Column erected.

1844 U.S. dentist Horace Wells pioneers use of nitrous oxide (laughing gas) as an anaesthetic during surgery; First effective Factory Act in Britain.

1845 Potato crop failure causes mass starvation in Ireland; Inventions of self-raising flour and rubber bands in England.

1848 Safety pin first seen; First W H Smith book stall, at Euston station.

Charles Dickens wrote Oliver Twist in 1838, Nicholas Nickleby a year later

Pierre Renoir, later one of the leading Impressionist painters, was born in 1841

Victoria came to throne in 1837 and married cousin Prince Albert in 1840

KARL Marx, the founder of communism, is one of the most influential thinkers of all time — his memory revered by some and loathed by others.

Marx was born in Trier, Germany, in 1818 and educated at the universities of Bonn and Berlin.

In 1842 he became editor of the Cologne newspaper Rheinische Zeitung. But his articles attacking the government caused a storm and he was forced to resign.

Marx moved to Paris, where he developed his communist beliefs after further studies in philosophy, history and economics.

During this period he struck up what was to be a lifelong friendship with Friedrich Engels.

The two men discovered they had each formed almost identical views on the necessary conditions for a revolution by the workers.

They began a collaboration to spell out the principles of communism and to organise an international working-class movement dedicated to those principles.

In 1845 Marx was told to leave Paris because of his revolutionary activities. He went to Brussels, where he began organising a network of revolutionary groups called Communist Correspondence Committees.

In 1847 these committees, which had been set up in European cities, formed the Communist League.

Marx and Engels set out a statement of principles, a document known as the Communist Manifesto after its publication in February 1848.

The manifesto, printed in London, was the first systematic statement of modern socialist doctrine.

Its central thesis is that history is dominated by the struggle between the oppressed working classes and their oppressors in the ruling class. Marx came to the conclusion that the current ruling class — the capitalists — would be overthrown by a worldwide working-class revolution.

This revolution would then see the dawn of a classless society.

The manifesto's publication came in the same year as revolutions in France, Italy, Austria, Hungary and Germany.

The Belgian government became alarmed and banished Marx. He went first to Paris, then to Germany. In Cologne he set up a communist newspaper.

In 1849 Marx was arrested and tried on charges of inciting armed rebellion. He was acquitted, but expelled from Germany.

Marx returned to France for a few months but was barred from there too. He moved to London, where he spent the rest of his life.

In England Marx devoted himself to writing a number of works now seen as classics of communist theory, including Das Kapital.

For a time he was a correspondent for a New York newspaper, but he spent most of his time studying and researching in the library of the British Museum.

Marx's lack of income meant that he and his family lived in considerable poverty, often surviving on handouts from Engels.

In 1852 the Communist League dissolved and Marx set about forming another worldwide revolutionary group.

His efforts were rewarded in 1864 when the First International, a federation of workers' groups, was established in London.

Marx was dogged by ill health in later years and died in 1883.

California gold rush

GOLD was discovered close to the Sacramento River in early 1848 — causing a frenzy that would send more than 250,000 prospectors to California.

It began when Swiss-born trader John Sutter started building a sawmill on his land.

On January 24 his carpenter John Marshall found gold. Sutter and Marshall agreed to become partners and keep their discovery secret.

But news spread and they were soon besieged by thousands of fortune-seekers living in huge makeshift camps with little sanitation or law or order. The prospectors quickly overran Sutter's land, stealing his goods and livestock. By the next year, 1849, about 80,000 ''Forty-niners'' had stampeded to the California goldfields. By 1853 there were 250,000.

The gold finds were initially large, but the most easily-reached deposits were quickly exhausted. In total nearly $2billion in gold was taken from the earth.

One of the by-products of the 1848 Gold Rush was the invention of jeans — designed as work trousers to be worn while prospecting.

For Sutter the discovery of gold was a disaster. The U.S. courts ruled he had no ownership rights on the land. By 1852 he was bankrupt.

1830 saw the construction of Bristol's Clifton Suspension Bridge, designed by master engineer Isambard Kingdom Brunel, who also turned his hand to railways and ships

THE Sun

esday, February 15, 1848   **One penny**   **THOUGHT: ON YOUR MARX**

RED & BURIED

Stirring up trouble . . . Karl Marx's sinister pamphlet calls for rebellion

● Communist Karl Marx urges workers to revolt

A SINISTER pamphlet which incites workers to rise in revolt is circulating in the pubs of London, The Sun can reveal.

The document — called the Communist Manifesto — says the time is ripe for bosses to be overthrown.

The manifesto, written by German troublemaker Karl Marx and his sidekick

By ANN ARKIST and LEN INN

Friedrich Engels, openly calls on people to join the rebellion, declaring: "Workers of the world unite — you have nothing to lose but your chains."

Groups of "communists", men and women dedicated to revolution, are already established across Europe.

Rebels Without A Pause — Page Two

Stirring up rubble . . . two ageing prospectors search for gold in California

● Thousands rush west after huge gold find

THOUSANDS of fortune-hunters were flocking to California last night after two lucky workers discovered gold.

The pair dug up flakes of the precious metal as they built a sawmill close to a river.

They tried to keep their find a secret — but news quickly leaked out. Now hordes

By LUKE ANUGGET

of would-be millionaires are heading for the area after hearing that huge quantities of gold can simply be picked out of the dirt.

Scores have already arrived with picks and shovels and are setting up makeshift camps.

There's Gold In Them Thar Hills — Page Nine

53,079 DAYS TO GO

In 1852, New York mechanic and inventor Elisha Otis produced the first lift. Later his sons took over the business — becoming the Otis Elevator Company

. . . Timeline . . .

1849 Charles Dickens writes David Copperfield; Hat-makers Thomas and William Bowler sell their first "bowler".

1850 Launch in the U.S. of the Pinkerton Detective Agency; First department store opens, in Paris.

1851 The Great Exhibition in London; American Herman Melville pens Moby Dick; American inventor Linus Yale patents his lock;

Telegraph begins operating between London and Paris.

1852 American Elisha Otis invents the lift in Yonkers, New York; First screw-top bottles patented in Paris.

1853 Explorer Dr David Livingstone's expedition to cross Africa — he reaches Victoria Falls; Crimean War breaks out, Russia against Britain, Turkey and France; Scot Alexander Wood invents the hypodermic syringe.

Two developments in 1853: explorer Dr Livingstone (above) reached the Victoria Falls on his mission to cross Africa. Meanwhile the hypodermic syringe was developed by a Scot

1854

FLORENCE & THE CRIMEA

FLORENCE Nightingale is one of the great women of history — the founder of modern nursing and a legend for her life-saving efforts in the Crimean War.

She was born into an educated family and grew up in Derbyshire, receiving a classical education from her father.

In her 20s she travelled in Europe and Egypt, studying health care, and in 1853 took charge of the Hospital for Invalid Gentlewomen in London.

That year saw the outbreak of the Crimean War — in which England, France and Turkey joined forces against Russia in a dispute over the treatment of Christians in the Turkish empire.

Thanks to the invention of the telegraph, Britons for the first time had access to up-to-date Press reports from the front. And the news of the appalling conditions which the wounded had to endure at the barracks hospital in Scutari, Turkey, caused a scandal.

Florence was friendly with Britain's Secretary of War, Sir Sidney Herbert, and volunteered to lead 38 nurses to care for the soldiers.

Once in Scutari, they found the victims lying on the abandoned barracks' filthy floor. Men were dying all around them.

There were no toilets and sanitation was impossible. The men ate their one meal a day with their hands because there were no knives or forks. Some days they simply went hungry. Within a week, Florence and her nurses had set up a kitchen and were feeding men from their own supplies. She enlisted any help she could get from the able-bodied and dug latrines, cleaned the barracks and ensured laundry was done.

The wounded were properly fed and properly nursed.

Florence personally tended to the men, carrying a lamp on her rounds after dark. She even made sure that, for the first time, wounded soldiers received sick pay.

The death rate among the wounded plummeted, from 60 per cent when Florence arrived to two per cent within six months. By the end of the war in 1856, by which time another makeshift hospital had been set up at Balaclava, it was down to just one per cent.

Aside from the lives she saved in the Crimea, Florence earned her place in history by establishing nursing as a valued and respected profession. It had previously been seen as a menial task done by untrained personnel.

In 1860 she founded the Nightingale School and Home for Nurses at Saint Thomas's Hospital in London — the beginning of professional training in nursing.

She won many honours and in 1907 was the first woman to receive the Order of Merit. In 1915, five years after her death, the Crimean Monument in Waterloo Place, London, was erected in her honour.

Charge of Light Brigade

THE Charge of the Light Brigade was one of history's great military blunders — but it was not the abject disaster that is commonly believed.

The charge, lasting only 20 minutes in all, was the result of a communications mix-up during the 1854 Battle of Balaclava in the Crimean War.

British commander Lord Fitzroy James Raglan told the Cavalry Brigade, led by Lord George Lucan, to recapture three Russian gun emplacements.

Raglan sent Captain Lewis Nolan to give the order to Lucan.

But Lucan could not see the emplacements — and when he asked where they were Nolan angrily waved his hand in their direction . . . as well as at the main Russian position.

Lucan, prone to panic under pressure, then ordered the Light Brigade, led by his brother-in-law Lord James Cardigan, to advance on the MAIN Russian guns instead of the three emplacements.

They rode down a valley and came under heavy fire.

Nolan was killed by shrapnel while galloping past Cardigan trying to tell him he was going the wrong way.

The Light Brigade managed to force the Russian cavalry back a significant distance before having to withdraw because they were heavily outnumbered.

The popular myth that the Charge was a disaster grew after it was immortalised in a poem by Alfred, Lord Tennyson.

But in fact the Russians, including their commander General Liprandi, were hugely impressed by the Britons' courage.

And the Russian cavalry refused to fight them for the rest of the war, even when they had a huge advantage in numbers.

THE Sun

Monday, September 4, 1854 — One penny — THOUGHT: CARRY ON, NURSE

118 KILLED IN ATTACK

Cardigan undone at Balaclava

Hero . . . Lord Cardigan

AROUND 118 of our brave Army boys died as heroes yesterday during a triumphant charge against the Russians at Balaclava.

They were among 661 men of the Cavalry Brigade, led by Lord Cardigan, who stormed the Cossack guns despite being heavily outnumbered.

The Light Brigade advanced at high speed towards the enemy batteries despite coming under heavy fire.

Cardigan himself rode first through their gun emplacements — then his men drove the Russians back.

They were finally forced to retreat because of the Russian numbers.

Among the victims was Captain Lewis

From RON WAY
in the Crimea

Nolan, who was killed by a shell splinter as he galloped past Cardigan trying for some reason to attract his attention.

Last night it was revealed that six solders have been awarded the new Victoria Cross for bravery.

Even the Russians were amazed at Our Boys' courage and are said to be refusing to fight them any more.

The total British casualties were 118 dead, 127 wounded, 45 taken prisoner and 362 horses killed — mainly by artillery fire.

Was It A Stitch-Up? See Pages 6 and 7

ANGEL OF THE CRIMEA
Nurse Florence saves hundreds

By HELEN EARTH

A BRITISH nurse was hailed a heroine last night for saving hundreds of lives in the Crimea.

Florence Nightingale has almost single-handedly cut the death rate from 60 per cent to just **TWO** at Our Boys' makeshift hospital at Scutari, Turkey.

And the dedicated angel has become known as "The Lady With The Lamp" because she does her rounds of the wards at night, long after the rest of her staff are asleep. Brainy Florence, 34, from Derbyshire — pictured above during another late-night check on wounded men — volunteered to help out after reading Press reports in London of the appalling conditions our soldiers were having to endure.

She hand-picked 38 nurses to go with her — and they were sickened when they arrived at the hospital and saw its terrible state first-hand.

DECENT

Since then they have transformed the place, introducing proper sanitation, regular meals and decent standards of nursing.

One military expert said last night: "Miss Nightingale is a most extraordinary woman."

And a spokesman for Britain's Secretary of War Sir Sidney Herbert — a personal friend of Florence — said: "No one else could have done this but her."

Flo-getter — Pages Four and Five

1859

DARWIN'S THEORY

The world's first oil well — sunk on August 27, 1859, at Titusville, Pennsylvania. Oil wasn't the only thing that sprung up — so did the town of Oil City, which now has a population of 12,000

... Timeline ...

1855 The Bunsen burner is invented by German Robert Bunsen.

1856 Livingstone becomes the first European to cross Africa; Four Australian colonies achieve self-government; Birth of Sigmund Freud, father of psychoanalysis.

1857 Cable under the Atlantic gives Europe and U.S. instant communication by telegraph.

1858 Indian Mutiny shakes British rule — East India Company abolished; Bernadette Soubirous sees vision of Virgin Mary at Lourdes, France; Pencils with rubbers on the end first seen; First electric burglar alarm installed in Boston, U.S.

1859 First oil well drilled, in Pennsylvania. John Stuart Mill publishes On Liberty; Tightrope walker Blondin crosses Niagara Falls watched by 25,000 people.

Bunsen burner, still used in labs all over the world, dates back to 1855

CHARLES Darwin, born in 1809, was the first scientist to produce a detailed theory of evolution. And his concept caused uproar when it was published in full in the 1859 book On The Origin Of Species.

Nowadays it is accepted as fact, although it was still hotly debated as many as 80 years after the book came out and is still disputed in some religious circles.

Darwin was born into a rich family in Shrewsbury, Shropshire. One grandfather was the pottery and china tycoon Josiah Wedgwood, the other a famous doctor.

Darwin studied medicine at Edinburgh University for two years before going to Cambridge University, aiming to become a clergyman. There he met a naturalist, John Stevens Henslow, who encouraged his interest in studying natural phenomena.

Darwin's life changed soon after he graduated at 22. He joined the survey ship HMS Beagle on a scientific expedition around the world, working as an unpaid naturalist (his wealth allowed him the luxury of never having to earn a living).

He was able to study geological formations and wildlife in many countries — and noted that certain species seemed related to those elsewhere, while still being slightly different.

Many also bore remarkable similarities to the fossils of extinct creatures.

Back in England in 1836, Darwin read an essay written 28 years earlier by an economist, who stated the world's food could never sustain the rate of population growth.

Darwin combined this theory with his own beliefs about the links between species and concluded that because the world is incapable of supporting all life born into it, the young of each species compete intensely to survive.

The survivors are inherently fitter or better adapted to their conditions than the others.

They pass on their superior traits to their offspring, thus ensuring that by "natural selction", as Darwin called it, each species is refined over many thousands of years.

Darwin spent 20 years developing this theory, during which time he also concluded that all related organisms have the same ancestors.

This flew in the face of the then-accepted concept of "catastrophism", which stated that the Earth was periodically hit by enormous natural disasters which wiped out plants and animals and that each time life began again from scratch.

Modern-day life forms, the theory asserted, survived only by being placed aboard Noah's Ark during the great flood. Fossils were the remains of all life prior to that.

Darwin's On The Origin Of Species caused massive controversy because its logical conclusion was that man, too, had evolved over time from "lower" species and had not been created as the Old Testament had said.

Despite the furore, contemporaries respected his work and realised its importance. The book sold out on its first day and went through six editions afterwards.

Darwin married his first cousin Emma Wedgwood in 1839 and they had ten children, three of whom died as babies.

After the publication of "Origin" on November 24, 1859, he spent the rest of his life writing books which expanded on points made in his original.

Darwin died in Downe, Kent, on April 19, 1882, and was buried with honour in Westminster Abbey.

French daredevil Blondin (real name Jean-Francois Gravelet) crossed Niagara Falls on a tightrope several times, the first occasion in 1859. To top that, he did it blindfold

Big year for kids: 1858 saw invention of pencils with rubbers on end

ARE YOU A CHIMP OFF THE OLD BLOCK?
SEE PAGES 4 AND 5

Monkey nutter

Barmy boffin Darwin reckons we are all descended from apes

MAD scientist Charles Darwin caused fury last night by claiming we're all descended from APES.

Darwin, 50, makes a string of outrageous allegations in his controversial book On The Origin Of Species, which sold out on its first day yesterday.

Darwin **SCOFFS** at the "Adam and Eve" theory of mankind's creation. He says the real answer lies in the **FOSSILS** he once studied on a sailing trip.

The barmy boffin, from Shrewsbury, reckons all animals "evolve" — becoming more and more refined and advanced over thousands of

By JEAN POOLE

years. This is all thanks to "natural selection" which means only the fittest and best examples of a species survive to breed and pass on their successful characteristics.

Darwin avoids mentioning man in his book, concentrating on plants and animals. But experts say he **MUST** believe in mankind being merely advanced apes, or his theory doesn't hold water.

Furious scientists last night insisted Darwin did not have a shred of real evidence.

And Church chiefs said he was belittling the Bible and the importance of man over animals.

Buffoon as a baboon . . . how he'd look

Alice with the Mad Hatter and March Hare in Alice's Adventures in Wonderland, by Lewis Carroll (1865). The illustration was by Punch magazine cartoonist John Tenniel

...Timeline...

1860 Rebuilding of Houses of Parliament finished after devastating fire in 1834; Florence Nightingale launches nursing school; Pony Express launched in U.S.; Birth of crack-shot Annie Oakley, later a star of Buffalo Bill's touring Wild West Show; Abraham Lincoln elected President.

1861 Lincoln sworn in as President; American Civil War breaks out; First trams in London.

1862 Victor Hugo writes Les Miserables; American Richard Gatling invents the machine gun; London's Westminster Bridge opens.

1863 World's first underground rail network opens — it's the Tube in London; John D Rockefeller builds oil refinery in Ohio and goes on to become one of world's richest ever men; First National Hunt steeplechase at Market Harborough, Leics; Maori uprising against British in New Zealand.

1864 Sheffield reservoir bursts its banks and kills 250.

1865 British surgeon Joseph Lister invents antiseptic; Salvation Army founded; Lewis Carroll publishes Alice's Adventures in Wonderland.

The Gatling Gun of 1862

Lincoln was assassinated in 1865, a year after this photo

Reconstruction of the Houses of Parliament in London was finished in 1860. Two years later Westminster Bridge was built alongside it, spanning the River Thames

1865

SLAVERY & CIVIL WAR

SLAVERY played a central role in the history of the United States, existing from the early 1600s, and indirectly led to the Civil War which finally brought about its abolition in 1865.

Over those 250 or so years up to 11 million Africans were kidnapped from their homes, packed aboard ships in appalling conditions and taken across the Atlantic to strange new countries they had never heard of.

Only about six per cent were imported into the United States. Most went to Brazil or the Caribbean.

The slave trade sprang up mainly as living conditions improved back in England. People had previously sold themselves into servitude in exchange for a passage to America, where they believed life was better.

Their numbers dried up and landowners turned to Africans — small numbers of whom had been shipped over by the Portuguese since as early as the 1530s.

Almost no one in America raised a moral objection, coming as they did from societies in which the rich routinely exploited the poor.

Twenty slaves were bought in Jamestown, Virginia, in 1619. By 1680, seven per cent of the state's population were slaves.

Their primary function was to toil on plantations producing tobacco, sugar, coffee and cotton.

Their treatment and conditions were often barbaric. They were beaten and whipped to subdue them. Women were raped.

Even the more benevolent masters constantly meddled with their slaves' lives — and it was this they hated most. But attitudes to slaves gradually softened, particularly among second-generation owners who grew up with them.

By the late 1770s there were widespread doubts over the whole concept. The government introduced measures which resulted in slavery being banned in northern states, or slaves being guaranteed freedom by a certain age.

All slave imports were outlawed in 1808. But by then only a tiny percentage of the 1.2million in America were born in Africa anyway. The slave population continued to rise sharply.

There were various failed slave uprisings. About 1,000 a year escaped to the North and many more tried before being recaptured.

By the 1830s, America was divided into the slave South and the free North. Southerners argued that slavery was essential to maintain their quality of life.

A bitter dispute then erupted when the North insisted that new territories being settled to the west must be "free soil" — or slave-free.

The South considered this limit on their expansion westwards to be meddling in their affairs. And seven states left the Union in 1860 when Abraham Lincoln was elected President on a "free soil" platform.

Civil War erupted in 1861 with the slave population at four million — the vast majority in the South.

Lincoln's Emancipation Proclamation on January 1, 1863, declared that any slaves in the rebel Confederate states would be considered free. This meant that a Union victory would end slavery.

The Union's win at Gettysburg in July 1863 proved the turning point of the war and the Confederates surrendered in 1865.

Lincoln was assassinated. But on December 6, 1865, his Emancipation Proclamation was made law in the 13th Amendment to the Constitution. Slavery was no more.

The genius of Pasteur

THE pioneering work on bacteria by the biologist and chemist Louis Pasteur led to Pasteurisation and vaccines against a string of diseases. He was born on December 27, 1822, in Dole, France, and later became a professor in Lille. The local area made wine and beer, which soured quickly. Pasteur realised they were affected by bacteria — which died if the liquids were heated.

This "Pasteurisation" technique was then applied to milk, with dramatic results — making safe a drink which until that point often made people sick. Milk, wine and beer are still Pasteurised today.

Pasteur went on to prove that humans and animals could build up a defence against diseases if inoculated first with a weak dose of the same disease. He developed anthrax and rabies jabs. Pasteur died in 1895 and had a state funeral.

Biologist Pasteur at work in his laboratory

THE Sun

ursday, December 7, 1865   **Penny farthing**   **THOUGHT: ABOUT TIME**

GENIUS PASTEUR MAKES MILK SAFE

MILK will soon be completely safe to drink, it was revealed last night.

A new process dreamed up by scientist Louis Pasteur kills the bacteria which makes people ill.

Professor Pasteur, 43, has proved that if you heat milk to as much as 70°C for about half an hour, it destroys harmful bugs without damaging the liquid. The Prof says the process, to be called Pasteurisation after him, also stops wine and beer going off.

Pasteur, based in Paris, found fame when he discovered how bacteria — or "germs" — can produce disease.

A Government spokesman said last night: "If true, his claims would have a major impact on milk drinking."

BORN FREE

Joy after U.S. ends 260 years of slavery

A **FORMER** slave holds his baby daughter in his arms last night — the first generation of his family born free.

The moving moment at a small town in Virginia came hours after America's historic announcement that finally ended almost 260 years of slavery.

By NEIL NOMOORE

The 13th Amendment to the U.S. Constitution, voted through yesterday, frees **FOUR MILLION** black people — although their future is now far from certain.

The amendment reads: "Neither slavery nor involuntary servitude, except as a punishment for crime whereof the party shall have been duly convicted, shall exist within the United States, or any place subject to their jurisdiction." The amendment becomes law eight months after the assassination of President Abraham Lincoln, who battled for the end of slavery.

And it comes seven months after the last Confederate troops surrendered to end the Civil War, which had become a conflict over the future of slavery — a barbaric practice Britain abolished 60 years ago.

FULL STORY OF AN HISTORIC DAY
– Pages 4 and 5

THE END OF SLAVERY

600,000

SACRIFICED TO SET MEN FREE

Killing fields . . . Union soldiers cut down at Gettysburg two years ago. Around 48,000 men lost their lives during the Civil War's bloodiest battle, and President Lincoln made his moving address while dedicating the cemetery there later that year

THE END OF SLAVERY

By JOHN E REBBE

UR million slaves were free
night — after 600,000
s were sacrificed in one of
nkind's bloodiest wars.

he black men, women and
dren were rejoicing after the
Amendment to the United
es constitution was voted
ugh, abolishing slavery.

is the result the world hoped for
the American Civil War broke
five years ago following the elec-
of tragic Abe Lincoln as Presi-
on an anti-slavery platform.

e war started when the southern
slavery states — South Carolina,
issippi, Florida, Alabama, Georgia,
siana, Texas, Virginia, Arkansas,
essee and North Carolina — broke
y from the Union in protest.

eir Confederate forces then de-
d war on the North by seizing
Union's **Fort Sumter** in Charleston,
h Carolina, on April 12, 1861.

Rebs 'strangled' from all sides

e "Yankees" retaliated by march-
30,000 men towards the Confeder-
capital at **Richmond,** Virginia.

t they were stunned when the
-clad southern "rebs" under the
iant General Thomas J "Stone-
" Jackson defeated them in the
Battle of Bull Run at Manassas,
inia, and sent them packing back
Washington.

e Union called up 500,000 more
uits and developed a war strategy
vn as the Anaconda Plan. It in-
ed squeezing the Confederate
s from all sides, splitting them up
seizing control of the Mississippi
r and blockading their coast to
them off from European supplies.

string of horrific battles followed,
uding:

ion general Ulysses Grant captur-
the Confederate strongholds of
Henry and **Fort Donelson** in
essee in February 1862.

e bloody **Battle of Shiloh,** Tennes-
that April which saw 20,000 killed
out a win for either side.

e **Seven Days'** Battles between
25 and July 1, in which the
iant southern General Robert E
forced 100,000 Yankees to retreat
a a second bid to take Richmond.

e **Second Battle of Bull Run** in
ust, which saw Lee drive another
on army out of Virginia. Lee then
ded Maryland before being forced
vithdraw at the **Battle of Antietam**
Harpers Ferry, West Virginia.

at December Lee routed a Union
y at **Fredericksburg,** Virginia, and
May 1863 did the same at
ncellorsville, Virginia.

en came the worst battle of all —
the war's turning point. Lee,
ng to invade the North, entered
nsylvania with 75,000 men — and
untered General George Meade's
00 Union troops at **Gettysburg.**

uring the three-day battle, from
1 to July 3, the Union lost 23,000
, the Confederates 25,000.

e southerners were forced to re-
t to Virginia and could from then
only try to defend while being
ngled from all sides.

the same time in the west, 42-
-old Grant took **Vicksburg,** Missis-
i, giving him control of the
ississippi River as planned.

st year he took charge of the
on army in the East and directed
les in Virginia which saw tens of
usands killed at the **"Wilderness",**
tsylvania and **Cold Harbor.**

June he had pinned down Lee at
rsburg, Virginia, and the siege
t on for ten months.

'Our foe fought so valiantly'

eanwhile the Union's General Wil-
Sherman captured **Atlanta,** Geor-
and marched 300 miles to
nnah burning everything en route.

rant captured Richmond on April 3
year after the **Battle of Five Forks**
Lee, 59 — hit by a shortage of
lies and a string of desertions —
endered six days later.

rant said later: "I felt like any-
g rather than rejoicing at the
nfall of a foe who had fought so
and valiantly for a cause."

onfederate General Joseph Johnston
endered to Sherman in North Car-
23 days later. Two other reb
ies in Louisiana and Texas surren-
in May and the war was over.

General Grant . . . felt no joy in South's defeat

General Lee . . . led Confederates with courage

Bloody charge . . . Union cavalry attack before defeat at First Battle of Bull Run. Map shows war's major battle sites

A tragedy Abe did not live to see it

THE ending of slavery is
President Lincoln's greatest
triumph — eight months
after his murder.

He had always been
against slavery — and three
years ago his Emancipation
Proclamation told the Confederates he planned to free
all their slaves.

Earlier this year Mr Lin-
coln called the proclamation
"the central act of my administration and the greatest event of the 19th
Century."

And he spoke of Ameri-
ca's "new birth of freedom"
during his historic address
at the Gettysburg cemetery
four months after the battle
there. He said:

❛ Four-score and seven
years ago, our fathers
brought forth on this conti-
nent a new nation, con-
ceived in liberty and
dedicated to the proposition
that all men are created
equal.

Now we are engaged in a
great civil war, testing
whether that nation or any
nation so conceived and so
dedicated can long endure.
We are met on a great
battlefield of that war. We
have come to dedicate a
portion of that field as a
final resting place for those
who here gave their lives
that this nation might live.

Task

It is altogether fitting and
proper that we should do
this. But, in a larger sense,
we can not dedicate, we can
not consecrate, we can not
hallow, this ground.

The brave men, living and
dead, who struggled here,
have consecrated it, far
above our poor power to
add or detract.

The world will little note,
nor long remember, what
we say here, but it can
never forget what they did
here. It is for us the living,
rather, to be here dedicated
to the unfinished work
which they who fought here
have thus far so nobly
advanced.

It is rather for us to be
here dedicated to the great
task remaining before us —
that from these honoured
dead we take increased devotion to that cause for
which they gave the last
full measure of devotion.

That we here highly re-
solve that these dead shall
not have died in vain —
that this nation, under God,
shall have a new birth of
freedom and that govern-
ment of the people, by the
people, for the people,
shall not perish from
the Earth. ❜

Mr Lincoln was shot in
the back of the head at
point-blank range by crazed
actor John Wilkes Booth at
a Washington theatre in
April. Booth, a pro-slavery
Confederate, was killed by
Union troops at a Virginia
farm 11 days later.

45,935 **DAYS TO GO**

1874

IMPRESSIONIST PAINTERS

The comic-looking pennyfarthing, invented in 1871, had no gears and instead used a huge front wheel for greater speed

THE Frenchman Claude Monet was a genius who co-founded the Impressionist movement which changed the face of art.

More than 100 years on, he is still among the world's favourite painters. In early 1999 a record-breaking three-quarters of a million fans flocked to a three-month Monet exhibition at the Royal Academy in London.

Monet, born in Paris in 1840, grew up in Le Havre and began to study drawing in his teens.

He was encouraged by the French painter Eugene Boudin to paint outdoors and by the age of 19 he was painting full-time in Paris.

There Monet got to know other young artists including Pierre Renoir and Camille Pissarro.

His early landscapes were conventional enough and well-received at official exhibitions.

But as his style developed it became much less traditional.

He and his colleagues began breaking rule after rule — causing fury among the establishment.

Monet maintained his practice of painting outside, instead of in a studio.

He also chose to depict the world around him rather than historical scenes or figures, as was the tradition.

His technique was to convey a realistic "impression" of a scene at that moment, by omitting detail and using broad, broken strokes of bright colours to achieve a spontaneous look.

The turning point for Monet came in 1874 when he, Renoir and Pissarro — rejected by the establishment — staged their own exhibition in Paris. Among the paintings

Pissarro founded the movement with Monet. This is his Banks of the Oise (1878)

on display there was Monet's classic 1873 work The Poppy Field as well as his Impression: Sunrise.

Critics seized upon the title of the latter and sneeringly called the movement, which they considered slapdash and second-rate, "Impressionism". It was a description which stuck.

Traditionalists may not have liked Monet, but the public did. By the mid-1880s he was famous and relatively rich.

He bought a house in 1890 at Giverny, near Paris, and built a water garden there.

From 1906 until his death in 1926 he painted scenes from the garden.

They include the famous Waterlilies — huge canvases, several of which are on display at the Orangerie in Paris.

Modern-day Monet fans flock to his garden, now open to the public.

. . . Timeline . . .

1866 Outlaw Jesse James, then 19, robs his first bank in Missouri.

1867 Prime Minister Benjamin Disraeli introduces Second Reform Bill in Britain, giving millions more the vote; Johann Strauss writes The Blue Danube; 40 drown as crowds flock to frozen Regents Park lake in London and ice breaks; America buys Alaska from Russia for $7.2million; Barbed wire patented in U.S.; Alfred Nobel demonstrates his new invention, dynamite, at quarry in Redhill, Surrey.

1868 William Gladstone is PM; Last public execution in England.

1869 Football Association founded; Leo Tolstoy pens War and Peace; Chewing gum and margarine patented; Suez Canal opened; Union Pacific Railway completed in U.S.; Tea clipper Cutty Sark launched.

1870 The Red Cross Society is founded in Britain.

1871 Henry Morton Stanley, who works for New York newspaper, begins search for Livingstone, lost in Africa; Russian teacher produces periodic table of elements; George Eliot writes Middlemarch; Rugby Football Union founded; Pennyfarthing bicycle invented; Royal Albert Hall opened; Unions legalised; Three-day inferno in Chicago kills 250 and makes 95,000 homeless.

1872 Stanley finds Livingstone alive, utters the understated greeting: "Dr Livingstone, I presume?" and nurses him back to health; One of world's great mysteries as U.S. ship Marie Celeste found deserted of its ten crew and adrift in the Atlantic; First FA Cup Final, at Kennington Oval, London, sees the Wanderers beat the Royal Engineers 1-0; Britain grants Cape Colony self-government; Doughnut patented.

1873 First colour photographs; Typewriters get QWERTY keyboard.

1874 Disraeli forms his second government.

The doughnut, which was patented in 1872

London's Royal Albert Hall opened in 1871, at a time when William Gladstone (right) was Prime Minister

THE Sun

Friday, March 27, 1874   **Penny farthing**   THOUGHT: BAD IMPRESSION

MONET FOR OLD ROPE

Mr blobby . . . the splodges of colour on Monet's Poppy Field make you think your eyes have gone funny. Yet his paintings are set to fetch a fortune

Blurred paintings scandal

By LEN SCAPE

EXCLUSIVE

BIZARRE modern artist Claude Monet is set to make a fortune — from paintings a CHILD could have done.

The Frenchman, 34, simply dabs splodges of colour all over the canvas, claiming that it gives the viewer an "impression" of a scene.

His blurred painting The Poppy Field, which shows his wife and son wandering about the countryside, is nothing more than a few hundred blobs of red, blue and green.

Yet it took pride of place at a recent exhibition organised by Monet and his shadowy "impressionist" sidekicks Pierre Renoir and Camille Pissarro in France.

The new movement is a smash-hit with trendy art fans in Paris. But most decent art experts have shunned it. Respected critic M Louis Leroy, of the journal Le Charivari, sneered last night: "Wallpaper in its embryonic state is more finished than that."

That's telling him, Mr Leroy! But don't take his word for it, folks — judge for yourself.

We've printed The Hay Wain by English genius John Constable so you can see what a proper painting looks like.

● Can **YOU** do better than Monet? Send us your paintings — any old rubbish, no matter how blurred — to Show Me The Monet, The Sun, 1 Virginia Street, London.

He's Got A Framing Cheek — See Pages 10 and 11

Real painting . . . Constable's Hay Wain looks in focus

45,113 DAYS TO GO

1876

Fans of the new sport of lawn tennis, invented around 1875, enjoy a game of mixed doubles despite seemingly constricting Victorian outfits. This picture is from 1883

. . . Timeline . . .

1875 Austrian Siegfried Marcus invents the internal combustion engine; Snooker invented in India; Captain Matthew Webb becomes first person to swim the Channel; Lawn tennis is invented.

1876 Mark Twain writes Tom Sawyer; Queen Victoria proclaimed Empress of India by Prime Minister Benjamin Disraeli; Five million die in famine in southern India; Turks put down Bulgarian rising with great cruelty; First British trademark, for Bass Pale Ale.

Captain Matthew Webb became first person to swim across the Channel in 1875

Queen Victoria was made Empress of India by her PM, Benjamin Disraeli, in 1876

BELL & THE PHONE

THE telephone is simply one of the most important inventions in history — allowing instant communication between homes, towns and countries.

Its inventor Alexander Graham Bell was born in Edinburgh in 1847 into a family of scholars.

Even at 18, he was working on the idea of transmitting speech. He was a talented pianist and the seed of his telephone idea was planted when he heard a chord struck on one piano echoing faintly on a piano in another room.

It proved sound could be transmitted through vibration.

Bell emigrated to America in 1871 and became a teacher of deaf-mutes while continuing his experiments with sound.

His initial plan was to develop an advanced form of telegraph, which would allow more patterns to be transmitted down a wire at the same time than with Morse Code.

But his idea became much more ambitious and led to a much greater breakthrough. He began to realise that steel "reeds" could carry the vibrations which make up speech and convert them into an undulating current around a magnetic field which could be sent down a wire.

The telephone was born in June 1875 when Bell's assistant Thomas Watson plucked one of these reeds in his room — and it vibrated a reed in Bell's room.

Bell built a transmitter and receiver. On March 10, 1876, as he and Watson prepared to test the devices, Bell spilled acid on himself.

He called for help. Watson, by the receiver, heard his crackling voice say: "Mr Watson, come here. I want you." It was the first telephone message.

Bell knew his discovery was important and predicted the widespread use of telephones. His device was unveiled to scientists at the 1876 Centennial Exposition in Philadelphia, Pennsylvania. They were agog — and there was chaos as they rushed around to confirm that Bell, sitting in one room, really WAS speaking out of a receiver in another.

By 1913, further technological advances had given the phone a 1,000-mile range. By 1956 a cable under the Atlantic allowed calls between Europe and America.

Custer's last stand

CUSTER'S last stand, at the Battle of the Little Bighorn, is one of the most famous stories of the Wild West.

Born in Ohio in 1839, George Armstrong Custer went to military academy before joining the Union army in the Civil War as a second Lieutenant.

Within two years he had been given command of a cavalry brigade and fought at the epic Battle of Gettysburg which ultimately decided the fate of the war.

After the Union won the war he became Lieutenant Colonel of the 7th Cavalry and fought the Cheyenne indians in Kansas. His last fateful assignment, in 1876, was to protect gold miners and railway surveyors who were using land owned by the Sioux in Dakota Territory, now Montana.

He fought them for three years on and off before the U.S. Army decided to crush the Indians once and for all using huge numbers.

Custer's regiment was sent in to scout ahead of the main force — but he decided to attack the Indians himself, hopelessly underestimating their numbers.

The Little Bighorn Battlefield is now a National Monument.

Mark Twain (left) wrote Tom Sawyer in 1876. Photo shows statues of Tom with Twain's Huckleberry Finn

THE Sun

...nday, June 26, 1876   *Penny ha'penny*   **THOUGHT: IT'S FOR YOU**

Indians massacre cavalry regiment at Little Bighorn

...IS was the terrifying scene of ...nage last night as U.S. Cavalry ...ef George Custer and 264 of his ...n were surrounded and massa-...d by Indians.

...Hero Lieutenant Colonel Custer, ..., and his regiment were wiped out ...er being overwhelmed by up to

From SUE INJUN
in South Dakota

4,000 Sioux and Cheyenne at the Battle of the Little Bighorn.

The savages were led by their bloodthirsty chiefs Crazy Horse and

Sitting Bull. Custer is believed to have attacked the Indians at the Little Bighorn river in Dakota Territory without realising that he was hopelessly outnumbered.

He and his men from the 7th U.S. Cavalry had been sent to the region to protect gold prospecters who had

been repeatedly attacked in the Sioux territory of the Black Hills.

Last night military experts were baffled by why Custer, pictured right, went ahead with the attack. One said: "He seems to have totally disregarded his orders."

Full Story — Page Seven

GIVE US A BELL

Hello? Hello? Bell tests phone yesterday

Miracle of 'telephone'

By DI LINGTONE

AN amazing gadget unveiled yesterday could soon allow a person to talk to a friend in a different house.

The "telephone" can already transmit the sound of a voice from one room to the next.

And Scottish inventor Alexander Graham Bell reckons it could be used over much longer distances.

The telephone involves a transmitter and receiver. Words spoken into the transmitter travel along a wire and are heard in the receiver.

The gizmo caused a sensation yesterday at a Philadelphia technology exhibition. Bell said: "The day will come when friends converse with each other without leaving home."

My Ding-a-ling — Page Two

Wanted killer Billy The Kid (left) was shot dead in 1881 by Sheriff Pat Garrett (right) in New Mexico. The notorious Gunfight at the OK Corral happened the same year

...Timeline...

1877 First Wimbledon championships; First England v Australia cricket test; Thomas Edison records himself shouting "Mary had a little lamb" into new phonograph machine in U.S.

1878 First degrees for women at London University; The CID is launched.

1879 Zulus at war with British; American James Ritty invents cash register; First Woolworths opens, in Utica, New York; 80 die as Tay Bridge collapses in Scotland, sending train plunging into river; Novelist EM Forster born; England's first football international, they beat Wales 2-1 in London; Debut for Blackpool's illuminations.

1880 Edison invents electric light; Russian Peter Tchaikovsky composes 1812 Overture; Start of first Boer War — Transvaal defeats Britain; Australian bushranger Ned Kelly hanged; First phone book, in London, lists 255 numbers; Birth of deaf, blind mute Helen Keller, who becomes teacher and scholar.

1881 Outlaw Billy The Kid (William Bonney) shot dead aged 22 by Sheriff Pat Garrett in Fort Sumner, New Mexico; Wyatt Earp, his brothers and Doc Holliday shoot dead three gunslingers at the OK Corral in Tombstone, Arizona; Assassination of Czar Alexander II of Russia; London's Natural History Museum opens.

1882 Aussie cricketers beat England, Newspaper claims English cricket is dead and produces urn containing its ashes — Ashes Tests born; Treasure Island by Robert Louis Stevenson published; Britain's first electric trams run in Leytonstone, East London.

1883 Estimated 36,000 killed as volcanic eruption on isle of Krakatoa leads to 100ft tidal wave swamping Sumatra and Java.

1884 Fountain pen invented by American L E Waterman; First Oxford English Dictionary; Evaporated milk is patented in St Louis, Missouri.

1885 Pasteur produces inoculation against rabies; Gilbert and Sullivan write The Mikado; First successful appendix removal, in Iowa, U.S.

A star of Gilbert and Sullivan's Mikado, which debuted in 1885

Lord William Beresford earns the VC for a brave rescue in the Zulu War of 1879

1886
INVENTION OF THE CAR

NO invention has had a greater impact on the modern world than the car — and many people believe life would be impossible without one.

Roads have transformed the landscape of much of the world and dictate how cities and their suburbs are built.

Some countries' economies survive or fall on the performance of their motor industry.

But the world has paid a price for the freedom the car has brought — in environmental damage, crime and road deaths.

Karl Benz, a German engine driver's son born on November 25, 1844, was the father of the car as we know it.

Steam-powered automobiles had been in use since the late 1700s — but they were absurdly slow and frequently had to stop to build up a head of steam.

Benz had trained as a draughtsman and engineer.

His breakthrough was to build a tricycle-like carriage and attach to it a petrol-driven internal combustion engine.

He built the four-stroke engine himself, based on a decade-old design by another German engineer, Nikolaus August Otto.

Benz's car made its public debut on July 3, 1886, when stunned crowds watched it being driven around the streets of Mannheim.

The following year another German engineer Gottlieb Daimler produced a car and went into business manufacturing them.

Around the turn of the 20th Century, steam-powered cars were still more popular than petrol-driven ones.

But the public gradually caught on that the internal combustion engine was capable of driving the machine faster and for much longer distances.

The turning point came in America in 1908 when Henry Ford's company made the Model T — the first mass-produced car affordable by ordinary people.

Nicknamed the Tin Lizzy, 15 million Model T cars were sold before production stopped in 1927.

Meanwhile Benz, now a father of five, lived long enough to see the impact of his invention on the world.

In 1926 his firm joined forces with the Daimler company to form Daimler-Benz.

It is now Germany's largest industrial firm and makes Mercedes-Benz cars.

Benz died on April 4, 1929.

THE car's popularity owes much to an invention by a Scottish VET. John Dunlop, born in 1840, was 37 when he decided to make a kiddies' tricycle more comfortable by replacing its solid rubber tyres with an air-filled tube fixed to the wheel rim.

The invention was a huge success, thanks to the enormous popularity of the bicycle in those days.

Dunlop set up a company to make them both for bikes and for the newly-invented car — and thus gave birth to the multi-national company we know today.

American inventor Thomas Edison with the phonograph which he successfully used to record his voice in 1877. He invented the electric light three years later

THE Sun

Sun EXCLUSIVE

NOW WE'RE MOTORING

nday, July 5, 1886   1½d   THOUGHT: LOOKS DRAUGHTY

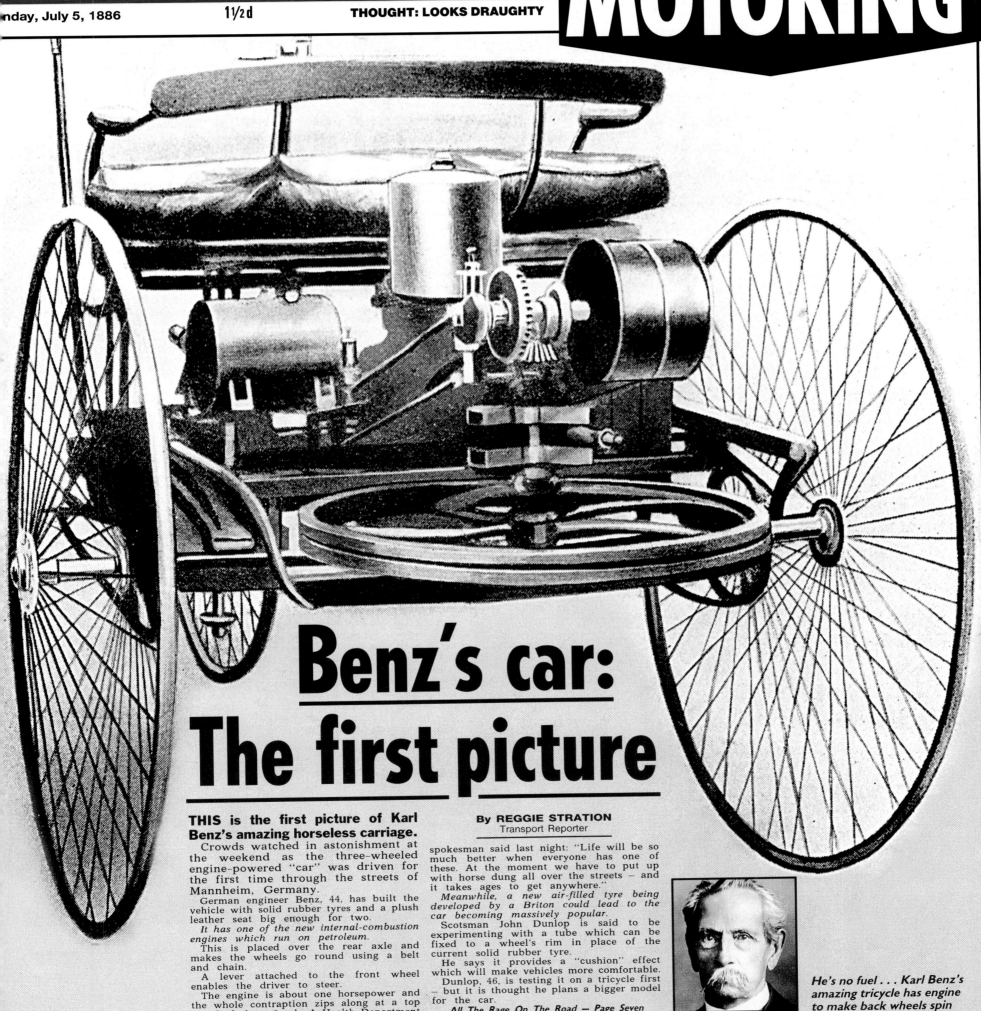

Benz's car:
The first picture

THIS is the first picture of Karl Benz's amazing horseless carriage.

Crowds watched in astonishment at the weekend as the three-wheeled engine-powered "car" was driven for the first time through the streets of Mannheim, Germany.

German engineer Benz, 44, has built the vehicle with solid rubber tyres and a plush leather seat big enough for two.

It has one of the new internal-combustion engines which run on petroleum.

This is placed over the rear axle and makes the wheels go round using a belt and chain.

A lever attached to the front wheel enables the driver to steer.

The engine is about one horsepower and the whole contraption zips along at a top speed of about 9mph. A Health Department

By REGGIE STRATION
Transport Reporter

spokesman said last night: "Life will be so much better when everyone has one of these. At the moment we have to put up with horse dung all over the streets – and it takes ages to get anywhere."

Meanwhile, a new air-filled tyre being developed by a Briton could lead to the car becoming massively popular.

Scotsman John Dunlop is said to be experimenting with a tube which can be fixed to a wheel's rim in place of the current solid rubber tyre.

He says it provides a "cushion" effect which will make vehicles more comfortable.

Dunlop, 46, is testing it on a tricycle first – but it is thought he plans a bigger model for the car.

All The Rage On The Road — Page Seven

He's no fuel . . . Karl Benz's amazing tricycle has engine to make back wheels spin

...Timeline...

1886 Thomas Hardy's The Mayor of Casterbridge published; Coca-cola invented; Statue of Liberty is unveiled in New York; Gold found in Transvaal.

1887 Sherlock Holmes makes first appearance in book by Arthur Conan Doyle; The gramophone is patented.

1888 Kodak makes simple box camera; Payphone invented; German Heinrich Hertz discovers radio waves; Britain annexes Zulu lands; Dutch artist Vincent Van Gogh paints Sunflowers; Start of the reign of Kaiser William II in Germany; Birth of soldier TE Lawrence, later dubbed Lawrence of Arabia; Drinking straws patented in U.S.

1886 saw invention of Coke and the unveiling of the Statue of Liberty, New York

Pipe-smoking detective Sherlock Holmes (below) first appeared in an 1887 novel

1888

JACK THE RIPPER

THE murderer known as Jack The Ripper is the most famous serial killer of all time. The monster's diabolical crimes — carried out in the cold, dark, murky streets of Victorian London — still have a horrible fascination.

The Ripper is known to have killed at least five prostitutes in the East End in 1888 in a little over two months.

Many crime writers and researchers claim he murdered other women — as many as a dozen more, some believe.

The five killings the Ripper is generally accepted as having carried out took place within a mile of each other in Whitechapel, Spitalfields, Aldgate and the City.

His first victim was Mary Ann Nichols, a 44-year-old alcoholic murdered on August 31, 1888, in a narrow street called Bucks Row in Whitechapel.

Victim number two was Annie Chapman, 45, killed on September 8 in Hanbury Street.

Three weeks later — on Sunday September 30 — the Ripper struck twice on the same day. He murdered 45-year-old Elizabeth Stride in Berner Street and Catherine Eddowes, 46, at Mitre Square, Aldgate.

His fifth victim was Mary Jane Kelly, 25. She was kiled on November 9 in the single room she rented at Miller's Court.

All five women were prostitutes. All but one was killed outdoors. Most are thought to have been drunk when murdered.

The Ripper seized the women by the throat and strangled them until they were unconscious.

He then lowered them to the ground and cut their throats before mutilating their bodies. There was no evidence of sexual contact. Most surgeons who examined the bodies believed that the killer must have had some degree of medical knowledge.

During the Ripper's reign of terror a number of letters were sent to the police and the Press by people claiming to be him.

One letter, received on September 27 by a news agency, was signed Jack The Ripper — the first use of the nickname. But experts now believe none of the letters were written by the murderer.

The crimes were committed in an age before forensic science or fingerprinting. The only way to prove someone was a murderer was to catch them in the act or get them to confess.

The Ripper was never caught. The killings just suddenly stopped.

Over the years the Ripper case has continued to fascinate — and various studies have produced a number of suspects.

In 1894 Chief Constable Sir Melville Macnaghten wrote a confidential report in which he named his main suspect.

It was a barrister named M J Druitt, who committed suicide shortly after the fifth murder. Unfortunately Macnaghten's evidence is mostly circumstantial and in some areas he simply got facts wrong.

In 1903 a retired detective who worked on the case said he thought the Ripper was multiple wife poisoner Severin Klosowski. But modern studies have rejected him as a serious candidate.

Other theories have been more outlandish. In 1970 a work was published which claimed the killer was Prince Albert Victor, the grandson of Queen Victoria.

Self-portrait of Van Gogh with bandaged ear, and his 1888 work Sunflowers

THE Sun

rsday, November 15, 1888 · Penny ha'penny · **THOUGHT: FIND THE FIEND**

Is THIS Jack The Ripper?

FACE OF No1 SUSPECT IN HUNT FOR BEAST

By TERRY BULCRIMES

HE looks like any respectable gentleman you might pass in the street — but this may be the face of Jack The Ripper.

The fiend has already struck at least five times in London's East End. All his victims were women. All were murdered and horribly butchered.

Police are convinced he **WILL** strike again unless he is caught. This picture has been put together from the testimony of witnesses who saw a man wandering the streets close to at least one of the murder scenes.

Do you know the face? Is he a friend or perhaps even a relative? If you do recognise him contact the police immediately.

Terror Grips The East End — Pages Two and Three

LONDON SERIAL KILLER

TERROR GRIPS

By TERRY BULCRIMES
Chief Reporter

THE women of London's East End were last night living in terror of the crazed killer Jack The Ripper.

The fiend has struck five times in just ten weeks. All his victims are women. All have had their throats slashed. All have been horribly mutilated after death.

The murders took place in the "evil quarter-mile" — an area around Whitechapel which has been described as the most dangerous in London.

Detectives probing the murders have now pieced together the last known movements of the five victims:

THE CASE OF *Mary Ann Nichols*

The first was prostitute Mary Ann Nichols, 44, sometimes known as Polly.

She lived at a variety of doss houses in Spitalfields. Most are used by prostitutes — with four or five people sharing a room. Sometimes men and women share a bed.

One of the last sightings of Mary was about 11pm on Thursday August 30. She was walking along Whitechapel Road looking for customers. Just after midnight she left the Frying Pan pub and returned to a doss house at Thrawl Street.

The manager has told police he threw her out just after 1am for not paying her rent. As she left she told him to save her a bed, adding: "I'll soon get my doss money."

At about 2.30am one of Mary's pals, Emily Holland, bumped into her on Whitechapel Road. Holland said last night: "She was very drunk and staggered against the wall."

Mary told Emily she had earned her rent money three times but had spent it all on booze. She said she was going to look for one more customer, then return to the doss house with the money.

Just over an hour later Mary's body was found in Bucks Row by Charles Cross and Robert Paul, on their way to work.

Cross felt the body and discovered it was still warm. Paul believed he felt a faint heartbeat. The two men called for help and a constable named PC Neil arrived.

He went to get Dr Rees Llewellyn who lives nearby. The doctor examined the body by the light of a single street lamp and pronounced Mary dead.

Dr Llewellyn later told an inquest he had no doubt she had been killed where she lay. Her throat had been slashed with a long-bladed knife.

The injury had been inflicted "with great violence". Her body had also been slashed several times with the same knife, possibly by a left-handed attacker.

THE CASE OF *Annie Chapman*

The Ripper's second victim, prostitute Annie Chapman, 45 — nicknamed "Dark Annie" — was killed eight days later.

She also lived in one of the Spitalfields doss houses. Annie spent the evening of September 7 drinking there, and at 1.30am was summoned by manager Timothy Donovan, demanding rent she owed.

He said last night: "I told her, 'You can find money for your beer and you can't find money for your bed'. Annie walked out, promising to return soon with money."

At 5.30am a woman called Elizabeth Long noticed Annie standing with a man outside 29 Hanbury Street. Long heard him say: "Will you?" and Annie replied: "Yes".

The man had his back to Long. He was about 40, with a dark complexion and deerstalker hat. She said: "He may have been a foreigner. He looked what I should call shabby genteel." Moments later carpenter

Albert Cadoch, of 27 Hanbury Street, walked into his back yard. From the other side of the 5ft fence he heard a woman's voice say: "No". Then something fell against the fence.

About 6.30am Annie's body was found in the yard of No29. Dr George Phillips, called to the scene, said: "The body was terribly mutilated and the throat deeply severed."

The Ripper had removed Annie's internal organs, placing some on one of her shoulders. Dr Phillips believed the injuries may have been inflicted by a knife used by slaughtermen or by medics performing post-mortems.

He said the incisions suggested the killer had "great anatomical knowledge" and spent 15 minutes to an hour mutilating Annie.

THE CASE OF *Elizabeth Stride*

The third and fourth victims were both killed on the same day, September 30. The first found was Elizabeth Stride, 45, sometimes called Long Liz.

She came to London in July 1866 from her home country, Sweden, where she had already been a prostitute.

Elizabeth recently lived with a man named Michael Kidney. Their relationship was extremely stormy, with her disappearing for weeks on end on drinking binges.

On September 25 Kidney saw Elizabeth for the last time. When he returned from work that evening there was no sign of her. He

told police he was not worried, as she had vanished before. He added: "It was drink that made her go away. She always returned without me going after her."

Days before her death a charity worker met Elizabeth in a Spitalfields doss house. She was chatting to other prostitutes about the Ripper and one said: "No one cares what becomes of us. Perhaps some of us will be killed next."

At 11pm on September 29 two labourers bumped into Elizabeth outside the Bricklayer's Arms opposite Berner Street. She was leaving with a short man with a moustache.

Shouted

One labourer told police: "He was hugging and kissing her, and as he seemed a respectably-dressed man, we were rather astonished at the way he was going on at the woman."

Less than an hour later, labourer William Marshall saw Elizabeth in Berner Street.

He noticed her kissing a man in a sailor's hat outside No63. He heard the man say: "You would say anything but your prayers."

Shortly after 12.35am PC William Smith saw Elizabeth with a young man on Berner Street. He was about 28, wearing a dark coat and a deerstalker and carrying a parcel.

Just minutes later a man named Israel Schwartz saw a man stop and speak to Elizabeth in a gateway in Berner Street.

The man tried to pull her into the street, then pushed her to the ground. She shouted out. The man called to a second man on the other side of the road. Schwartz walked off.

Another witness saw Elizabeth about this time talking to a stout man. He heard her

say: "No, not tonight, some other night." 1am jewellery salesman Louis Diemsch[utz] drove his pony and cart into Dutfield's Y[ard] on Berner Street. But at the entrance [the] pony refused to go forward.

Diemschutz investigated and found El[iza]beth's body. He could not see in the p[itch] darkness and at first thought she was dr[unk] or asleep.

He went to get two friends to help rouse the woman. On returning they dis[cov]ered her throat had been cut.

Police believe Diemschutz may have [dis]turbed the Ripper, forcing him to flee be[fore] he could mutilate her. Elizabeth's body [was] still warm when Diemschutz found her [and] his pony continued to behave oddly, a[s if] someone was hiding in the yard.

A post-mortem revealed Elizabeth's th[roat] had been slashed just like the other vict[ims]

THE CASE OF *Catherine Eddowes*

A few hours later the mutilated bod[y of] Catherine "Kate" Eddowes was discover[ed.] Eddowes, 46, lived with market labo[urer] John Kelly in another Spitalfields doss ho[use.] In the last few months he had found it h[ard] to get work and he and Eddowes went [hop] picking in Kent to raise money.

In September she returned and told a [...] "I've come back to earn the reward for [...] apprehension of the Whitechapel murd[erer]

Suspect . . . Mary Jane Kelly was with fat m[an]

Suspect . . . witnesses saw foreign-looking [...]

Ripper hunted over 5 murder[s]

LONDON SERIAL KILLER
THE EAST END

Street of horror . . . Bucks Row, where the mutilated body of Mary Ann Nichols was found

Victim . . . Catherine Eddowes and the man that she was seen talking to in the street

...k The Ripper). I think I know him." The
...nd warned her to be careful that she did
...end up being murdered herself, but she
...ied: "Oh, no fear of that."
... 8am on September 29 Eddowes pawned
...air of Kelly's boots for half a crown.
...bout 12 hours later she was drunk and
...acting a crowd in Aldgate High Street by
...ating a fire engine.
...e was arrested by PC Louis Robinson
... put in a cell at Bishopsgate to sober up.
...ortly after midnight Eddowes was heard
...ing in her cell. A little later she called
... to ask when she could go home.
...e officer on duty told her she could go
...n she was able to take care of herself.

Slashed

...e yelled back: "I can do that now." At
...Eddowes was allowed to leave.
...s she was released from the cell she
...d a PC what the time was. He replied:
...o late for you to get anything to drink."
...e said: "I shall get a damn fine hiding
...n I get home."
...s she left the police station she said:
...odnight, old cock."
... about 1.35am Eddowes was spotted
...ide Mitre Square by three witnesses. She
... standing talking to a man, with her
...d on his chest. He was about 30, 5ft 7ins
...a fair complexion and a moustache.
...me 12 hours later a PC Watkins found
...owes dead in Mitre Square.
...r face and body had been mutilated.
... of her right ear, the tip of her nose and
... of her liver had been sliced off. The
...r had slashed her throat. The post

mortem said some of Eddowes' organs had
been removed in a manner needing "a great
deal of medical knowledge".

THE CASE OF
Mary Jane Kelly

The Ripper's most recent victim, killed a
week ago, was the youngest. Mary Jane Kelly
was 25, with blonde hair and blue eyes.
One friend called her "a pleasant girl,
well-liked by everyone. When in liquor she
was very noisy, otherwise she was a very
quiet woman."
Mary once worked in a high-class brothel
but in August moved into a small single
room at 13 Miller's Court, off Dorset Street.
It had two windows, one of which could be
reached through to unbolt the door.
At 11pm on Thursday November 8 Mary
was seen drunk in the Britannia pub with a
seemingly-respectable, well-dressed man with
a dark moustache.
Within an hour Mary Ann Cox, 31, saw her
with a stout man in Dorset Street. He was
35 or 36, 5ft 5ins, in an overcoat and hat
and carrying a bucket full of beer.
Mrs Cox followed them into Miller's Court.
They stopped outside Mary's room and as
Mrs Cox walked past to her own room she
said goodnight. Mary replied drunkenly:
"Goodnight, I am going to sing." A few
minutes later Mrs Cox heard Mary singing a

song called It Was Only A Violet I Plucked
From My Dear Mother's Grave. At 1am Mrs
Cox went out. She could hear Mary singing
and saw a light on in her room.
An hour later Mary stopped George Hutchinson in Commercial Street and asked for
money. He said he had none and she replied:
"I must find some money."
Hutchinson watched her walk up the street
towards a man who put his hand on her
shoulder as she passed. The man said something at which Mary laughed.
Hutchinson heard Mary say: "All right"
and the man added, "You will be all right
for what I have told you." The man then put
his right hand on Mary's shoulder and they
walked towards Dorset Street.
The man, about 35, 5ft 6ins with a dark
complexion and moustache, had a small
parcel in his left hand.

Response

Hutchinson walked behind Mary and the
man for a while until they stopped at the
entrance to Miller's Court.
Hutchinson heard Mary say: "All right, my
dear. Come along. You will be comfortable."
At 3am Mrs Cox returned home. There was
no sound or light coming from Mary's room.
Later a neighbour heard someone cry "Oh,
murder!" but thought it was a prank.
Shortly before 11am Thomas Bowyer, a
rent collector for Miller's Court, knocked on
Mary's door. When he received no response
he pushed aside Mary's curtain and found
her mutilated, naked body on the bed.
Police found Mary's clothes neatly folded
on a chair and her boots in front of the fire.

Surgeon Dr Thomas Bond told the inquest
Mary's breasts had been cut off and her
organs removed and placed around the room.
Her face was hacked beyond recognition.
*After more than two months the police
admit they are no nearer to catching the
Ripper — though they and local news agencies and newspapers have been sent scores of
letters from people claiming to be him.*
Most are obvious fakes — but some may
not be. One of the most chilling was sent to
London's Central News Agency just before
the Stride and Eddowes murders. It read:

❝ Dear Boss, I keep on hearing the police
have caught me but they won't fix me
just yet.
I have laughed when they look so clever
and talk about being on the right track.
I am down on whores and I shant quit
ripping them till I do get buckled.
I love my work and want to start again.
You will soon hear of me with my funny
little games.
My knife's so nice and sharp I want to get
to work right away if I get a chance.
Good Luck. Yours truly, Jack The Ripper. ❞

*On October 1 the agency received another
postcard with similar handwriting, reading:*

❝ I was not codding dear old Boss when I
gave you the tip, you'll hear about Saucy
Jacky's work tomorrow, double event this
time. Number one squealed a bit couldn't
finish straight off. Jack The Ripper. ❞

On October 16 investigators were sent a
small cardboard box containing a human
kidney similar to the one removed from
Catherine Eddowes.

35,078 DAYS TO GO

...Timeline...

1889 Bra invented; Eiffel Tower unveiled in Paris.

1890 Two hundred Sioux indians massacred at Wounded Knee, South Dakota — last major battle with U.S. army; First electric chair execution, in New York; Basketball invented by a Canadian.

1892 Edison co-invents the peep-show Kinetoscope (moving pictures). German Rudolph Diesel invents diesel engine.

1893 New Zealand is first country to give women vote; Norwegian Edvard Munch paints The Scream.

1894 Marconi invents wireless; Blackpool Tower, Manchester Ship Canal and London's Tower Bridge open.

1895 French Lumiere brothers invent film projector; King C Gillette invents razor; Heinz make baked beans; Playwright Oscar Wilde jailed in gay scandal.

1896 X-rays invented; First modern Olympic games, in Athens; Walter Arnold, from Kent, first British driver fined for speeding (8mph in 2mph zone).

1897 Bram Stoker's Dracula published; The WI is founded, in Canada.

1898 Kellogg's launch top breakfast cereal, the Cornflake.

1899 Premiere of Edward Elgar's Enigma Variations; Second Boer War starts in South Africa; Aspirin patented.

1900 Birth of Queen Elizabeth, Queen Mum; Sigmund Freud's Interpreta-

Teddies, named after President 'Teddy' Roosevelt, first appeared on scene in 1902

tion of Dreams launches psychoanalysis.

1901 Queen Victoria dies, Edward VII crowned; First Nobel prizes.

1902 Polish scientist Marie Curie discovers the element radium, to treat cancer; Marmite appears; Treaty of Vereniging ends Second Boer War; Teddy bears invented after President Theodore "Teddy" Roosevelt refuses to kill bear on hunting trip; First borstal, at Borstal, Kent.

1903 The Great Train Robbery released, first proper film.

Oscar Wilde, brilliant Irish playwright, was jailed in 1895

The Eiffel Tower was first seen in Paris in 1889

Marie Curie discovered radium, for cancer treatment, in 1902

1903

MAN'S FIRST FLIGHT

AIR travel is so commonplace and so essential to the modern world it is hard to believe its development came about entirely during the 20th Century.

As early as the 15th Century Leonardo da Vinci studied the mechanics of flight, though his designs were of machines with flapping, birdlike wings.

The French brothers Joseph and Jacques Montgolfier invented and flew in a hot-air balloon in 1783 — having first sent up a sheep, a duck and a chicken to see if they survived.

But the self-propelled aircraft took a lot longer to develop.

English pioneers Sir George Cayley and William Henson made important steps forward in the early 1800s. Cayley established the principle that the wings would provide lift and a separate device would provide thrust.

Henson then designed in 1847 an Aerial Steam Carriage — a steam-powered monoplane with propellers, wheels, a fuselage and rudder. The only trouble was it would not fly.

Later inventors attempted in vain to take off in a variety of weird and wonderful designs — many hopelessly fragile and with flapping wings.

American Samuel Pierpont Langley managed to shoot a steam-powered aircraft into the air in 1896 over Virginia — but it never successfully carried a pilot.

In the 1890s, German engineer Otto Lilienthal made, designed and successfully flew hang gliders. They were hard to control and indeed he was eventually killed flying one — but his work inspired the American brothers Orville and Wilbur Wright.

The Wrights, from Dayton, Ohio, were skilled engineers who had for a decade built and sold bicycles. In 1896 they turned their attentions to flight.

Rejecting other engines, they made their own 12-horsepower model. This, with their home-made propellers plus a strong, light fuselage and wings and an efficent means of steering, proved the winning combination.

They tested their "Flyer" biplane on December 17, 1903, in the open space of Kill Devil Hills near Kitty Hawk, North Carolina. It had a 39ft wingspan and weighed 750lb including the pilot.

Orville went up first — and his 12-second flight earned him a place in history.

By 1905 the brothers had built their third Flyer, the first plane that could be manoeuvred in the air and stay up as long as the fuel held out.

Aviation then rapidly expanded, especially when its military advantages were realised during World War One.

By the 1920s the first airlines were carrying post, and new aircraft were able to cross continents and oceans.

The 1930s saw the development of more efficient all-metal monoplanes.

Aircraft played a vital role during World War Two, when another milestone was reached with the development of the jet engine.

This enabled planes to fly much faster — and gave rise to the huge expansion of commercial air travel.

Wilbur Wright died of typhoid in 1912 and did not live to see the mark he made on the world.

Orville did. He died in 1948 — a year after the American test pilot Chuck Yeager first broke the sound barrier.

The Suffragettes

EMMELINE Pankhurst's Suffragette movement won women the vote — though the struggle began a century earlier.

Mary Wollstonecraft's 1792 work A Vindication of the Rights of Woman launched the campaign, but in the following century its powerful opponents included Queen Victoria and her Prime Ministers.

Emmeline, wife of pro-women's rights lawyer Richard Pankhurst, founded the Women's Franchise League in 1889. Five years later it won married women the right to vote — in local elections only.

In 1903 Emmeline founded the Women's Social and Political Union. Its increasing militantcy involved bombing, arson, vandalism, picketing and harassment.

Emmeline's daughter Christabel was jailed in 1905. Emmeline herself was repeatedly imprisoned — and went on hunger strike in jail.

Suffragette Emily Davison died after throwing herself under the King's horse at Epsom in 1913.

In 1918 Parliament gave certain women the vote, then all women in 1928 — the year Emmeline died. Britain had its first woman in the Cabinet in 1929 and its first woman PM, Margaret Thatcher, in 1979.

THE Sun

Friday, December 18, 1903   1d   THOUGHT: YOU CAN FLY, ORVILLE

Air we go . . . Orville went first   Next up . . . his brother Wilbur

ALL WRIGHT

ON THE FLIGHT

Plane in the air nearly a minute

OVERJOYED Orville Wright makes history yesterday as the first human to fly.

American Orville, 32, stayed in the air for 12 seconds and covered 120ft in the rickety-looking biplane he built with brother Wilbur.

Then 36-year-old Wilbur had a

By HEATH ROWE and **STAN STEAD**

go in the propellered plane, which has a 12-horsepower engine.

And he went one better than Orville — staying up for a full 59 seconds and covering a whopping 852ft at Kill Devil Hills near Kitty Hawk, North Carolina.

Magnificent Men — Pages 4 and 5

FLEW THE JURY
Would YOU go up in an aeroplane?
YES: RING 20
NO: RING 21

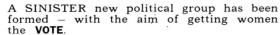

anatical . . . Pankhurst

SINISTER 'WOMEN'S RIGHTS' PLOT

A SINISTER new political group has been formed — with the aim of getting women the **VOTE**.

The Women's Social and Political Union is the brainchild of radical Emmeline Pankhurst.

Mrs Pankhurst, a 46-year-old widow, is said to be plotting a series of spectacular demonstrations in a bid to win publicity.

Some of her followers, who call themselves

By MILLIE TANT

"suffragettes", say they will parade through the streets and even smash windows to draw attention to themselves.

Mrs Pankhurst's husband, the firebrand lawyer Richard Pankhurst, was an outspoken supporter of women's rights. He died five years ago.

Mrs Pankhurst has been lobbying for women's

rights for more than 10 years, but up to this point her efforts have not gained her public notoriety.

The new group's aggressive tactics are said to have been urged on Mrs Pankhurst by her daughter Christabel Harriette, 23.

A Government source last night insisted that Mrs Pankhurst and her friends were wasting their time.

He scoffed: "Votes for women? It's about as likely as a man travelling to the moon."

50 Great New Knitting Patterns — Page 12

1912

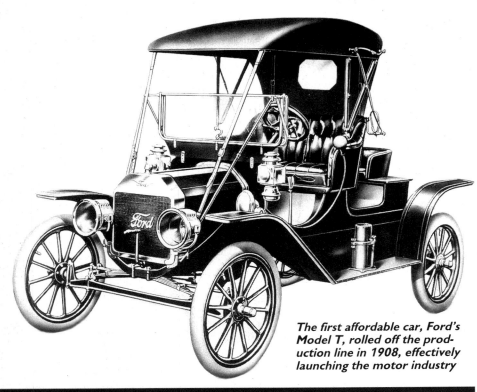

The first affordable car, Ford's Model T, rolled off the production line in 1908, effectively launching the motor industry

...Timeline...

1904 Early telephone answering machine invented; Entente Cordiale between Britain and France; FIFA, international football body, established.

1905 Albert Einstein publishes Theory of Relativity; first All Blacks rugby tour of England; Juke box invented; Cadbury's dairy milk chocolate launched; British New Guinea becomes Australian, renamed Papua.

1906 Four square miles of San Francisco levelled by earthquake, 700 dead; Liberal government elected in Britain; First cartoon film is produced; First Grand Prix, at Le Mans, France.

1907 American William Hoover buys rights to vacuum cleaner and cleans up financially; New Zealand gains its independence from Britain; Picasso's Les Demoiselles d'Avignon launches cubism in art; First washing machine in U.S.; Boy Scouts formed in Britain; Earthquake kills more than 1,000 in Kingston, Jamaica, and destroys city; First ever Mother's Day.

1908 Henry Ford produces Model T — first affordable, mass-produced car; General Motors formed.

1909 Apache chief Geronimo dies (last Indian chief to go to war on settlers); Persil washing powder launched; First toilet paper on roll; U.S. Commander Robert Peary reaches North Pole; Frenchman Louis Bleriot is first to fly across channel; Britain's first department store, Selfridges, opens in London; First double-decker buses, in Widnes, Cheshire.

1910 Reign of George V begins; Robert Scott and Roald Amundsen begin planning their race for the South Pole; American Dr Hawley Harvey Crippen murders wife in London, is caught fleeing with his lover to the U.S. and hanged; First Father's Day in America.

Many died when large area of San Francisco was laid waste by 1906 earthquake

1911 Air conditioning invented by American WH Carrier; China becomes a republic.

1912 Scott's team reach South Pole but Norwegians beat them by six days — Scott dies with entire party on return journey but records how frost-bitten Lawrence Oates left tent after saying "I am just going outside and may be some time" in order not to hinder their progress; First airmail; Albert Berry makes first parachute jump from plane, over Missouri; Girl Guides founded in America.

Scott of the Antarctic died in race to South Pole (1912)

1909 saw death of Geronimo, the famous Indian chief

Albert Einstein published Theory of Relativity (1905)

TITANIC DISASTER

THE sinking of the Titanic on its maiden voyage with the loss of 1,523 lives was one of the worst, and certainly the most famous, shipping disaster of all time.

The 46,000-ton luxury liner had been thought unsinkable because its hull comprised 16 watertight compartments — and four could be flooded at one time without the ship going down.

But at about 11.39pm on April, 14, 1912, the ship hit an iceberg as it sailed from Southampton to New York and sank 95 miles off Newfoundland, Canada, within three hours.

The Titanic, of the White Star Line, was carrying 2,228 passengers and crew and travelling at 20.5 knots when lookouts spotted an iceberg 500 yards dead ahead rising 60ft above the water.

The ship veered hard to port to avoid it, but still struck it a glancing blow, which loosened the joins between the hull's steel plates and allowed water to flood in.

Crucially, FIVE of the watertight compartments were breached.

By midnight the ship's designer Thomas Andrews, who was on board, had told the Captain Edward Smith that the Titanic would only stay afloat for two hours.

Water was by now pouring through the Titanic and it was starting to sink.

A distress call to the nearest ship, the Californian, fell on deaf ears because its radio operator was asleep.

At 12.05am the order was given to muster the passengers and crew and uncover the lifeboats — but even if they were filled there was only room for 1,178 of the 2,228 on board.

Twenty minutes later women and children were ordered into the boats. The band played lively ragtime tunes to try to quell panic.

Meanwhile the Cunard liner Carpathia received a distress call and began steaming to the scene from 58 miles away.

At 12.45am the first lifeboat was put in the water. In the rush to escape, it took only 28 people despite its capacity of 65.

More lifeboats were put in the water over the next half-hour, all below capacity.

By 1.30 the Titanic was listing to one side and panic was setting in. Shots were fired in the air by one of the ship's officers to warn people from jumping willy-nilly into the lifeboats.

An urgent new distress call read: "We are sinking fast. Women and children in boats. Cannot last much longer." A succession of lifeboats were lowered into the water, becoming fuller and fuller. By 2.05am the last was ready to leave, with room for just 47 people. More than 1,500 people were still aboard.

To prevent a rush Second Officer Herbert Lightoller brandished his pistol and the crew locked arms around the lifeboat, letting only women and children aboard.

Captain Smith told his crew, "It's every man for himself" and returned to the bridge to await his doom.

Ship designer Andrews was seen staring into space in the first-class smoking room. A priest heard a last confession from 100 passengers.

Passengers and crew then began jumping into the icy sea — and many drowned.

At 2.18am survivors heard a huge roar as all moveable objects inside the liner rushed towards the now-submerged bow.

The lights went out and the Titanic broke in two.

The broken-off stern section settled back on to the surface before filling with water and tilting upright. It then sank.

At 3.30am the Carpathia arrived to pick up survivors. Second Officer Lightoller was the last rescued, five hours later.

He wrote of the Titanic's sinking: "Slowly and almost majestically the immense stern reared itself up, with propellers and rudders clearing the water, till at last she assumed the exact perpendicular.

"Then, with an ever quickening glide, she slid beneath the water of the cold Atlantic.

"Like a prayer as she disappeared, the words were breathed, 'She's gone'."

The dead included the American millionaires John Jacob Astor and Benjamin Guggenheim.

The disaster led to many maritime reforms, including providing a lifeboat space for everyone on a ship and new regulations insisting on ships keeping a full-time radio watch.

The wreck of the Titanic was not found until 1985. Tests on steel used for the hull showed that it became brittle in extremely cold conditions, such as on the night of the disaster.

Further investigations showed that the rivets were weak and may well have contributed to the joins between the steel plates coming apart on impact.

● THE 1997 movie Titanic won 11 Oscars and is the biggest-grossing film ever.

THE Sun

Monday, April 15, 1912   1d   THOUGHT: GOD REST THEIR SOULS

Claimed by the deep . . . Titanic skipper Edward Smith went down with his ship

They sailed across the Atlantic on the ship that was 'unsinkable' . . . last night 1,523 passengers and crew were lost and the Titanic was at the bottom of the ocean. Read the harrowing story on Pages 2, 3, 4, 5, 6, 7, 8, 9 and Centre Pages.

30,497 DAYS TO GO

1916

BATTLE OF THE SOMME

Tarzan first appeared in a 1914 book. This photo is from a Tarzan movie made in 1948

...Timeline...

1913 South African government introduces laws to reserve 87 per cent of land for whites; Emmeline Pankhurst jailed for inciting supporters to plant bombs; Suffragette Emily Davison dies after throwing herself in front of King's horse at Epsom Derby.

1914 Assassination of heir to Austrian throne leads to outbreak of World War One; Britain and France occupy German colonies in West Africa; Battle of the Marne; Germany beats Russia at Battle of Tannenberg; Englishman ED Swinton invents the tank; Tarzan of the Apes by Edgar Rice Burroughs published; Panama canal opens; Suffragette Mary Richardson slashes painting The Rokeby Venus at London's National Gallery; First successful blood transfusion, in Brussels.

1915 Dardanelles Campaign — British try to force passage to Constantinople; Germans sink Cunard liner Lusitania off Ireland, drowning more than 1,100; Frank Sinatra born; Radio-telephone carries speech across the Atlantic; Cricket legend WG Grace dies; Birth of a Nation, first movie epic; Germans start submarine campaign to blockade British Isles; Britain's worst rail disaster sees 227 killed at Gretna Green, Scotland.

1916 Battles of the Somme, Gallipoli and Jutland; Boer leader Jan Smuts leads an anti-German drive from Kenya into Tanzania; English composer Gustav Holst finishes his Planets suite; Easter uprising in Dublin — British army executes 15 republicans.

Cricket's Dr WG Grace died aged 67 in 1915. A legend, he scored 126 centuries

THE battle of the Somme was one of the most savage conflicts the world has seen — and one of the great tragedies of the 20th Century.

The attack itself was supposed to hand the Allies victory over Germany in World War One by ending the stalemate of trench warfare on the western front.

Anglo-French forces were to launch a massive infantry assault which would punch an enormous hole in the German lines.

This breakthrough was then to be exploited by the cavalry, who would ride through the gap and attack the enemy's rear.

The assault began with a huge artillery attack on the German lines. Thousands of British and French guns fired 1.6million shells.

The intense noise of the barrage could be heard in London.

On the morning of July 1, 1916, British engineers exploded two mines which had been planted beneath the German lines, tearing gaping holes in the enemy trenches.

Two minutes later, at 7.30am, British and French troops attacked along a 25-mile front.

The thick mud and the heavy equipment that the British Tommies had to carry made an advance at more than a walk impossible.

Most of the Germans had survived the artillery barrage by sheltering in deep concrete shelters.

As the advance began the Germans emerged from these shelters, set up machine-guns on prepared platforms and poured fire into the British ranks. The result was nothing short of a massacre.

Lance Corporal H Bury was a signaller who was ordered to stay behind as his battalion attacked.

He said later: "We were able to see our comrades move forward only to be mown down like meadow grass. I felt sick at the sight of this carnage and remember weeping."

A few British units managed to reach the enemy trenches and storm the concrete blockhouses that defended the German lines. Most were driven back by counter attacks. The French, attacking on the left, had run forward in an open formation and so suffered lighter casualties.

They were able to capture some lightly-manned German trenches. But they were forced to fall back when the British attack failed.

The first day of the Somme saw more British casualties than any other single day in the Great War.

In total there were 19,240 killed, 35,494 seriously wounded and 2,152 missing. The Ulster Division — which attacked the heavily-fortified German right — alone lost 5,600 men, most before noon.

Nine Victoria Crosses were awarded.

The offensive on the Somme continued for another four months.

When it finally ended in November the Allies had advanced ten miles at most at a cost of 600,000 men. Of these casualties 400,000 were British Empire troops, the remainder French. The Germans suffered 450,000 casualties.

The great offensive to end the war had failed. There was to be two more terrible years of bloodshed before the killing finally stopped.

The British Army's 39th Siege Battery firing their howitzers in the Fricourt-Mametz Valley during the Battle of the Somme, one of history's bloodiest encounters. The tank was invented by an Englishman in 1914. Our photo, right, is a 1917 model

The Cunard passenger ship Lusitania was sunk by a German ship off Ireland in 1915 with the loss of more than 1,100 lives. The fact that many among the victims were Americans is thought to have hastened the United States' entry into the war

THE Sun

Monday, July 3, 1916   1d   THOUGHT: PRAY FOR THEM

SLAUGHTER

Bravest of the brave . . . British Tommies crawl along a trench towards No Man's Land yesterday

60,000 of Our Boys cut down on first day at Somme

ALMOST 60,000 British soldiers were killed or seriously wounded on the first day of the suicidal attack on the Somme, it was revealed last night.

As Our Boys advanced towards the German trenches they got bogged down in the mud or tangled up in barbed wire, making them sitting ducks for enemy machine-guns.

The Tommies fell in their thousands, but were made to keep advancing into the jaws of Hell. A few heroic units reached

By SUN FOREIGN DESK

the enemy lines but were driven back by counter attacks.

Saturday's assault was supposed to be an easy victory.

For six days our guns had bombarded the German trenches, firing six million shells in a barrage you could hear back in London.

CONFIDENT

The generals thought that any of the enemy who had survived would be too stunned to offer serious resistance.

And the commanders were so confident they ordered the

troops to march forward slowly in parade-ground style across No Man's Land.

But the Germans were neither dead nor demoralised.

The slaughter only stopped when darkness fell.

The victims of this terrible folly came from all walks of life. Some were from the cream of upper-crust society.

Others were miners' sons, farm boys – or groups of friends who had enlisted in "Pals" battalions.

British general Sir Henry Rawlinson was so horrified by the massacre that he wanted to abandon the offensive.

But last night British commander Sir Douglas Haig refused. The attack will go on.

MORE DRAMATIC PICTURES FROM THE FRONT - Pages 2, 3, 4, 5, 6 & 7

27,002 DAYS TO GO

Treasures of Tutankhamen (left) were found by Briton in 1922. Two years earlier, Mahatma Gandhi (right) launched non-cooperation movement against British in India

1926
BAIRD & THE TV

TELEVISION is one of the great scientific advances of the 20th Century and has changed the face of the developed world.

It was invented by Scotsman John Logie Baird (born in 1888), who initially funded his experiments by working as a shoe-shine boy and a razor-blade salesman.

He based his system on a mechanical device called a Nipkow disk, which was built in the late 1800s — but improved it significantly by applying new technology.

His prototype TV, called a "televisor", was housed in an old tea chest.

It comprised a motor, some lenses and a Nipkow disk made from a circle of cardboard cut out of a hat box and using a darning needle as a spindle.

It was all glued together with sealing wax and string.

In October 1925 Baird stood a ventriloquist's dummy called Stooky Bill in front of his cameras and attempted to transmit the image from one end of his attic flat in London to the other.

It worked — and an ecstatic Baird dashed from his apartment to find a real person to use in place of the dummy.

He found a teenage office boy called William Taynton and bribed him to stand in front of his lights for long enough that his flickering picture could be transmitted on to the 4ins by 2ins screen.

Taynton was thus the first person ever shown on TV.

By the following January, Baird had developed his system so that it could show significant movement.

He invited members of the leading scientific body the Royal Institution to his flat in Frith Street, Soho, and showed them moving human faces.

They were hugely impressed and Baird went on to win financial backing from private investors as well as a transmitting licence from the Post Office.

In 1927 he managed to send a transmission from London to Glasgow. The next year he sent pictures to Hartsdale, New York — the first transatlantic broadcast.

The advent of all-electric television devices eventually overtook Baird's mainly mechanical model — although he continued to make breakthroughs during the remaining years of his life.

Among them were the first ever colour pictures, which he demonstrated to a 3,000-strong audience on a 12ft by 9ft screen at a London theatre in 1938.

Much of today's television technology is still based on Baird's pioneering work. He died in 1946 — and in the late 1940s and 1950s televisions began to become enormously popular.

Colour pictures were the major advance of the 1960s, and the 1970s saw the introduction of the video recorder.

Nowadays the vast majority of homes in the developed world have a TV — and satellites and digital technology have ushered in a huge array of channels.

Experts in the field predict that in the very near future TVs will be linked to the home computer and telephone, thus becoming an essential tool for both entertainment and communication.

Screens are likely to be much larger and with better-quality pictures — but far thinner and hung on the wall like a painting.

. . . Timeline . . .

1917 America declares war on Germany; Russian Revolution overthrows government and puts Bolsheviks in power, led by Vladimir Lenin.

1918 Armistice ends World War One; The "Red Baron", legendary German fighter ace Baron Manfred von Richthofen is shot down and killed; American John Browning invents the automatic rifle; The 19,600-tonne USS Cyclops goes missing with a crew of 300 in Bermuda Triangle; Russian Czar Nicholas II and family shot by Bolsheviks; Lenin is also shot by assassin but recovers; Britain gives women over 30 the vote.

1919 British scientist Ernest Rutherford splits the atom; Paris peace conference thrashes out international settlement after World War One; First nonstop flight across Atlantic; British troops massacre more than 300 Indian civilians at Amritsar; African National Congress demonstrates against pass laws in Transvaal; Dutchman Piet Mondrian paints Abstraction.

1920 Indian Mahatma Gandhi launches peaceful non-cooperation movement against British rule; Prohibition in America bans alcohol; Band aid plasters invented in U.S.; Rupert Bear's first appearance in Daily Express.

1921 Lenin introduces New Economic Policy in Russia; Charlie Chaplin writes, directs and stars in The Kid.

1922 British archaeologist Howard Carter discovers treasure-packed burial place of Egyptian king Tutankhamen (3,500 years old); TS Eliot's The Wasteland is published; First 3-D movie appears — viewer needs coloured glasses; James Joyce writes Ulysses; Egypt becomes independent from Britain; Irish Free State founded; First football pools; Mussolini becomes Italian prime minister.

1923 Massive earthquake kills 132,000 in Japan; First neon advertising signs; Tuberculosis vaccine developed in France; Mars Bar invented; First FA Cup final at Wembley — Bolton Wanderers beat West Ham 2-1.

1924 Labour Party in power for first time; J Edgar Hoover takes over the FBI; Lenin dies; Malcolm Campbell breaks first of nine land and water speed records, achieving 146mph on land in Bluebird; American Edwin Hubble discovers galaxies; George Gershwin writes Rhapsody In Blue; Hitler writes Mein Kampf; Clayton F Summy publishes his song Happy Birthday To You; Climbers George Mallory and Andrew Irvine disappear on Everest.

1925 F Scott Fitzgerald writes The Great Gatsby; Mussolini progressing towards dictatorship in Italy.

1926 General strike rocks Britain; Escapologist Harry Houdini dies after a punch in the solar plexus; Safeways supermarket launched in America; Women get vote at 21 in Britain; First pop-up toasters in U.S.

Lenin, founder of Bolsheviks and Russian Revolution leader (1917)

British scientist Ernest Rutherford, first man to split the atom in 1919

In 1921 Benito Mussolini became Italian PM — later a dictator

1923 saw the invention of the Mars Bar, still a top-selling snack today

THE Sun

Wednesday, January 27, 1926 — 2d — THOUGHT: VISIONARY

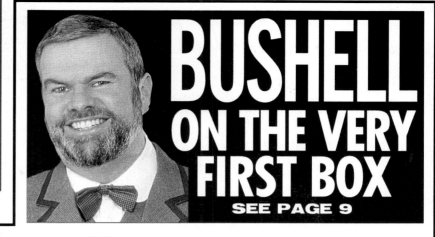

BUSHELL ON THE VERY FIRST BOX
SEE PAGE 9

WATCHA

Genius . . . Darwin

SORRY CHARLES

un chumps ver chimps

edition of The Sun dated
nber 25, 1859, and head-
"Monkey Nutter" we may
inadvertently given the
ssion that we believed
es Darwin's theory of
ion to have been unsound.
has been drawn to our
ion that our use of the
"mad" and "barmy" may
ast doubt on Mr Darwin's
stion that mankind's an-
s were apes.

family have also indi-
to us that by superimpos-
r Darwin's head on the
of a monkey we may have
tingly left him open to
le.

now accept Mr Darwin's
y of evolution is almost
ly true and apologise
umously to him for any
rassment caused.

Genius . . . Monet

SORRY CLAUDE

e had wrong mpression

e Sun of March 27, 1874,
a previous Editor, The
mplied that the paintings
ench artist Claude Monet
have been done by a

article, headlined Monet
Old Rope, suggested that
se Mr Monet's paintings
"blurred", he was earning
y under false pretences.
compared his Impression-
work The Poppy Field
ourably with John Con-
's The Hay Wain, which is
blurred.

also invited readers to
in paintings better than
Monet's.

Sun now accepts that Mr
t was one of the finest
s of all time.
are happy to set the
straight.

Scientists stunned as 'televisor' beams live pictures on to a screen

By DICKY PICTURE

A MAN has invented a miracle gadget called a "televisor" — out of an old tea chest, some bits of cardboard and string.

It has a postcard-sized screen which shows live, moving images sent from a camera nearby.

Scottish inventor John Logie Baird caused amazement when he demonstrated the contraption yesterday at his flat in London's Soho.

And scientists were last night speculating that homes everywhere might one day have a "TV" and receive pictures from all over the world.

DUMMY

Baird, 36, has been working on the project for years. He revealed that his big breakthrough came last October when he successfully beamed the image of a ventriloquist's dummy called Stooky Bill on to the screen.

He said: "The image of the dummy's head formed itself on the screen with what appeared to me an almost unbelievable clarity.

"I had got it! I could scarcely believe my eyes and felt myself shaking with excitement."

Smarter Than The Average Baird — Centre Pages

It was working earlier . . . inventor John Logie Baird stares pensively at his ingenious televisor device

TODAY'S TV PROGRAMMES IN FULL – TURN TO PAGE 8

TV TODAY

ONE TO WATCH
Stooky Bill Show
BBC1 7.30pm

BBC1   BBC2   ITV   Ch4   Ch5

7.30pm STOOKY BILL SHOW
Several seconds of action from John Logie Baird's ventriloquist's dummy (repeat).

Sky One	Sky Sports 1	Sky Sports 2	Sky Sports 3

Moviemax	Sky Premier	Sky Cinema

UK Living	Bravo	Discovery	UK Gold

Eurosport	Home & Leisure	Sky News

Garry BUSHELL
ON THE NEW BOX

I'm tellying you, this is the future

Give 'em a caning . . . our dapper Garry will pour bile on TV shows . . . just as soon as they make some

I HAVE seen the future — and it's work. This new-fangled television will surely introduce a new and respected profession, the television critic.

But the BBC will need many programme ideas to fill their eventide schedules. Here are my suggestions:

ONLY FOOLS & HORSES — costermonger Derek Trotter travels around Peckham on a three-legged donkey selling stolen trinkets.

He lives in Ramsay McDonald Terraces with his uncle Albert and younger brother Rodney the Dullard. Favourite saying: "This time next year we'll have 2s 6d."

T.F.I. FRIDAY — a jolly celebration of all the latest Music Hall turns, presented by the offensively ginger Christopher Evans. To feature performances by Marie Lloyd, Gus Elen and perhaps that young upstart Des O'Connor.

WISH YOU WERE HERE — holidays for the jobless. This week: how to preserve your boot leather while walking from Jarrow to London.

FILM '26 — Jonathan Ross previews all the latest moving pictures. Includes mimed interviews (plus subtitles) with Charles Chaplin and the Keystone Cops.

GOODNIGHT SWEETHEART — in which a young chap with a time machine leads a double life between the metropolitan sophistication of 1926 and the harsh privations of the Boer War (With apologies to H.G. Wells.)

Garfield Sparrow shocks Victorian England with his premature rendition of the Black Bottom.

Q.V.C. — a shopping channel hosted by the young Arthur Negas, offering the very finest bargains in snuff boxes and titfers.

AN AUDIENCE WITH JIMMY TARBUCK — hear the jokes today he'll still be telling in the 1990s.

THE PEELERS — a thrice-weekly drama set among the dashing Bobbies of Sun Hill. Watch them track down Jack The Ripper and set about those hooligan General Strikers.

TOMORROW'S WORLD — all the latest scientific advances, hosted by Fern Ancient-Briton and Phillipa Sapling.

The venerable Peter Snow is on hand to debunk outlandish theories like space travel and splitting the atom as the hokum they undoubtedly are.

CORONATION STREET — a soap opera, to be set amongst surly Northern proletarians who keep coal in their baths and eat raw pigeons alive.

The star should be Kenneth Barlow, a relatively young man of 57 who beds an improbable number of wenches such as Ena Sharples, 19, and Minnie Caldwell, 17.

EASTENDERS — laugh along with Oswald Mosley and his jolly blackshirts.

KISS ME KATE — adult comedy, contains shock scenes of people embracing on the lips.

THE PLANETS — see our solar system represented by a selection of fruit. You'll believe the moon is edible!

TOP GEAR — the latest in pennyfarthing bikes demonstrated by Jeremy Clarkson.

CASUALTY — with Florence Nightingale.

QUESTION TIME — Your chance to hurl rotting fruit at politicians on soap boxes.

THE JERRY SPRINGER SHOW — shocking American programme featuring social outcasts. This week: I Skipped Church To Go Fishin' and I Dated A Girl Who Was No Better Than She Should Be.

LAST NIGHT'S TV

★ WHAT utter balderdash! If this is the best John Logie Baird can do then I confidently predict the public will never turn their backs on the Music Hall. In his first broadcast, Mr Baird transmitted a picture of a ventriloquist's dummy.

In the second he showed a slip of a boy sitting stock still. I would rather watch horse manure set hard in the sunshine. What Mr Baird must do to liven television up is bring in some variety acts *(Continued at Queen Victoria Tavern, Albert Square).*

24,441 DAYS TO GO

Left, Mickey Mouse in Steamboat Willie (1928). Centre, Salvador Dali painted one of his most famous works in 1931. Al Capone (right) was by 1930 crime boss in Chicago

1933
THE RISE OF HITLER

...Timeline...

1927 Charles Lindbergh flies non-stop, solo across the Atlantic; Al Jolson's movie The Jazz Singer is the first "talkie"; Technicolor invented; Wings wins Best Picture at first Oscars; Baseball legend Babe Ruth hits record 60 home runs in season; Harlem Globetrotters basketball team founded.

1928 Alexander Fleming discovers penicillin at Queen Mary's Hospital in London; Paul Robeson sings Ol' Man River in the musical Showboat; DH Lawrence's racy Lady Chatterley's Lover published; Invention of sliced bread in U.S.; Brylcreem invented — it's the best thing since sliced bread; Walt Disney's Steamboat Willie introduces Mickey Mouse; British engineer Frank Whittle dreams up the jet engine; Joseph Stalin launches five-year plan to expand Soviet industry.

1929 Wall Street crash helps trigger Great Depression of 1930s; St Valentine's Day massacre makes Al Capone crime boss of Chicago; Tintin makes first appearance, as does Popeye.

1930 Ras Tafari crowned emperor of Ethiopia and takes name Haile Selassie; Debut of the Marathon bar (now Snickers); Cricket's Don Bradman, then 21 and probably the greatest batsman ever, hits 10 centuries on first tour of England; New York's Chrysler building opens; Stalin has total command in USSR; The planet Pluto is discovered.

1931 Spanish surrealist Salvador Dali paints famous limp watches in The Persistence of Memory; Republic declared in Spain after King Alfonso XIII abdicates; New York's Empire State Building opens; Scrabble invented; Statute of Westminster makes British dominions self-governing; Capone gets 11 years' jail for tax evasion.

1932 Democrat Franklin D Roosevelt becomes U.S. President and tells depression-hit country: "The only thing we have to fear is fear itself"; Electron microscope invented.

1933 Prohibition ends; Harold "Kim" Philby begins spying for Soviets.

Left, Chrysler Building in New York opened in 1930

Right, the Empire State Building was opened in 1931

Al Jolson, Jazz Singer (1927)

ADOLF Hitler plunged the world into the most devastating war in history — and masterminded the systematic murder of more than six million Jews.

Hitler was born in Austria in 1889. After leaving school he dreamed of being a great artist. But he fell on hard times after failing to gain entry to art school.

In 1913 he left Austria for the German city of Munich.

At the outbreak of World War One in 1914 Hitler volunteered for service in the German army. He served throughout the war in the trenches and was decorated for bravery.

After Germany's defeat Hitler was recruited by the army to infiltrate and spy on a number of small right-wing political groups.

One of these was the German Workers' Party. Hitler discovered that its members shared his nationalist and racist views.

He quickly became the spokesman for the group which he renamed the National Socialist German Workers Party — or Nazis for short.

His new role revealed a talent for public speaking and in July 1921 he was chosen as the growing party's Fuhrer, or absolute leader.

In November 1923 he and 600 armed followers tried to seize power by force. They marched through Munich, intending to overthrow the Bavarian provincial government.

But the police opened fire, killing 16 of Hitler's followers. He was jailed for five years for treason.

Hitler served only a year — and spent his time writing Mein Kampf (My Struggle). The book spelled out his hatred of the Jews and insisted Germany needed to expand — by conquest if necessary.

By the time Hitler was released he had decided that the Nazis could only come to power through the ballot box.

In May 1924 they stood for elections for the first time, winning 32 seats. And their fortunes improved as the worldwide economic depression reached Germany.

The swift rise in inflation and unemployment sparked panic and the government fell.

In September 1930 the Nazis scored their great electoral breakthrough. They won 107 seats in the German parliament, making them the second largest party.

The economic crisis deepened and Hitler seemed the one politician confident of providing the solution to the problem.

His insistence that his programme for national revival could save Germany began to strike a chord with many desperate citizens.

In the elections of July 1932 the Nazis won 230 seats. But the German president, 85-year-old World War One commander Paul von Hindenburg, stood in their way.

Hindenburg, who disliked Hitler because he was not a gentleman, refused to appoint him Chancellor.

But after another inconclusive election Hindenburg was forced to choose between what he saw as the lesser of two evils.

He could appoint a left-wing Government and risk a socialist revolution, or he could appoint a right-wing coalition under Hitler.

The President's advisers insisted they could control the Nazis — Hitler would be a mere figurehead.

On January 30 Hindenburg gave in and made Hitler Chancellor.

Within months the Right-wingers' boast of being able to control Hitler was proved hollow as he assumed the powers of a dictator.

Cricket's great crisis

THE "bodyline" Test series of 1932-3 was probably cricket's greatest crisis. England developed a tactic of bowling very fast, short-pitched balls on the leg side, which would rise up and threaten to hit the batsman.

The idea was that the batsman, trying to defend himself, would hit the ball into a pack of fielders waiting for a catch on the leg side.

The policy was mainly introduced to counter Aussie batting sensation Don Bradman, perceived to be weaker against a short, fast ball.

England, captained by the arrogant Douglas Jardine, devastated the Aussie batting on the tour Down Under, thanks mainly to the fast bowling of Harold Larwood.

Several Aussie players were injured — and angry telegrams flew between both countries, even threatening the future of England-Australia tests.

In one the MCC insisted bodyline was not "unsportsmanlike." On the day Hitler came to power the Aussies sneered back in a telegram: "We appreciate your difficulty in dealing with the matter without having seen the actual play."

England won the series 4-1. Bodyline later petered out.

THE Sun

Tuesday, January 31, 1933   2d   THOUGHT: FACE OF EVIL

Jardine . . . great skipper

'BODYLINE' IS BLASTED

WHINGEING Aussies complained to England's cricket chiefs AGAIN yesterday over our Test team's brilliant "bodyline" bowling.

They bleated that the MCC don't realise how dangerous bodyline is because they are not in Australia to see it.

Our top paceman Harold Larwood, under Douglas Jardine's superb captaincy, has put England 2-1 up in the series Down Under — and bruised a string of slow-footed Aussies.

Bradman 'Scared' — See Back Page

Nazi piece of work

GERMAN LEADER COULD START WAR

THE Sun SPEAKS ITS MIND

A SINISTER shadow has fallen over Europe — in the shape of the new German Chancellor Adolf Hitler.

Hitler has until now cut a faintly comic figure with his Charlie Chaplin moustache and absurd posturing.

But the joke suddenly turned sour yesterday as the 43-year-old former jailbird and his Nazi bully boys were handed the reins of power.

Hitler preaches a perverted gospel of hatred, violence and racism.

His vile anti-semitic outbursts and the beatings inflicted on Jews by the brown-shirted yobs who follow him have sickened all decent, civilised people.

But now what is to stop the insane rantings and thuggery being transformed into a more murderous persecution?

His calls for Germany to rebuild its army and retake the territory it lost at the end of the Great War have been described as a fantasy.

But now what is to stop him engulfing Europe in a sea of blood as he tries to turn that fantasy into reality at bayonet-point?

The German nation voted for Hitler because he promised to banish the spectre of unemployment which has left six million people on the dole.

But The Sun foresees a day in which the world will curse those who used their vote so thoughtlessly.

Let us pray we are proved wrong.

Who do you think you are kidding, Mr Hitler? – Pages Four and Five

One of the century's most dramatic photographs shows the Hindenburg (1937) exploding over New Jersey, killing 36. Incredibly 61 people survived. The cause is still unknown

...Timeline...

Hemingway (left), wrote For Whom The Bell Tolls in 1940. Centre, Orson Welles in Citizen Kane (1941). Right, Ingrid Bergman with Bogart in Casablanca, Best Picture in 1944

1934 Flying Scotsman is first loco to break 100mph mark; Mussolini meets Hitler; Cat's eyes invented by Briton Percy Shaw; First drive-in movie theatre in New Jersey; Bonnie and Clyde (Clyde Barrow and Bonnie Parker) die in police ambush in Louisiana after robbery and murder spree; First launderette opens in Fort Worth, Texas.

1935 Italians under Mussolini invade and annexe Ethiopia; "Monopoly" patented; First portable hearing aid.

1936 Death of George V — King Edward VIII abdicates to marry divorcee, George VI becomes King; Black athlete Jesse Owens takes four golds at Berlin Olympics watched by furious Hitler; Germany reoccupies Rhineland region on French-Belgian border; Civil war breaks out in Spain; Fire destroys Crystal Palace; Jarrow march — 200 jobless men walk from Tyne and Wear to London; First Spitfire prototype takes to the air; Germans invent V-2 rocket.

1937 Hindenburg disaster — huge German airship explodes just before landing in New Jersey, killing 36; Nylon invented; Spaniard Pablo Picasso paints Guernica, inspired by bombing of the town by German planes working for Franco's forces; San Francisco's Golden Gate Bridge opens; 999 becomes Britain's emergency phone number.

1938 Hitler forces Austria to form union with Germany, the "Anschluss"; Two brothers named Biro invent the ballpoint pen in Argentina; Munich crisis — France and Britain agree to let Germany partition Czechoslovakia; Superman makes his first appearance in comic; John Logie Baird demonstrates colour TV; Disney's first full-length colour cartoon, Snow White and the Seven Dwarfs, screened.

1939 Germany invades Poland, leading ultimately to World War Two; Helicopter invented by American Igor Sikorsky; Nescafe coffee is launched; The tallest man ever, American Robert Wadlow, measures 8ft 11ins on his 21st birthday; General Franco becomes dictator in Spain after civil war; Batman makes his comic-strip debut.

1940 Winston Churchill replaces Neville Chamberlain as PM; France signs armistice with Germany; Flight from Dunkirk; Battle of Britain; Ernest Hemingway writes For Whom The Bell Tolls; British scientists develop radar; Gone With The Wind, made the previous year, sweeps board at the Oscars.

1941 Germany's ally Japan attacks U.S. fleet at Pearl Harbour, Hawaii — America enters war; German army under Irwin Rommel attacks British in North Africa; Luftwaffe Blitz on British cities; Black-out leads to worst year ever for deaths on British roads — 9,149; Jet aircraft developed in England and Germany; Orson Welles' Citizen Kane released — often since voted best movie ever.

1942 Japanese seize Singapore, British troops surrender; British defeat German army at El Alamein in Egypt; American Navy defeats Japanese at Midway Island in the Pacific; Sir William Beveridge's Beveridge Report proposes welfare state for Britain; Coal mine explosion kills 1,572 in China — worst-ever pit tragedy.

1943 German Sixth Army fails to capture Stalingrad in USSR and retreats; Germans and Soviets fight largest tank battle in history at Kursk; Germans and Italians driven from North Africa.

1944 D-day landings — Allies liberate France and begin to retake Europe; Casablanca, starring Humphrey Bogart, is Best Picture at Oscars; Aaron Copland composes Appalachian Spring.

1945 Germany defeated; Allied troops reach German concentration camps and realise scale of Nazi massacre of Jews; American scientist Robert Oppenheimer builds atom bomb; America drops A-bombs on Hiroshima and Nagasaki, Japan — 130,000 killed at Hiroshima, 40,000 at Nagasaki; Two million Europeans emigrate to Australia thanks to assisted passage scheme; Britain gets a welfare state; Labour wins power; Five American bombers vanish on training flight in Bermuda Triangle.

1945

WORLD WAR TWO

VE Day marked the fall of Hitler's Nazi regime and the end of the European theatre of World War Two.

The war began on September 1, 1939, as the German armies invaded Poland. Two days later Britain and France declared war in support of their Polish allies.

But they were unable to offer any help to the Poles, who were over-run in just four weeks.

The Russians, who had signed a non-aggression pact wth the Nazis, invaded Poland from the east.

In April 1940 the Germans occupied Denmark and Norway. Then Hitler turned to western Europe.

In May 1940 the Nazis swept into Belgium and Holland. Within four days Holland surrendered and German tanks were about to encircle French and British forces defending Belgium.

By May 26 the British had been pushed into a narrow beachhead around Dunkirk. The next day Belgium surrendered as 338,266 Allied soldiers were rescued from the beaches of Dunkirk.

On June 5 Germany's ally Italy declared war on Britain and France. The French surrendered on June 25, just seven weeks after the offensive began.

By the summer of 1940 Hitler's only remaining enemy was Britain, whose new Prime Minister Winston Churchill vowed to fight on.

Hitler aimed to finish off Britain with air power alone and in August 1940 the Battle of Britain began.

But British fighter planes, notably the Spitfire, were more than a match for the Germans. Hitler postponed the invasion indefinitely, effectively conceding defeat.

In April 1941 German armies invaded Yugoslavia and Greece. In June Germany and her allies Romania and Hungary attacked Russia along a 2,000-mile front with three million troops.

The German army enjoyed its usual success at first, reaching the outskirts of Leningrad by September and Moscow by November. But by then the Russian winter had set in. Snow was blocking some roads, turning others into seas of mud, bringing tanks to a standstill.

In the south of Russia the Germans were still advancing. By July 1942 they had reached the city of Stalingrad. Russian dictator Joseph Stalin warned his generals that they must defend it to their last man.

In January 1943 the Russians counter-attacked and encircled the Germans, whose General Paulus surrendered with 200,000 men.

Stalingrad was the beginning of the end for the German army, which from then on could mount only a fighting retreat from Russia.

The Nazis had also tasted defeat in North Africa, where the forces of General Irwin Rommel had been decisively defeated by Britain's General Bernard Montgomery at El Alamein in November 1942.

By September 1943 the British and Americans — who had entered the war at the end of 1941 — invaded Italy.

On June 6, 1944, the Allies invaded Normandy. A little over two months later Paris was liberated.

Early in February 1945 British and American forces crossed into Germany. In April Russian forces began their advance on Berlin.

Hitler committed suicide in his Berlin bunker on April 30. A week later the German army agreed to surrender unconditionally. The news was announced on May 8.

The conflict in Europe was over, although World War Two would not end until Japan surrendered three months later.

The war cost the lives of an estimated 55million people, more than half of those civilians.

Alongside these were the victims of Hitler's obscene racial hatred.

Some six million Jews, gipsies, homosexuals and other "undesirables" were systematically exterminated by the Nazis.

Churchill the orator

WINSTON Churchill made many memorable speeches throughout his life. Here are extracts from a few during World War Two:

"I would say to the House ... 'I have nothing to offer but blood, toil, tears and sweat'." (May 13, 1940)

"We shall fight on the beaches, we shall fight on the landing grounds, we shall fight in the fields and in the streets, we shall fight on the hills; we shall never surrender." (June 4, 1940)

"Let us brace ourselves to our duties and so bear ourselves so that if the British Empire and its Commonwealth last for a thousand years men will still say, 'This was their finest hour'." (June 18, 1940)

"Never in the field of human conflict was so much owed by so many to so few." (August 20, 1940, referring to RAF after Battle of Britain).

True Brits . . . thousand of delighted revellers celebrate outside Buckingham Palace yesterday while a sailor and his pal clamber up a bus stop for a better view of the fun

WE'VE DONE IT

BRITAIN threw a massive party yesterday as our six-year battle with Hitler's evil Nazi regime finally ended in victory.

Millions of overjoyed revellers flocked into the streets to celebrate VE Day as the nation rejoiced from Land's End to John O'Groats.

In London many thousands stood beneath the balcony of the Ministry of Health to hear a moving speech by Prime Minister Winston Churchill. He began by saying: "God bless you all. This is your victory!"

Instantly the crowd roared back: "No — it's yours!"

Mr Churchill smiled and went on: "It is the victory of the cause of freedom in every land.

DANCING

"In all our long history we have never seen a greater day than this. Everyone, man or woman, has done their best. Everyone has tried.

"Neither the long years, nor the dangers, nor the fierce attacks of the enemy, have in any way weakened the independent resolve of the British nation. God bless you all." Many revellers were

By ROSIE FUTURE

still singing and dancing in the streets of London early today.

Others remained outside Buckingham Palace, paying tribute to the Royal Family.

In hundreds of other towns and cities there were similar scenes of jubilation.

But all the celebrations were tinged with sadness — for the thousands who died fighting for freedom in the face of terrible tyranny.

And there was also the realisation that the job is not yet done. In the Japanese we have another fiendish foe who must now be defeated.

MORE AMAZING VE DAY PICTURES — See Pages 2, 3, 4, 5, 6 and 7

Contrast in car design: Britain launches Mini in 1959. Meanwhile the '59 Cadillac epitomises the "cars with fins" the Americans produced throughout 1950s

1963

LIFE OF JOHN F KENNEDY

PRESIDENT John Fitzgerald Kennedy's assassination was perhaps the most shocking single event of the 20th Century.

People still recall where they were the moment they heard the news on November 22, 1963.

The murder produced the fiercest "conspiracy" debate in history — one still raging today.

JFK, born into a rich Boston family in 1917, led an extraordinary life.

He studied at Princeton and Harvard universities before becoming a hero during World War Two.

Kennedy won a U.S. Navy and Marine Corps Medal thanks to his life-saving leadership after the torpedo boat he commanded was rammed by a Japanese destroyer in the Pacific in August 1943.

Kennedy entered politics as a Democrat representative in 1947 and became an accomplished writer, winning the Pulitzer prize in 1956.

In 1960 Kennedy, then 43, became the youngest person and the first Catholic elected U.S. President. He was immensely popular, especially among the young who admired his vitality and commitment to peace. Three major events stand out from his short Presidency:

❶ The 1961 Bay of Pigs fiasco, where he backed an invasion of Cuba by rebels aiming to oust Communist leader Fidel Castro.

About 1,500 Cuban exiles landed at the Bay of Pigs, ready to move inland, only to find Castro's forces waiting for them. Air support promised by the CIA never arrived and the rebels were taken prisoner.

❷ Kennedy's finest hour, in 1962, when he prevented nuclear conflict through his tough handling of the Cuban missile crisis at the height of the Cold War.

A U.S. spy plane had spotted a Soviet nuclear missile positioned in Cuba, within range of Florida.

Kennedy ordered the Soviets to remove any missiles and after days of tense negotiation with PM Nikita Krushchev, the Soviets did so.

❸ In 1963, America, the Soviet Union and Britain agreed to a ban on all nuclear tests above ground. Kennedy believed the deal, signed on August 5, was his greatest achievement. Two and a half months later he was dead.

The conspiracy theory

THE conspiracy theory surrounding JFK's assassination is essentially as follows: Kennedy's commitment to peace and rooting out corruption offended powerful organisations on both sides of the law. The CIA, FBI, big business, the mafia and anti-Castro Cubans are said to have conspired to kill him.

The mafia — and the banks and industries it illegally controlled — wanted JFK dead because he had launched a crackdown on organised crime with his brother, Attorney-General Robert Kennedy.

The CIA and FBI hated the Kennedys, who had realised how out-of-control the two organisations had become. The anti-Castro Cubans felt betrayed by JFK over the Bay of Pigs fiasco.

Conspiracy theorists even implicate the U.S. military. They were said to have hated Kennedy for his liberalism, his signing of the nuclear test treaty and his perceived plans to halt U.S. involvement in Vietnam.

The mafia, in cahoots with the CIA, are said to have hired a top hitman to publicly execute JFK. Lee Harvey Oswald was then framed.

Among the more outlandish theories is that policeman J D Tippet, shot by Oswald, was somehow in on the plot. Various forensic arguments are used to support the theory, most famously the shots and gunsmoke allegedly seen coming from a "grassy knoll" near the motorcade route which prove the bullets did not come solely from the warehouse where Oswald was.

Fuel was added to the fire when Oswald, who had been charged with murder and was being moved between jails as millions watched on TV, was himself shot dead by nightclub owner Jack Ruby.

Anti-conspiracists argue that there in not a shred of genuine evidence supporting a plot and that the forensic "evidence" and witness statements have been distorted to suit the theory.

They also point out that Oswald, a Communist who once defected to the Soviet Union, was an attention-seeking oddball with ultra-Left-wing beliefs — and a trained marksman perfectly capable of shooting Kennedy without help.

The official investigation was carried out by a commission led by Supreme Court Chief Justice Earl Warren. His verdict, published on September 27, 1964, was that there was no conspiracy.

But a House of Representatives committee in 1979 acknowledged that a conspiracy was likely and that a second assassin might have been involved.

...Timeline

1946 Launch of the bikini; First electronic computer, big as garage, unveiled at Pennsylvania University; Scrabble's debut; Nazi chiefs hanged at Nuremberg.

1947 Invention of microwave in U.S.; Subbuteo football invented; India and Pakistan independent; Palestine divided into Jewish and Arab states — first Arab-Israeli war.

1948 Berlin airlift begins; "Iron Curtain" shuts off eastern europe; Racist National Party wins power in South Africa; Mahatma Gandhi assassinated.

1949 Britain recognises Irish independence; Chinese revolution, Communists in power; NATO launched.

1950 First credit card in States (Diners Club); Korean War begins; England's football stars lose 1-0 to America.

1951 Churchill is PM again, forms his first peacetime Government.

1952 Queen Elizabeth II crowned; Agatha Christie's Mousetrap play opens in London and is still going.

1953 New Zealander Edmund Hillary and Tensing Norgay climb Everest; DNA discovered; Tetley introduce tea bag; Ian Fleming invents James Bond in Casino Royale.

1954 Frank Sinatra wins Oscar in From Here To Eternity; Roger Bannister runs first four-minute mile, in Oxford; Elvis Presley releases first single That's All Right (Mama); JRR Tolkien publishes Lord of the Rings.

1955 The Pill invented; Rock Around The Clock is huge hit; Ruth Ellis is last woman hanged in Britain; Disneyland opens in California; First McDonald's opens in Des Plaines, Illinois; Warsaw Pact signed.

1956 Suez crisis — Britain and France fail to take Suez canal from Egypt; First PG Tips "chimp" ad.

1957 Russians launch first Sputniks; Treaty of Rome ushers in the EEC; Leonard Bernstein writes West Side Story.

1958 Air disaster in Munich kills eight Manchester United players; Brazilian Pele wins first of three World Cup winner's medals; BBC launch Grandstand and Blue Peter.

1959 Briton Christopher Cockerell invents the hovercraft; Fidel Castro takes control of Cuba; Mini launched; Microchip invented.

1960 ITV's Coronation Street launched; Police kill 69 black demonstrators at Sharpeville, South Africa.

1961 Russian Yuri Gagarin becomes first human in space; Spurs win league and cup double, first team to do so.

1962 Cuban missile crisis; Actress Marilyn Monroe dies of overdose.

1963 Beatles' biggest hit I Wanna Hold Your Hand; Baptist Minister Martin Luther King leads 250,000 on anti-racism march in Washington — famous "I have a dream" speech; TV's Doctor Who launched.

Russian cosmonaut Yuri Gagarin became the first human being in space in 1961

Marilyn Monroe, greatest sex symbol of century, died in 1962

Brazilian star Pele leaps for ball in 1958 on the way to his first World Cup victory

MOMENT THE EARTH STOOD STILL

THIS was the devastating moment yesterday when President Kennedy was shot dead by a sniper. The man the world knew as JFK was hit by two bullets, the second a fatal shot to the head, as he rode through Dallas, Texas, in a limo with wife Jackie at his side. Last night a Communist was arrested over the assassination. Read the full tragic story on Pages 2, 3, 4, 5, 6, 7, 8, 9 and the Centre Pages.

Jackie cradled JFK in her arms and cried: Oh no

Pride of his nation . . . smiling JFK rides through Dallas with Jackie yesterday. Moments later the bullets stru

JACKIE Kennedy wailed "Oh no" and cradled her dying husband's bloodied head as their car sped to hospital after yesterday's horror.

Moments earlier JFK, 46, was shot by a sniper who fired a rifle from a sixth-floor window as the open-topped Presidential limousine passed by in Dallas.

Crowds lining the road screamed in terror and ducked to the ground after hearing two or three shots as the President's motorcade approached an underpass.

The first bullet hit Mr Kennedy in the neck. He slumped to his left and Jackie, 34, lent over to help him.

Moments later a second shot hit him in the head, causing massive injuries.

The motorcade, which was taking the Kennedys to a VIP lunch, instead raced them to the Texas city's Parkland Hospital.

Doctors tried desperately to save Mr Kennedy with blood transfusions and he clung to life for 20 minutes. He never regained consciousness and was pronounced dead at 1pm (7pm British time).

Less than two hours later Vice President Lyndon Johnson, 55, was

By SUN FOREIGN DESK

sworn in as the 36th President. Mr Johnson, who had been sitting one car behind the Kennedys in the motorcade, took the oath of office before a judge aboard the Presidential plane Air Force One at Love Field airport, Dallas.

Widow Mrs Kennedy was by his side, her stocking still saturated with the blood of her husband, whose body was by now aboard the plane.

Police launched a massive hunt for the killer.

A photographer who saw the assassination said the shots came from the sixth-floor window at the Texas School Book Depository building near the underpass.

Distraught

And he claimed he saw the rifle's muzzle being pulled inside the window immediately afterwards.

Police who raided the building found the remains of fried chicken and some paper beneath the ledge of the window where they believe the sniper opened fire. A spokesman said: "Apparently the person had been there quite a while."

The first bullet went through Mr Kennedy and into the back of Texas

Governor John Connally, who sitting in front of him.

He had an operation last night was in a serious condition. A do said that although he "was not of the woods, his vital signs good."

Distraught Texas senator R Yarborough told how he heard or three shots as he sat two behind the Kennedys in motorcade.

He held back tears as he said could see a Secret Service man the President's car leaning on car with his hands in anger, ang and despair.

"You could tell something a and tragic had happened."

An hour after Mr Kennedy's de his body was taken from the hosp via the emergency entrance.

Mrs Kennedy walked out looked around, dazed and in shock, before climbing into the senger seat of the ambulance hol her husband's body.

It drove off towards Love F with its curtains drawn.

Air Force One arrived back Washington last night.

Mrs Kennedy, who joined her band on his visit to Texas to d up political support, returned to White House to be with her grie children Caroline, six, and John,

Horror . . secret serviceman climbs on rear of car

Grim ceremony . . . Johnson, with Jackie (right), is sworn

Oswald . . . did he shoot from sixth floor of building where he worked?

Warehouse man held by police

THIS is Lee Oswald, the man arrested yesterday for the murder of President Kennedy.

Communist Oswald, 24, was seized after a struggle with a policeman at a cinema in Dallas, Texas, three miles from the scene of the murder.

He was caught just over an hour after the assassination.

Defected

Oswald is also suspected of shooting dead another police officer, named only as J D Tippet, who confronted him yesterday during the hunt for the President's killer.

Oswald, a married dad of one, is known to have worked at the Texas School Book Depository, the Dallas warehouse from which the sniper opened fire.

He is also known to have defected to the Soviet Union before returning to the States last year.

TV reports last night described him as chairman of a Fair Play For Cuba committee.

...per's lair . . . Texas School Book Depository, which JFK was passing as he was shot yesterday. Cops found debris there left by assassin

QUEEN'S DISTRESS

THE Queen yesterday led tributes to President Kennedy — loved around the world for his energy and commitment to peace.

In a message to widow Jackie she said: "I am so deeply distressed to learn of the tragic death of President Kennedy.

"My husband joins me in sending our heartfelt and sincere sympathy to you and your family."

And in a message to new President Lyndon Johnson she said: "I am shocked and horrified to learn of the tragic death of President Kennedy.

"On behalf of my peoples, I send my sincere sympathy to the government and to the Congress and to the people of the United States." **Lyndon Johnson** himself said: "This is a sad time for all people. We have suffered a loss that cannot be weighed.

"For me it is a deep personal tragedy. I know the world shares the sorrow that Mrs Kennedy and her family bear. I will do my best. That is all I can do. I ask for your help — and God's."

Prime Minister **Sir Alec Douglas-Home** said JFK was "greatly loved and admired by all."

Speaking later on TV he added: "He had more power than had ever been given in history to a mortal man, and he used it always for high purposes and always to make the world a better and safe place for ordinary men and women to live in." **Sir**

Winston Churchill said: "This monstrous act has taken from us a great statesman and a wise and valiant man. The loss to the United States and to the world is incalculable."

Soviet foreign minister **Andrei Gromyko** expressed his "shock and greatest sympathy towards the American people."

Former Premier **Harold Macmillan** said: "Jack Kennedy meant to so many people in every country understanding, hope and faith in the future of the people of the United States."

French President **Charles De Gaulle** said: "President Kennedy died as a soldier, under fire, for his duty and in the service of his country."

...een . . . sent 'sincere sympathy'

Sir Winston . . . 'a monstrous act'

12,206 DAYS TO GO

. . . Timeline . . .

1964 Leonid Brezhnev takes over from Nikita Khrushchev in USSR; Peter Allen and John Malby executed for murder, last ever in Britain; Elizabeth Taylor and Richard Burton marry for the first time; Muhammad Ali knocks out Sonny Liston to become world heavyweight champ; Palestine Liberation Organisation is set up to unite Palestinian refugees; Jimmy Savile presents first Top of the Pops on BBC TV; Worst-ever soccer disaster sees more than 300 fans killed during riot over refereeing decision in Lima, Peru.

1965 U.S. enters war against communist North Vietnam in earnest; Race riots in Watts, Los Angeles, leave 34 dead; White regime in Zimbabwe declares independence; UK abolishes capital punishment; Soccer's Stanley Matthews knighted; Ten footballers guilty of match-fixing; Post Office Tower opens in London.

1966 Aberfan disaster in Wales — 116 children and 28 adults die as slag heap engulfs school; Xerox markets useable fax machine; The Sound of Music is Best Picture at Oscars; Indira Gandhi becomes Indian PM; Moors murderers Ian Brady and Myra Hindley get life; Gangster Ronnie Kray shoots dead rival George Cornell in the Blind Beggar pub in Whitechapel, East London.

Julie Andrews in The Sound of Music, Best Movie in 1966. Right, London's Post Office Tower opened in 1965

1966
WORLD CUP VICTORY

ENGLAND'S World Cup victory in 1966 was the nation's greatest sporting achievement. The squad had the benefit of home advantage, but their early tournament games were less than inspiring.

In the First Round group phase they scraped a 0-0 draw with Uruguay, struggled to put two past a poor Mexico side and ground out a dull 2-0 victory against France.

In the quarter-finals things did not get much better. England's match against Argentina was marred by the South Americans' cynical fouling and the sending-off of their petulant captain Rattin.

But even with the Argentinians down to ten men, England struggled. Then with 13 minutes to go, West Ham's Geoff Hurst headed home to put England in the semi-finals.

In the match against Portugal, England at last began to hit something approaching top form. After half an hour Bobby Charlton put his side one-up — adding a second 11 minutes from the end. Portuguese striker Eusebio scored a consolation penalty.

England were favourites to win the final. But the Wembley crowd were shocked into silence when the Germans scored after 13 minutes. It took England just six minutes to draw level, though — Hurst heading home from a free kick taken by England and West Ham captain Bobby Moore. At half-time it was 1-1.

The second half opened quietly, with neither side willing to take risks.

With less than 13 minutes left, West Ham's Martin Peters scored after a corner. But with less than a minute to go German defender Wolfgang Weber stabbed home an equaliser after a goalmouth scramble.

In extra-time England got the upper hand. After 100 minutes, Geoff Hurst met a cross with a thunderous shot that sent the ball cannoning on to the underside of the crossbar and then bouncing down.

The jubilant England players raised their arms — but had the ball crossed the goal-line? The referee was unsure, but his Russian linesman signalled a goal.

The desperate Germans now threw everything into attack, leaving themselves exposed in defence.

In the dying seconds Moore got the ball and put Hurst clean through.

TV commentator Kenneth Wolstenholme, referring to the crowd encroaching on the pitch, said: "They think it's all over". And as Hurst's fierce left-foot shot hit the back of the net, he added: "It is now!"

A year later team manager Alf Ramsey became Sir Alf.

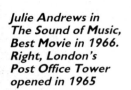

Richard Burton and Elizabeth Taylor married twice, the first time in 1964

Muhammad Ali, then Cassius Clay, lands another blow on Sonny Liston as he wins the world heavyweight championship in 1964

THE Sun

nday, August 1, 1966   4d   THOUGHT: HANS OFF, IT'S OURS

ARISE SIR ALF

Support new Sun campaign Pages 4 & 5

WORLD CUP 1966

MOORE THE MERRIER

By SAUL OVER

BOBBY Moore and his World Cup heroes were last night hailed as the greatest England team ever after their sensational 4-2 victory over West Germany.

Captain marvel Bobby and the rest of the lads were yesterday still celebrating Saturday's historic Wembley win.

And the entire nation was joining in with the biggest knees-up since VE Day.

REWARD

There was scarcely a house in England where the talk was not of hat-trick hero Geoff Hurst, battling Bobby Charlton, magnificent Martin Peters and the nail-biting finish in extra-time.

Today The Sun launches a campaign to give manager Alf Ramsey and his lads the reward they deserve. We reckon that's nothing short of a knighthood for him — and MBEs for all the players.

More great pictures on Pages 2, 3, 4 and 5 PLUS a super 16-page World Cup Final souvenir pullout

11,121 DAYS TO GO

1969
THE MOON LANDING

The Beatles, biggest pop band ever, released their classic Sergeant Pepper album in 1967

...Timeline..

1967 Doctor Christiaan Barnard does first heart transplant, in Cape Town; Queen launches QE2; Torrey Canyon oil disaster, 50,000 tons of crude fouls Cornish coast; Malcolm Campbell's son Donald dies at Coniston Water, Lake District, attempting another water speed record in Bluebird; Lee Harvey Oswald's assassin Jack Ruby dies in hospital; Six Day War between Israel and Arabs; Beatles release Sergeant Pepper's Lonely Hearts Club Band; Three astronauts burned to death on launch pad at Cape Kennedy inside Apollo I.

1968 Martin Luther King and JFK's brother Robert, by then a presidential hopeful, both assassinated; Major anti-Vietnam War protests in U.S.; Bob Beamon's long jump at Mexico Olympics smashes world record and stands for 23 years; Student riots in Paris; West Indian cricket legend Gary Sobers hits six sixes off one over, first time ever; Warsaw Pact invasion ends fledgling reforms in Czechoslovakia; American troops slaughter 175 villagers at My Lai, Vietnam, in killing frenzy — the Lieutenant in charge is later jailed for murder.

1969 Three-day Woodstock rock festival becomes lasting symbol of hippie era; Vertical take-off Harrier jump-jet invented in Britain; Sony make first practical video recorder; BBC1 now in colour; Britons get vote at 18; The Sun is launched.

In 1968, West Indian Gary Sobers hit sixes off six consecutive balls, a record

Martin Luther King and (right) Robert Kennedy were both assassinated in 1968

AN awestruck world was able to watch mankind's greatest-ever technological achievement on live TV.

And as American astronaut Neil Armstrong became the first man on the moon he uttered one of history's most famous misstatements.

He planned to say: "That's one small step for a man, one giant leap for mankind" — but forgot the "a" in the heat of the moment.

The moon landing, at around 4am British time on July 21, 1969, was the culmination of the 12-year space race between the Soviet Union and America.

The Soviets launched the first satellite, the unmanned Sputnik 1, in October 1957. Sputnik 2 went up a month later, with a dog called Laika aboard. She died when her oxygen ran out.

The U.S. launched its first satellite, Explorer 1, in January 1958.

The next major breakthrough came when the Soviets put the first man into space. Yuri Gagarin, 27, orbited Earth once on April 12, 1961.

The 1960s saw a string of missions, significant among them America's Apollo 8, which in 1968 became the first manned spacecraft to orbit the moon.

Then came the historic Apollo 11 mission. Astronauts Neil Armstrong, Edwin "Buzz" Aldrin and Michael Collins launched from Cape Canaveral, Florida, on July 16, 1969.

The spacecraft consisted of the command module Columbia and the small lunar module Eagle. Collins stayed in the Columbia while Armstrong and Aldrin landed the Eagle on the moon shortly before 11pm American time on July 20.

Armstrong descended the ladder first, uttered his immortal remark and planted an American flag.

Aldrin followed and the pair worked for 2½ hours setting up scientific instruments, collecting samples and taking photos.

They finally lifted off after 21 hours and 36 minutes, to rendezvous with Collins and return to Earth.

In the 1970s the U.S. and USSR joined forces for the Apollo-Soyuz Test Project (ASTP) — which saw U.S. and Soviet crafts dock in space.

In 1981 America launched the Space Shuttle, the first reusable manned vehicle.

The Soviet station Mir was put into orbit in 1986 and for more than a decade enabled astronauts from around the world to spend prolonged periods in space.

Since the start of the space race more than 5,000 manned flights, satellites and probes have been launched.

The immediate future of space exploration is likely to favour robot missions over costly manned ones.

The world's space agencies aim to study Mars and Europa — one of Jupiter's moons.

Europa is thought to have a vast ocean beneath its icy surface which could contain life.

Other missions will study asteroids and comets.

The NASA orbiter Cassini will reach Saturn in 2004. The agency is considering sending others to survey Mercury, Uranus, Neptune and eventually Pluto.

The crew of Apollo 11, left to right, Neil Armstrong, Michael Collins and Edwin 'Buzz' Aldrin. Armstrong became the first man on the moon, Aldrin the second

THE Sun

4am news

Monday, July 21, 1969   6d   THOUGHT: EARTH SHATTERING

One small step for man, one giant leap for mankind

THE HISTORIC WORDS EARLY TODAY OF ASTRONAUT NEIL ARMSTRONG AS HE BECAME THE FIRST MAN TO WALK ON THE MOON. READ THE FULL STORY OF THIS AWE-INSPIRING ACHIEVEMENT ON PAGES 2, 3, 4, 5, 6 & 7

6,451 DAYS TO GO

. . . Timeline . . .

1970 Guitar legend Jimi Hendrix dies after overdose; Beatles split up; Oil found in North Sea; John Wayne wins his only Oscar as Rooster Cogburn in True Grit; Five-day drama aboard crippled spacecraft Apollo 13 grips world — three astronauts finally touch down safely; Communist Khmer Rouge takes over Cambodia; Tonga and Fiji gain independence from Britain; Micro-computers being developed in U.S.

1971 Britain goes decimal; Arsenal win double; Brief war leads to East Pakistan becoming independent as Bangladesh; Space Hoppers for kids invented; Intel builds the microprocessor; 42 die in uprising at Attica jail, New York.

1972 Bloody Sunday in Londonderry, Northern Ireland — troops shoot dead 13 marchers; 11 Israeli athletes are killed by Arab "Black September" organisation at Munich Olympics — and swimmer Mark Spitz wins seven golds; America invents pocket calculator; Murderous dictator Idi Amin seizes power in Uganda; Miners' strike leads to power cuts and a state of emergency being declared.

1973 America pulls troops out of Vietnam; UK joins the European Commmunity; New York's World Trade Centre is finished; Sydney opera house opens; Yom Kippur War between Arabs and Israelis begins; Cut in Arab oil production causes oil crisis in U.S. and Europe; Marlon Brando wins Oscar in The Godfather and refuses to accept it.

1974 President Richard Nixon resigns after Watergate scandal exposed by two Washington Post reporters; BBC transmits Teletext data to TV sets; Lord Lucan vanishes; Muhammad Ali regains world heavyweight title at 32; Kojak hits TV screens; World's tallest inhabitable building, Chicago's 1,454ft Sears Tower, completed; Concorde's first commercial flight; Britain's James Hunt is Formula One champion; Helsinki convention on human rights adopted; Soweto uprising — police massacre blacks in demo over enforced use of Afrikaans language.

1975 Saigon falls, all Americans leave Vietnam; Franco dies and Spain becomes democracy; Pol Pot's reign of terror begins in Cambodia; Moorgate Tube station disaster in London leaves 41 dead.

1976 Viking probes touch down on Mars; Starsky and Hutch on British TV; Punk rock upsets establishment; Massive earthquake kills 250,000 in Tangshan, China; Briton John Curry wins Olympic figure-skating gold; Concorde's first commercial flight; Britain's James Hunt is Formula One champion; Helsinki convention on human rights adopted; Soweto uprising — police massacre blacks in demo over enforced use of Afrikaans language.

1977 Elvis Presley dies; Liverpool win European Cup; Kerry Packer's breakaway cricket series causes uproar; Star Wars is massive movie hit; Virginia Wade wins Wimbledon; Worst air disaster in history leaves 574 dead as two Boeing 747 jumbos collide at Tenerife airport; Queen's silver jubilee sees street parties — the Sex Pistols play on boat sailing up Thames in anti-Jubilee stunt, their God Save The Queen hits No2 in charts; Red Rum wins Grand National for third time.

1978 Camp David summit between Egypt and Israel, hosted by United States; Vietnam invades Cambodia and forces out Khmer Rouge; Space Invaders arcade game sweeps world; Anna Ford is first female newsreader on British TV.

1979 Tory Margaret Thatcher elected first British woman Prime Minister; Mother Teresa wins Nobel Peace Prize; Ayatollah Khomeini adopts Islamic constitution for Iran; Soviets invade Afghanistan; First Sony Walkman; Sebastian Coe sets world mile record, 3mins 48.95secs; Trevor Francis is England's first £1million footballer, signing for Nottingham Forest.

1980 John Lennon shot dead in New York; Iran-Iraq War breaks out; Bjorn Borg wins Wimbledon for fifth time; Mount St Helens erupts in U.S.; Ronald Reagan elected President; Born Free author Joy Adamson murdered at home in Kenya; Independent trade union, Solidarity, formed in Poland; Rhodesia, upon independence from Britain, renamed Zimbabwe; SAS storm the Iranian embassy, watched by millions on TV.

1981 AIDS is first recognised; First London marathon; Yorkshire Ripper Peter Sutcliffe jailed; BBC launch Only Fools and Horses; First laptop computer; Space shuttle Columbia makes its first flight; Prince Charles marries Princess Diana; Four rebel Labour MPs found the Social Democrats party; Reagan shot and wounded by John Hinkley; Brixton riots in London.

1982 ET is huge movie hit; Channel 4 is launched; British movie Chariots of Fire triumphs at Oscars; Sir Freddie Laker's Laker Airlines collapses.

Red Rum won National for third time in 1977

The King, rock legend Elvis Presley, died in 1977

Skater John Curry won gold in 1976

1982
WAR FOR THE FALKLANDS

THE sinking of the Argentine battleship Belgrano was the first major engagement of the war over control of the Falkland Islands in the south Atlantic.

The islands had been controlled by Britain since 1833 — but for decades Argentina had claimed sovereignty over them, despite the islanders themselves wishing to remain under British rule.

The first steps towards war came on March 19, 1982, when Argentine scrap metal merchants landed on South Georgia (an isle to the east of the main Falkland Islands) escorted by troops.

The British Government under Prime Minister Margaret Thatcher insisted they must leave.

But on April 2 the Argentine military junta led by General Leopoldo Galtieri sent thousands of troops to invade the Falklands.

A small detachment of Royal Marines was hopelessly outnumbered and surrendered.

The United Nations called on Argentina to withdraw, but over the next few days Galtieri rushed between 10,000 and 20,000 more troops to the Falklands.

Mrs Thatcher declared a 200-mile exclusion zone around the islands and began to assemble a naval task force to retake them.

On April 25, after attempts at a negotiated settlement had broken down, British commandos retook South Georgia.

The main British task force was still on its way.

Less than a week later British fighters shot down three Argentine aircraft over Port Stanley. On May 2 the British submarine HMS Conqueror sank the Argentine cruiser General Belgrano just outside the exclusion zone. Almost 400 crewmen died.

Two days later Argentine planes using Exocet air-to-surface missiles sank the British destroyer HMS Sheffield with the loss of 20 lives.

Over the next week two Argentine supply ships were sunk and a further 14 aircraft destroyed.

On May 21 British forces made an amphibious landing near Port San Carlos on East Falkland and marched south towards Darwin and Goose Green.

HMS Coventry was hit by Argentine bombers on May 25, killing 19 British troops.

Three days later 12 more British soldiers died when the MV Atlantic Conveyor was hit.

The 2nd battalion of the Parachute Regiment took Darwin and Goose Green, despite being outnumbered by more than 2-1.

On May 29 more than 250 Argentinians were killed and 1,400 captured in attacks on their positions. Two days later Port Stanley was surrounded.

An Argentine air attack hit the British landing crafts Sir Galahad and Sir Tristram on June 8, killing 50.

Over the next few days British troops took important strategic positions at Mount Longdon, Two Sisters, Mount Harriet and Mount Tumbledown.

On June 14 almost 10,000 Argentine troops surrendered in Port Stanley, effectively ending the war. The conflict lasted 72 days and claimed almost 1,000 lives — 236 British and 655 Argentine.

Tennis giant, Swede Bjorn Borg, won his fifth Wimbledon men's title in 1980

Sex Pistols punk band formed in 1976 and caused furore throughout late '70s

Prince Charles and Princess Diana kiss during their fairytale wedding of 1981. Left, Margaret Thatcher takes power in 19..

THE Sun

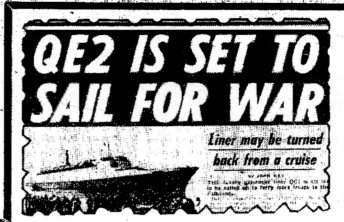

QE2 IS SET TO SAIL FOR WAR

Liner may be turned back from a cruise

BY JOHN KAY

We told you first

NINE days ago The Sun said that the QE2 was to be called up. Everybody denied it. Yesterday the Ministry of Defence confirmed it. If you really want to know what's going on in the war buy The Sun. We try harder. See Page 2

sday, May 4, 1982   14p   TODAY'S TV: PAGE 12

GOTCHA

SUNK AN Argie patrol boat like this one was sunk by missiles from Royal Navy helicopters after first opening fire on our lads

CRIPPLED THE Argie cruiser General Belgrano . . . put out of action by Tigerfish torpedoes from our super nuclear sub Conqueror

Our lads sink gunboat and hole cruiser

From TONY SNOW aboard HMS Invincible

THE NAVY had the Argies on their knees last night after a devastating double punch.

WALLOP: They torpedoed the 14,000-ton Argentina cruiser General Belgrano and left it a useless wreck.

WALLOP: Task Force helicopters sank one Argentine patrol boat and severely damaged another.

The Belgrano, which survived the Pearl Harbour attack when it belonged to the U.S. Navy, had been asking for trouble all day.

The cruiser, second largest in the Argy fleet, had been skirting the 200-mile war zone that Britain has set up around the Falkland Islands.

MAJOR

With its 15 six-inch guns our Navy high command were certain that it would have played a major part in any battle to retain the Falklands.

But the Belgrano and

BATTLE FOR THE ISLANDS

its 1,000 crew needn't worry about the war for some time now.

For the nuclear submarine Conqueror, captained by Commander Richard Wraith, let fly with two torpedoes.

The ship was not sunk and it is not clear how many casualties there were.

HMS Conqueror was built at Cammell Laird's shipyard in Birkenhead for £30million. She was launched in 1869 and *Continued on Page Two*

UNION BOYCOTTS WAR

UNION chief is telling seamen on two ships taken over by the Government: "Don't go to war—the union can't protect you."

The astonishing advice comes from George Cartwright the Communist leader of the National Union of Seamen at Felixstowe Port in Suffolk.

The Government has just requisitioned the Townsend Thoresen roll-on, roll-off vessels Baltic Ferry and Nordic Ferry.

'Folly'

The ferries will carry troops and battle equipment in support of the QE2.

Mr Cartwright told the 150 seamen: "Our advice is that it would be folly to go off on a dangerous adventure.

"I'm old enough to remember that one in three merchant seamen were killed in the last war.

"It is not a case of being unpatriotic. We are not at war and our advice is based on union practicalities.

"What we are saying is that if seamen put themselves under military command, they will no longer have our protection."

Question

"There is no question of politics being behind the recommendation. We were asked for our view

and gave our best advice."

He believes the majority of crew members will decide not to sail to the South Atlantic.

"So far I have heard from three seamen who want to go, the rest are non-commital or against joining the task force," Mr Cartwright said.

1986

First cast of EastEnders, which launched in 1985. Leslie Grantham played 'Dirty' Den Watts, landlord of the Queen Vic pub. Anita Dobson played his wife Angie

...Timeline...

1983 More than 1.5million die during war in Sudan; Ben Kingsley wins Best Actor Oscar in Gandhi; Top racehorse Shergar is kidnapped and never seen again; Skeleton of new dinosaur Baryonyx unearthed in Surrey quarry.

1984 IRA bombs the Tory Party's Brighton hotel during conference week, killing four; Disaster at Bhopal, India — 2,500 killed by leak of toxic gas from insecticide plant; The CD player arrives; Indian prime minister Indira Gandhi assassinated by Sikhs; New Zealand declared nuclear-free; Singer Marvin Gaye shot dead by his dad.

1985 Trouble at Liverpool football match ends in crush which kills 39 people at Heysel Stadium, Brussels; Blaze at Bradford's soccer ground kills 56; Boeing 737 bound for Corfu catches fire at Manchester Airport, killing 55; Two major earthquakes kill 8,000 in and around Mexico City; Bob Geldof's Live Aid concert raises millions for starving in Ethiopia; Mikhail Gorbachev takes power in USSR, brings in new spirit of openness ("glasnost") with West; The CD-rom arrives — it can store 270,000 sheets of text; British scientists in Antarctica first to discover hole in ozone layer; Sir Clive Sinclair launches the C5 electric buggy, it flops; BBC launches new soap opera, EastEnders.

1986 Chernobyl nuclear disaster in Ukraine kills 31 immediately and thousands later from radiation; U.S. space shuttle Challenger explodes just after lift-off above Florida, killing all seven astronauts; Philippines president Ferdinand Marcos forced to flee with wife Imelda — Corazon Aquino takes over; America bombs Libya for backing terrorists; Prince Andrew weds Sarah Ferguson; Mike Tyson, 20, becomes youngest world heavyweight boxing champ.

Catastrophic explosion on the Challenger shuttle killed seven astronauts in 1986

Devastation at Grand Hotel, bombed by the IRA in 1984 during Tory conference

FREDDIE STARR

FREDDIE Starr has been Britain's wildest comic of the last 25 years — and provided The Sun with one of its most memorable headlines, even though he always denied the story.

The comedian was born Frederick Fowell in Liverpool on January 9, 1943, the youngest of a bricklayer's five children.

As long ago as 1957 he appeared in the movie Violent Playground, as a troubled teenager.

He later formed various rock bands including Freddie Starr and Midnighters, who played at the Cavern nightspot made famous by the Beatles. Freddie turned to mimickry in the late 1960s, winning Opportunity Knocks and receiving a standing ovation at the 1970 Royal Variety Show.

The LWT series Who Do You Do, which ran from 1972 to 1976, established him as a major star and his comic impersonations of Hitler, Elvis, Mick Jagger and Norman Wisdom brought the house down.

The 1980s saw him fall out of fashion and become hooked on valium and cocaine. But his career was revived in the 1990s, with successful guest appearances on a string of shows — plus his own Audience With Freddie Starr and Another Audience With Freddie Starr.

In 1999, dad-of-five Freddie, 56, married third wife Donna, 29.

...and the hamster

HAMSTERS are short-tailed furry rodents with large cheek pouches for carrying food — and certain types make top pets.

The most common of these is the golden hamster which, in captivity, is clean and easily tamed.

It can produce up to 18 baby hamsters a year and has a gestation period of an amazing 2½ weeks. In the wild, hamsters are nocturnal creatures living in parts of Europe and Asia in elaborate, multi-chambered burrows and feeding mainly on grain, fruit and vegetables.

The common hamster is quite large, growing up to a foot long — plus tail.

Horror at the vicarage

THE Ealing Vicarage rape was one of the most shocking crimes of the 1980s. On March 6, 1986, a drunken gang armed with knives burst into the West London vicarage intent on robbery.

Gang leader Robert Horscroft, Martin McCall and brothers Andrew and Chris Byrne demanded money from vicar Michael Saward.

They then fractured his skull with a cricket bat while McCall and Chris Byrne subjected Mr Saward's virgin daughter Jill, 21, to a half-hour ordeal. Jill's then-boyfriend David Kerr was also savagely beaten. Deeply-Christian Jill waived her anonymity to help other rape victims but also tried three times to kill herself.

She is now a happily-married mum of three.

The gang were caught and jailed in 1987. Drug addict McCall was freed in 1993, Chris Byrne in 1991. Andrew Byrne died in 1990.

Horscroft was freed in 1996 and later begged Jill's forgiveness at a pre-arranged meeting. She told him: ''You already have it.''

Rock stars during 1985 Live Aid charity concert at Wembley for the starving in Ethiopia, footage of whom shocked the world a year earlier

Inventor Clive Sinclair hoped his C5 (1985) would change the world. It did not

FREDDIE STARR ATE MY HAMSTER

Comic put a live pet in sandwich, says beauty

kened . . . animal-loving Lea yesterday   Picture: PETER RALPH

Freddie . . . "It's lies"

EXCLUSIVE by DICK SAXTY

ZANY comic Freddie Starr put a live hamster in a sandwich and ATE it, model girl Lea La Salle claimed yesterday.

She said "I was sickened and horrified. He killed my pet.

"It's something I'll never forget. He put my hamster between two slices of bread and started eating it.

"He thought it was hilarious,"said Lea. "He just fell about laughing."

Lea, 23, said the incident—which Starr hotly denies—happened while the comic was staying with her and boyfriend Vincent McCaffrey in Birchwood, Cheshire. Freddie was performing at a Manchester nightclub.

Lea, a former Miss UK runner-up, said: "He used to get back in the early hours and demand something to eat.

"On about the fifth night, I told him to get something himself.

BITE

"He came back from the kitchen with a sandwich, and at first I didn't pay any attention to what was in it. I saw him take a bite.

"Then I saw part of my hamster Supersonic sticking out from between the bread!"

Supersonic was kept in an open-top glass cage near the kitchen, said Lea.

"I screamed when I

Continued on Page Seven

JEWEL IN MY CROWN

Vicar praises rape daughter

By MURIEL BURDEN

HE vicar whose daughter as raped by the "spider-en" gang praised the 21-ar-old girl's courage last ght.

With tears in his eyes he d: "She is the jewel in my own."

The vicar, whose skull was actured in the attack, was eaking from his hospital bed police were early today izzing FIVE men and a OMAN about the crime.

He said: "I am deeply impressed with the way my daughter and her boyfriend have responded to the situation."

Justice

The girl's boyfriend was also beaten unconscious during the attack in a West London vicarage.

Of the men, the vicar said: "I want to see justice done. I think this country is soft on justice.

"But not once have I felt hatred or felt vengeful I feel sad for them. They were a trio of derelicts.

"And if I am a Christian minister, preaching a gospel of reconciliation and hope for the outcasts of this world, I would have no gospel if I did not have that in my heart.

"Clergymen are supposed to be plaster saints. But I can say that in all honesty, not because I am a clergyman, but as a man who has been bashed up."

Thousands of messages and cards have been sent to the vicarage in six days since the attack.

The vicar added: "I will not be able to write personally to everyone. But I hope they will take this as my deep appreciation of their kind words and thoughts."

Two of the men being ques-

Continued on Page Two

SELLERS GIRL IS

Vicky . . . police hunt

CHARGED IN DRUG CASE

Page 5

3,704 **DAYS TO GO**

Smiling Soviet President Mikhail Gorbachev and U.S. President Ronald Reagan sign a historic treaty at the White House in 1987 banning intermediate-range nuclear missiles

1989
FALL OF COMMUNISM

...Timeline...

1987 U.S. President Ronald Reagan and Soviet leader Mikhail Gorbachev sign historic INF Treaty, cutting nuclear weapons; Herald of Free Enterprise ferry capsizes off Zeebrugge, Belgium, killing 193; Black Monday crash, October 19, wipes £50billion off stockmarket values; Work starts on Channel Tunnel; Church envoy Terry Waite kidnapped on mission to Beirut; German Mathias Rust, 19, lands his light aircraft in Red Square, Moscow; Hurricane rocks much of southern England.

1988 Pan Am jumbo jet blows up over Lockerbie, Scotland, killing 270; Inferno on Piper Alpha oil rig in North Sea kills 167; Golfer Sandy Lyle is first Briton to win U.S. Masters; George Bush elected U.S. President; Liberals and Social Democrats merge to become the Liberal-Democrats; British ski-jumper Eddie "The Eagle" Edwards is the star of the Winter Olympics, even though he comes last.

1989 Crush at Liverpool soccer match at Hillsborough, Sheffield, kills 95; Up to 2,600 people, mostly students, reported dead after Chinese troops are ordered to clear human rights protesters from Tiananmen Square, Beijing; Popular protests topple communist regimes in East Germany, Poland, Czechoslovakia, Bulgaria and Romania; 44 killed as plane crashes on M1 near Kegworth, East Midlands; Exxon Valdez oil tanker leaks 11 million gallons of oil into Prince William Sound, Alaska; Japanese emperor Hirohito dies; Major earthquake kills 67 in San Francisco; First flight of B-2 stealth bomber; U.S. invades Panama and deposes ruler General Manuel Noriega; Sky TV launched; FW de Klerk, who eventually brings apartheid to an end, becomes South African President.

Eddie 'The Eagle' Edwards in action at 1988 Olympics

THE dismantling of the Berlin Wall was the climax of six months in which the communist regimes of eastern Europe tottered and fell.

The seeds of this destruction were sown by the reforming Soviet President Mikhail Gorbachev.

Gorbachev came to power in 1985 with an unshakeable belief that the Soviet Union was doomed unless it could modernise.

His plans were symbolised by his twin slogans Glasnost, meaning openness, and Perestroika, meaning restructuring.

These words signalled immense changes for the Soviet Union — and for the eastern European nations which were its satellite states.

The first signs of the momentous times ahead came in 1988 when demonstrations in Czechoslovakia on the anniversary of the 1968 Soviet invasion went unchecked.

Then in Poland the Solidarity union demanded democratic reforms and the government approved partially free elections. Solidarity won all 161 seats.

In May the first breach in the infamous Iron Curtain occurred when Hungary opened its border with Austria.

In August a small number of East Germans began to escape to the West across the open border. The trickle soon became a torrent — by September 30,000 people had crossed into Austria.

At the end of August more than a million Latvians, Estonians and Lithuanians held demonstrations to demand independence from the Soviet Union. Similar protests began all over East Germany. In October, Hungary amended its constitution to abolish the Socialist party's "leading role" in society and legalise non-communist parties.

In the East German cities of Leipzig and Dresden, crowds of more than 300,000 demanded an end to communist rule. On November 1 the East German government gave in, by opening its border with Czechoslovakia.

After more demonstrations the East German government resigned.

On November 9 it was announced that exit visas would be granted to all East Germans who wished to visit the West. The border was now open. Overjoyed citizens flocked to the Berlin Wall and began pulling it down.

In Czechoslovakia the hardliners tried to hang on. On November 17 a huge pro-democracy demonstration in Prague's Wenceslas Square was broken up by force. But when this prompted even larger protests the government quit.

In Bulgaria the end of communism was peaceful and the government resigned in November.

In Romania there was a bloodbath. Dictator Nicolae Ceausescu was determined to preserve his rule at all costs. He ordered his security forces to shoot crowds of demonstrators, but the rebellion could not be stopped. When large numbers of soldiers sided with the rebels, civil war broke out.

On December 22 Ceausescu was captured trying to flee the country. Three days later he was executed after being found guilty of genocide.

China crushed its pro-democracy movement — and hundreds of demonstrating students were killed.

Wreckage of the nose cone of Boeing 747 jumbo jet, Pan Am Flight 103, which blew up over Lockerbie, Scotland, in 1988, killing 270 people in the air and on the ground

A lone pro-democracy student defies army tanks in Tiananmen Square, Beijing (1989)

WAR PLANE HITS FLATS

DOZENS of people were feared dead last night after a military jet crashed into a block of flats and started a massive blaze.

The pilot parachuted from the doomed plane as it dived towards an apartment complex in Atlanta, Georgia.

An eye-witness said: "You can see the flames lighting up the sky. We are sure there will be many dead and injured."

—See Page Two

IT'S WALL OVER

Berlin carnival as Iron Curtain falls

By TREVOR KAVANAGH and JOHN HELLINGS

THE hated Berlin Wall was thrown wide open last night — and hundreds of jubilant East Germans surged across to be greeted by champagne and fireworks in the West.

East Berliners crying with joy burst through checkpoints to celebrate their freedom with new-found friends on the other side.

The Wall — symbol of tyranny and a barrier between East and West for 28 years — was overwhelmed by crowds in carnival spirit.

It now seems certain to be pulled down. West Berliners chanted, "The Wall is gone, The Wall is gone" after Communist leaders announced they were removing the last restrictions on their citizens leaving East Germany.

Many East Berliners walked through to the West then **RETURNED** — just to prove their new freedom was real.

One woman came back and said: "Going to West Berlin was as good as going to Australia for me."

Crowds, whooping and cheering like soccer fans, converged on the Bornholmer Strasse crossing point.

Drivers in a half-mile queue of cars tooted their horns incessantly.

GUARDS

Pedestrians yelled: "We're off to the Kudamm" — West Berlin's main boulevard.

The eight crossing points were not supposed to be officially opened until today — but guards could do little.

West Berliners stormed Checkpoint Charlie to prove the freedom was two-way and shouted "We want in" at *Continued on Page Seven*

The brave who made it and those who didn't
—Pages 6 & 7

Sun picture exclusive

HERE is kids' TV presenter Michaela Strachan as you have never seen her before — and how she prayed you would **NEVER** see her!

The Sun today reveals how pretty Michaela — who hates being thought of as a sex object — once worked as a £15-a-night **STRIPPOGRAM** girl.

The children's favourite in Saturday mornings' Wide Awake Club, worked for Tantalising Telegrams in Surrey when she was 17!.

Michaela — now 23 — who last week told The Sun: "Sexist b*****ds make me sick," did saucy schoolgirl and naughty nurse routines.

Last night she gasped: "Oh God — I prayed these photos would never get out."

Michaela Strip-on — Centre Pages

THE PHOTO KIDS' TV STAR PRAYED YOU'D NEVER SEE

£54,000 LOTTO:—See Page 11 ● £31,000 BINGO:—See Page 20

3,232 DAYS TO GO

The jubilation of freed Beirut hostages Terry Waite and (inset) John McCarthy as they arrive back in England in 1991

...Timeline...

1990 Iraq invades Kuwait, sparking Gulf War with U.S., Britain and Allies; East and West Germany are unified; Poll tax riots in London; Margaret Thatcher ousted by rebellion in Tory Party — John Major takes over as Prime Minister; Nelson Mandela is released after 27 years in jail in South Africa as the apartheid regime is dismantled; Czechoslovakia is first once-communist country to establish democracy; Solidarity union chief Lech Walesa is elected president of Poland; Romanian president Nicolae Ceaucescu executed with wife in uprising; Most complete Tyrannosaurus Rex skeleton found in South Dakota; Hubble Space Telescope launched — it sends back spectacular, if fuzzy, photos of space; Observer journalist Farzad Bazoft hanged as "a spy" by Iraq.

1991 Allies liberate Kuwait; Soviet Union breaks up — Mikhail Gorbachev resigns, Boris Yeltsin takes power in Russia; Beirut hostages Terry Waite and John McCarthy are freed after years in captivity; Yugoslavia breaks up and erupts into civil war; Mirror Newspapers tycoon Robert Maxwell drowns after falling off yacht in Atlantic — massive pensions fraud uncovered; Rock singer Freddie Mercury, of Queen, dies of AIDS; William Kennedy Smith — nephew of Teddy Kennedy — cleared of rape after dramatic trial; Indian PM Rajiv Gandhi assassinated in New Delhi.

Margaret Thatcher, her eyes red with tears, leaves Downing Street for last time (1990)

Left, Freddie Mercury died of AIDS in 1991. Right, Nelson Mandela was freed in 1990

Tyrant Saddam Hussein, whose invasion of Kuwait triggered the war

1991
THE GULF WAR

IRAQI dictator Saddam Hussein started the Gulf War in August 1990 when his army invaded neighbouring Kuwait.

The Iraqis had claimed for generations that Kuwait should be part of their country — and border disputes between the two countries had led to a tense relationship.

By 1990 Iraq was heavily in debt from funding its eight-year war with Iran. Saddam claimed that Kuwait was taking oil from a field that was partly in Iraqi territory and failing to share the revenues.

He also accused Kuwait of pumping more oil than was allowed under an international agreement, thus pushing down the price of oil — Iraq's main export.

In the summer of 1990 Iraqi forces began to mobilise near the Kuwaiti border. America and the West were convinced this was merely sabre-rattling by Saddam.

But on August 2 Iraq invaded, its 150,000-strong army overpowering Kuwait's troops. The United Nations condemned Saddam and imposed an economic embargo on Iraq.

For weeks a diplomatic solution was pursued. But Saddam refused to pull out of Kuwait. At the same time a huge international force began to assemble in Saudi Arabia with the intention of retaking the country.

America sent 400,000 troops and 200,000 more came from Britain, Saudi Arabia, France, Kuwait, Egypt, Syria, Senegal, Niger, Morocco, Bangladesh, Pakistan, the United Arab Emirates, Qatar, Oman and Bahrain. In the early hours of January 17, 1991, the Allies launched Operation Desert Storm with a massive air attack on military and industrial targets within Iraq. This soon destroyed Saddam's air defences, giving the Allies control of the skies.

After almost six weeks of bombing and more than 100,000 flights by Allied planes Saddam's military forces were seriously depleted. He retaliated by attacking Israel and Saudi Arabia with Scud missiles.

On February 24 the Allies launched their land offensive. Tanks thrust into southern Iraq, then turned east — encircling the Iraqi forces in Kuwait. Thousands of Iraqi troops surrendered or deserted. Two days later Iraq announced it was pulling out of Kuwait.

On February 28 the Allies declared a ceasefire after Iraq accepted surrender terms laid down by the UN. Between 20,000 and 35,000 Iraqis are believed to have died during the Gulf War. Allied losses were 240 killed and 776 wounded.

The Allies launched Gulf War air offensive in January 1991

Bombed-out Iraqi trucks, cars, buses and armoured vehicles litter the road to Basra after an assault by Allied aircraft during the war. The Iraqis were retreating, and the attack was branded a 'turkey shoot'

A SEA OF WHITE FLAGS

've had enough! Soldiers of Iraq's crack Republican Guard surrender on the Saudi-Kuwait border yesterday

10,000 Iraqis give in
100,000 troops on run

TEN thousand Iraqi troops surrendered last night as Allied tanks stormed to the outskirts of Kuwait City.

They waved white flags in what U.S. Pentagon chiefs described as "the mother of all surrenders."

From TREVOR KAVANAGH at Allied Command HQ, Riyadh

One report said another 100,000 of Saddam's troops were fleeing the onslaught as tanks, headed by Britain's Desert Rats, roared into Iraq and Kuwait. And the Allies were "within hours" of retaking Kuwait

City in a desperate race to halt a massacre of innocent civilians.

Retreating Iraqis were said to be slaughtering children in a copy of Hitler's atrocities when he smelled defeat in 1945.

Desperate Saddam pleaded on Baghdad Radio with his troops in the desert: "Fight on, fight on, fight

Continued on Page Two

1997

Flames pour from the turrets at Windsor Castle during the devastating fire of 1992. More than 100 rooms were damaged, but a restoration was completed by 1997

...Timeline...

1992 President Bill Clinton elected; Silence Of The Lambs is Best Picture at Oscars, Anthony Hopkins as Hannibal Lecter is Best Actor; Windsor Castle ravaged by fire; Prince Charles and Princess Diana formally separate; Los Angeles riots — after white police are cleared of beating black motorist Rodney King — leave 58 dead and cause billions of dollars' damage.

1993 PLO leader Yasser Arafat and Israeli prime minister Yitzhak Rabin sign peace agreement in U.S.; Federal agents storm Branch Davidian cult's HQ in Waco, Texas, after 51-day siege and 81 people die.

1994 ANC wins first multi-racial election in South Africa — Nelson Mandela elected first black president; Manchester United win double; Newly-repaired Hubble telescope provides evidence of black hole; Channel Tunnel opens; National Lottery launched; American football legend O J Simpson tried for murders of ex-wife and her friend — it is televised worldwide.

1995 Serial killer Fred West hangs himself before facing trial — wife Rose later gets life for murders of women at their Gloucester "house of horror"; Israeli PM Rabin assassinated; Huge truck bomb planted by neo-Nazis blows up building in Oklahoma City, U.S., killing 168 people, 19 of them children; Earthquake at Kobe, Japan, kills 5,480; OJ cleared; Rogue trader Nick Leeson bankrupts Barings bank.

1996 Thomas Hamilton shoots dead 16 children and their teacher, then himself, at school in Dunblane, Scotland; Diana and Charles divorce, as do Prince Andrew and Fergie.

1997 Labour's Tony Blair elected PM, ending 18 years of Tory power; Britain hands over Hong Kong to China; Titanic is biggest box-office hit ever; Scientists in Scotland clone first mammal, Dolly the sheep; Elton John's Candle in the Wind tribute to Di is biggest-selling single ever; World chess champion Garry Kasparov beaten by computer over six games.

Serial killers Fred and Rose West. Fred killed himself in 1995 before his trial. Rose got life

Movie killer Lecter won Hopkins an Oscar in '92

In 1997, Dolly the sheep (right) became the first mammal cloned. On her left is another cloned sheep called Polly

OJ Simpson was cleared of two murders in 1995

THE PEOPLE'S PRINCESS

PRINCESS Diana, the most famous woman of the last 20 years, captured hearts everywhere with her model looks and vivacious personality. Her death in a car crash at the age of 36 stunned the world.

Born Diana Frances Spencer in 1961, she grew up on the Althorp estate in Northants after her father inherited the title Earl Spencer.

She was educated in Britain and attended finishing school in Switzerland before returning to London as a kindergarten teacher.

Diana, then 19, was catapulted into the limelight when romance blossomed with Prince Charles, 31.

They were married in July 1981 at St Paul's Cathedral in a fairytale ceremony screened worldwide.

They had two sons, William in 1982 and Harry in 1984, but Royal life took its toll and Diana fought depression and eating disorders.

The Princess suspected Charles was still obsessed by former love Camilla Parker Bowles. She felt trapped both by her loveless marriage and the stuffy Palace courtiers she loathed. She herself then had a five-year affair.

By the 1990s it was clear the marriage was dead. Diana and Charles separated in December 1992.

The same month saw the publication of the book Diana: Her True Story, which with the Princess's full but anonymous co-operation lifted the lid on her disastrous marriage and troubled Royal life. The separation gave Diana, who made Kensington Palace her full-time base, a new lease of life. She became a global fashion icon who mixed with the world's biggest stars.

She threw herself with greater gusto into the charity work which in the 1980s had seen her champion the homeless, drug addicts, deprived children and AIDS victims. She had in 1987 caused shock by holding an AIDS patient's hand at the height of paranoia about the disease.

Diana — patron of more than 100 charities and vice-president of the British Red Cross — made unannounced, unpublicised late-night visits to the sick in hospital. She campaigned for a ban on the manufacture and use of land-mines.

She and Charles divorced in August 1996. A year later she was killed with her boyfriend and their drunken chauffeur in Paris.

Diana's death brought forth a national outpouring of grief. Hundreds of thousands held vigils outside the London palaces and laid tons of flowers there.

Mourners wept in the streets for a woman they never met but who nonetheless had won their hearts.

A clearly-upset Queen addressed the nation on TV and called Diana — for many years a thorn in the Royal Family's side — "exceptional and gifted". Tony Blair called her "The People's Princess".

More than one million people lined the route of Diana's funeral in London on September 6, 1997. Millions more watched on TV.

She was buried on an island on the Althorp estate.

Sea of flowers, letters and other tributes laid by mourners outside the gates of Princess Di's London home Kensington Palace after her shocking death in 1997

THE **Sun**

Monday, September 1, 1997   28p

GOODNIGHT SWEET PRINCESS

The coffin of Princess Diana is carried home to a grieving Britain last night after one of the saddest days in our country's history. Di, 36, died around 16 hours earlier after a horrific car crash in Paris.

556 DAYS TO GO

John Major's premiership was rocked by Euro rows

Tory Edward Heath took Britain into EC in 1973

1998

Monica Lewinsky's sex revelations rocked Bill Clinton's presidency and his marriage in 1998

Pop star Victoria Adams got engaged to David Beckham in 1998 — and had his baby in 1999

James Major, the son of ex-Tory Premier John, became engaged to TV's Emma Noble in 1998

Luciana Morad announced she was pregnant by Mick Jagger in 1998 and had son in 1999

EU AND SINGLE CURRENCY

THE concept of a European Union grew out of the terrible destruction of World War Two. It has become an issue that has dominated modern British politics — and a bitter debate in which The Sun has played an influential role.

One side favours an integrated Europe with a single currency and central bank. The other backs a loose trading confederation whose members are allowed to keep their own currency.

After the war many statesmen believed a Europe with common economic goals would help avoid conflicts between nations.

The first step came in 1950 when ex-French Premier Robert Schuman unveiled a plan to pool the coal and steel resources of western Europe. This became the European Coal and Steel Community.

In Britain, neither the Labour nor the Conservative governments of the 1950s showed any interest in joining the communtiy.

Then in 1957 a trading body called the European Economic Community, or Common Market, was founded. It members were Belgium, France, West Germany, Italy, Luxembourg and Holland.

Ten years later this EEC joined the Coal and Steel Community to form the European Community.

Britain finally joined the EC in 1973 under Conservative Prime Minister Edward Heath. Denmark and Ireland joined the same year.

In 1975 Labour's Harold Wilson held a referendum on whether Britain should stay in the EC. His Government campaigned in favour of a Yes vote in the face of stiff opposition from Left-wingers. Some 67.2 per cent of Britons voted Yes while 32.8 per cent said No.

By the mid-1970s the economic benefits of increased trade opportunities led some politicians to begin to propose a new future for Europe.

Instead of a trading confederation, they envisaged a powerful, politically-based body which would take over many aspects of government from member states.

This community would preside over a single frontierless market using a single European currency. Countries would have their economic policies controlled by a central European bank. Many aspects of social policy would also be imposed.

A second group fiercely opposed such a politically and economically-unified Europe.

This group, now usually known as Euro-sceptics, vowed to fight the transfer of power from the individual citizens in the democracies of Western Europe. The Sun has been

Commission boss Jacques Delors led push for single Euro currency

at the forefront of this movement. During the 1980s membership of the European Community increased. Greece joined in 1981, Portugal and Spain in 1986. The former East Germany was later admitted as part of reunified Germany.

In 1987 the member states adopted the Single European Act, by which they declared their eventual intention to create a unified, free-trade market in western Europe.

For pro-integrationists, led in the late 1980s by European Commission President Jacques Delors, creating a single currency was vital.

Central to this ambition was the setting-up of the Exchange Rate Mechanism. This was designed to regulate currency exchange rates and promote monetary stability among member states, thus paving the way to a single currency.

Britain shunned the ERM until October 1990 when John Major — Chancellor in Margaret Thatcher's Tory Government — agreed to join to help the fight against inflation.

The climax of the move towards further integration came in December 1991 when Mr Major, by then PM, signed the Maastricht Treaty.

This provided for the introduction of a central banking system and a common currency. It committed member states to implementing a common foreign and security policy and turned the European Community into the European Union.

Mr Major negotiated an "opt-out" for Britain from the single currency and central bank.

On September 16, 1992, Britain was forced out of the ERM in humiliating circumstances when the value of the Pound plummeted against the German mark.

The day was initially known as Black Wednesday. But Britain's removal from the economic straitjacket of the ERM sparked a boom — and prompted City analysts to rename September 16 as White Wednesday.

The ERM debacle heightened the debate here about our role in the EU.

Central to this was the question of whether Britain should scrap the Pound and join a single currency. This suggestion has always been fiercely opposed by The Sun and its readers — and has caused bitter divisions within both Labour and Tory parties.

It dogged the Premiership of Mr Major (1990 - 1997) and eventually sparked an unsuccessful leadership challenge.

Many Tories blamed the party's split into pro and anti-EU factions for the 1997 General Election defeat.

On January 1, 1999, the single European currency, or the euro as it is known, came into being. Britain did not join. In the following six months the euro's value fell by more than 12 per cent.

Tony Blair's Labour Government currently believes it could be in Britain's interest at some time in the future — though not at present — to join the euro and scrap the Pound.

Mr Blair has promised that if, and when, his Government thinks the time is right he will hold a referendum, so giving the British people the final say.

THE Sun

Wednesday, June 24, 1998   28p   DEDICATED TO THE PEOPLE OF BRITAIN

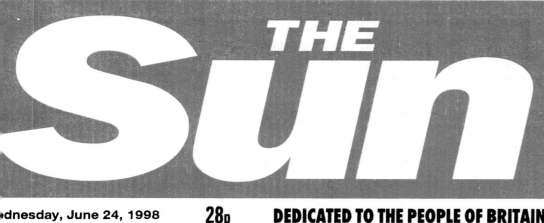

AMAZING COURAGE OF WILLIAM AND HARRY

By EARL SPENCER   See Pages 22 & 23

AS EURO LOOMS **Sun** ASKS CRUCIAL QUESTION

Is THIS the most dangerous man in Britain?

Gambling with our Pound . . . Premier Tony Blair seems determined to join the euro

PAGE ONE OPINION

IT IS the question we never dreamed we would ask.

But we have been forced to think the unthinkable. And today The Sun demands:

Is Tony Blair the most dangerous man in Britain?

In most respects he is a fine Premier. But he seems determined to scrap the Pound and take Britain into the European single currency.

And that, we believe, will be the biggest gamble any Prime Minister has ever taken.

The result could be disastrous for this country. That is why The Sun has vowed to fight it all the way.

Blair is a charming, persuasive politician. We like him.

He has the potential to be a truly great Prime Minister. He thinks fast and outflanks opponents with a smile that conceals a touch of steel. These are the qualities which

Continued on Page Six

COUNTDOWN to 3000

361,226 DAYS TO GO

They're back: Mammoth may be recreated (2001) and screen legends John Wayne and Greta Garbo could co-star in computer-generated film (2004)

2010

...Timeline...

2000 Production begins on the Skycar personal commuter aircraft — it carries four and cruises at 397mph, taking off and landing vertically; The mobile video-phone is launched — it has two-inch wide screen which shows caller.

2001 The woolly mammoth, extinct for more than 4,000 years, is recreated by scientists who fertilise an elephant egg with sperm extracted from the body of a mammoth frozen in Siberia.

2004 Long-dead actors Greta Garbo and John Wayne co-star in new movie — thanks to magic of computers which accurately recreate how they looked, move and spoke.

2005 New slimline TV system introduced which enables screen to be hung on wall like painting — "virtual paintings" can be screened on it when not in use for TV shows; American scientists cure baldness with miracle cream which restores missing hair and prevents further loss; John Wayne wins his second Oscar — for Best Computer-Generated Actor.

2006 Another telly advance — the intelligent TV which selects programmes to record, based on current watching trends in the owne home; Death of the CD as most mu fans subscribe to Internet libraries wh send music to the PC; An end to obesity as new diet pill convinces y body the lettuce leaf you're eating is cream or a steak.

2007 Last video recorder com off production line — D battles it out with the home PC as platform for watching movies and recc ing TV shows; Invention of the car which breathalyses the owner and refuses to start if driver's over the li

2008 New "smart drug" which enhances intelligence is veloped; Wristwatch video-phone goe into production in Japan.

2009 Fridge linked to the Internet orders delivery milk from local supermarket's website when it sees you've run out.

2010 Newspaper sales at reco low as readers switch t subscribing to each paper's website, printing out pages for a hard copy.

The mobile video-phone (2000) will show the caller's face at a rate of two frames a second. In 2008 you'll get one you wear like a watch

SKYCAR

Is this the future of everyday travel? The Sky Car, an aircraft which cruises at 400mph, seats four and is capable of vertical take-off and landing, will be made in 2000. Air traffic control might be a problem, mind

2020

...Timeline...

2012 America elects its first woman President.

2013 Cannabis legalised in Britain — it is subject to enormous Government tax; Asteroid watch set up by NASA to monitor objects in space posing a threat to Earth and divert them.

2014 Space shuttles opened to paying passengers — tickets are hugely expensive, but by leaving the atmosphere you can fly from London to Sydney in only two hours and to New York in 50 minutes.

2015 Massive volcano and earthquake in California kills one million people in Los Angeles and San Francisco, making many millions more homeless and plunging U.S. economy into depression; Cars which drive themselves first seen — they respond to all road emergencies faster than humans and use satellite navigation.

2016 Robots now carrying out domestic chores in 30 per cent of Britain's homes.

2018 Four "gated cities" for the rich open in Britain — an idea pioneered by the Disney Corporation in the 1990s at their squeaky-clean Florida town, Celebration. The cities have massive security, no crime or dirt and even the cats' claws are removed.

2020 Large areas of coastal Britain disappear as global warming melts the ice cap and sea level rises. New York, Boston and coastal New England also under water. Ironically Britain's temperature plummets as cold water flowing into the Atlantic slows down flow of the warm Gulf Stream.

...entists believe California is long overdue for an earthquake and volcano which could kill one million ...ople (see 2015). This scene is from the 1997 movie Volcano, about an eruption in central Los Angeles

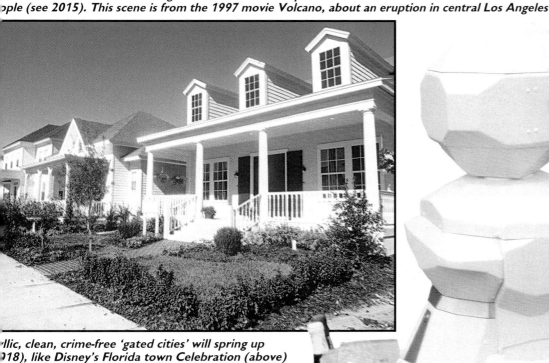

...llic, clean, crime-free 'gated cities' will spring up ...018), like Disney's Florida town Celebration (above)

...is could be New England in 2020 as melting ice ...o floods America's east coast and part of Britain

Robots will be commonly used for domestic tasks like shopping by 2016

By 2014, we may be buying tickets on space shuttle, slashing flying times around world

2040
UFOs AND ROSWELL

Time travel by 2030? Some believe H G Wells' prediction may come true. This photo is from the 1960 movie of his novel The Time Machine

...Timeline...

2021 NASA land the first man — and woman — on Mars.

2023 Scientists develop way to regenerate lost brain cells, curing Alzheimer's and other brain damage; New European rail network of 400mph trains allows travel between major cities at amazing speed — London to Paris in an hour.

2024 Home PCs powered by Intel Pentium IX processor are now as powerful as all the computers in California in the 1990s put together; Forty per cent of the world's workforce now working from home using PC.

2025 Man's brain linked to computer for first time — he interacts directly with the Internet and is immediately the most knowledgeable bloke on Earth; About 95 per cent of all body parts now replaceable using spare limbs and organs grown in "body banks"; Forty per cent of all cars, and 70 per cent of new ones, are now electric as old, smelly, dirty fossil fuel-burners are phased out.

2030 Cancer and heart disease cured, but still no end to the common cold; Scientists achieve time travel, transporting a matchbox-sized object back and forward by a minute.

2035 Advance in gene technology allows humans to grow back lost limbs — huge storm as it is revealed geneticists are secretly working on changing a man's DNA so he can grow wings.

2039 Robot developed which is more intelligent than human; Manned mission to Jupiter in nuclear-powered spacecraft is launched.

Astronauts could land on the surface of Mars, so far only explored by robot vehicles, by year 2021

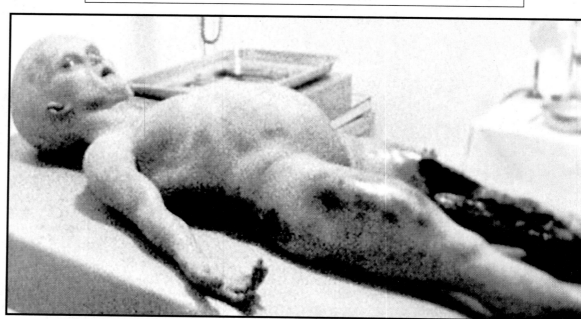

A strange-looking body from the 'alien autopsy' film said to have been taken after the alleged UFO crash at Roswell in July 1947. Despite claims that it is a dummy, many UFO theorists are still convinced by it

THE possibility of life on other planets has fascinated mankind for centuries. Numbers of UFO sightings have soared in the 20th Century and have given rise to a science-fiction industry encompassing film, literature and art.

Most scientists agree it is probable that in an infinite universe life must exist elsewhere, but the actual presence of aliens on or orbiting Earth is hotly debated.

The origins of "Ufology" lie in 22,000-year-old cave paintings in Les Eyzies, France — said to show saucer-shaped flying objects.

Passages from the Old Testament book of Ezekiel, describing a visit from heavenly beings using flying vehicles, have been interpreted as an alien encounter.

References are found in the literature of other ancient cultures. Some modern authors believe aliens influenced our evolution.

A newspaper in Nuremburg, Germany, reported in 1561 that mysterious red, blue and black shapes appeared in the sky and seemed to be in battle over the city. But the modern-day fascination

with UFOs began with the widespread sighting of mysterious "airships" in countries across the world in November 1896.

Cigar-shaped craft were seen first in California, then across the States. Flying discs were spotted by ships at sea. The sightings spread to Europe and then Australia.

During World War Two, pilots on both sides reported being "buzzed" by balls of light up to 5ft wide which performed astonishing manoeuvres impossible for human aircraft.

The objects, dubbed "Foo Fighters", were also tracked by radar.

In the summer of 1947 came the two most famous UFO incidents. On June 24, pilot Kenneth Arnold spotted objects in the sky "like saucers skipping across water" while flying in Washington State. The Press coined the term "flying saucers" — and reported sightings began to pour in.

Then came the incident at Roswell, New Mexico, on July 4. Air force radar tracked an object flying in a way impossible for man-made aircraft. It then vanished

from the screens. Locals reported seeing a UFO. Rancher Mac Brazel heard a loud explosion, went to the scene and found strange "otherworldly" debris there.

The military sealed off the area — and UFO theorists believe they recovered aliens there, both dead and alive.

Matters were further confused when the army at first said a flying saucer HAD been found, then said the debris was a crashed weather balloon.

Nearly 50 years later a film surfaced, purporting to show a post mortem being carried out on one of the bodies.

Ufologists claim the military covered up the incident — and some Roswell witnesses say they were threatened to keep quiet.

The U.S. air force held official investigations into UFOs from 1947 to 1969 and found the vast majority had simple earthly explanations.

In 1997 the CIA admitted that more than half the UFOs reported during the 1950s and 1960s were in fact its secret high-altitude spy planes.

Sightings and theories continue unabated, some of the most convincing from airline pilots who claim to have been buzzed by UFOs.

Countless people say they have been abducted by aliens and taken aboard spaceships, often for biological experiments.

Aliens are blamed for all kinds of mysterious phenomena — from crop circles to the unexplained mutilations of cattle worldwide.

Some believe B2 bomber was based on alien technology from Roswell

THE Sun 2040

WE ARE NOT ALONE

Announcement . . . Hague last night

By CHLOE SENCOUNTER

MAN has made contact with aliens, the world's leaders announced last night.

The biggest development in our history was revealed in simultaneous TV and radio broadcasts in all the major countries of the Earth.

NASA scientists have spent months deciphering radio signals sent to us from orbiting UFOs.

They have sent back a greeting using the aliens' language and the co-ordinates of a desert site in the United States where they hope a meeting will take place.

Prime Minister William Hague, 79, made the historic announcement at once on all of Britain's TV channels — Sky 1, 2, 3, 4, 5, 6, 7, 8 and 9.

Mr Hague, whose election last year ended 42 unbroken years of Labour rule, revealed that the aliens:

● Have studied Earth for 500 years, abducted people for embarrassing biological tests and infiltrated our parliaments disguised as humans.

● Have sent small spacecraft into our atmosphere "for a giggle."

● Crashed one at Roswell, New Mexico, in 1947, and are still wrangling with their insurers.

ET PHONES HOME
Sun souvenir edition

World leaders announce: Man has made first contact with aliens

Acknowledgements

● ● ● ● ● ● ● ● ● ● ● ● ● ● ● ● ●

THANKS to: Phil Leach, for making silk purses from sows' ears, Rachel Ward for her tireless and good-natured picture research, Sun photographer Steve Lewis and his team, Emma Holder, Colin Packham and Sean Clark for their computer skills and invaluable suggestions, Sun columnists Jeremy Clarkson, Garry Bushell and Jane Moore for their excellent contributions, Kathryn George and Roy Cooper for the graphics and Elaine Roberts for the Page Three Girl of the Year captions.

The following contributed ideas and other help for which we are grateful: Mark Fishman, Chris Stevens, Fergus Shanahan, David Yelland, Rebekah Wade, Andy Coulson, Paul Ridley, Paul Simpson (Editor of Focus Magazine), Becky Goddard, Myles Archibald from Harper Collins and Simon Clarke.

We also wish to thank certain other Sun staff: the Imaging Department, for working miracles with some of the pictures, Russell Dewey for his technical assistance and dedication, the Systems Department (in particular Lee Wells), the News Sub-Editors, the Art Desk and Page Builders, the Picture Desk, the Plate Room — and Carlos the carpenter for the glasses. Thanks also to Philip Skingley, of Spink and Co., dealers and auctioneers, 5 King Street, London SW1Y 6QS, for the wonderful coin book, to Dick Clark for the Roman pictures and to the historian Richard Vinen.

The Hastings Battle scenes came from English Heritage Special Events Unit, which is staging two events in 2000 not to be missed — the Battle of Hastings reenactment at Battle Abbey, East Sussex, on October 14 and 15 and the History In Action festival at Kirby Hall, near Corby, Northants, on August 14 and 15 (full details from English Heritage).

We are further indebted to the following picture agencies: Corbis; Hulton/Getty; The Bridgeman Art Library; Mary Evans Picture Library; Popperfoto; Rex Features; Moviestore; Science Photo Library. Some pictures by courtesy of the National Portrait Gallery, London; Mickey Mouse ©Disney Enterprises Inc.; Kennedy photo by Zapruder/Colorific!; The Beatles' Sergeant Pepper LP cover ©Apple Corps Ltd.

THE Sun THANKS A LOT, FOLKS!

DEDICATED TO JACK

HarperCollins*Publishers*   77-85 Fulham Palace Road   London   W6 8JB • First published 1999, reprinted 1999 • 10 9 8 7 6 5 4 3 2 1 • © The Sun Newspaper • All rights reserved